WELL-BEING AND WE

Edited by Thomas Falkenberg

By its very nature, school education is concerned with student well-being. Written by Canadian education scholars from a Manitoba-based research group, *Well-Being and Well-Becoming in Schools* aims to develop the notion that what we wish for our children is their well-being and well-becoming as they live their lives. This collection brings education scholars together to focus on a timely topic that has been of rapidly increasing interest to the research and education communities: student well-being and flourishing schools.

Contributors address a broad range of issues that arise from this position to create a rich and integrated understanding of the topic. Chapters focus on foundational issues, conceptual issues, socio-cultural and organizational issues, and pedagogical and curricular issues. Ultimately, *Well-Being and Well-Becoming in Schools* weaves together substantial ideas to create an integrative framework that will not only serve as a guide for further research, but also for school educational leaders and educators to implement the idea of making school education primarily about student well-being.

THOMAS FALKENBERG is a professor in the Faculty of Education at the University of Manitoba.

Well-Being and Well-Becoming in Schools

EDITED BY THOMAS FALKENBERG

UNIVERSITY OF TORONTO PRESS
Toronto Buffalo London

© University of Toronto Press 2024
Toronto Buffalo London
utorontopress.com
Printed in the USA

ISBN 978-1-4875-4350-1 (cloth)   ISBN 978-1-4875-4352-5 (EPUB)
ISBN 978-1-4875-4351-8 (paper)   ISBN 978-1-4875-4353-2 (PDF)

Library and Archives Canada Cataloguing in Publication

Title: Well-being and well-becoming in schools / edited by
   Thomas Falkenberg.
Names: Falkenberg, Thomas, editor.
Description: Includes bibliographical references and index.
Identifiers: Canadiana (print) 20230551815 | Canadiana (ebook)
   20230551874 | ISBN 9781487543501 (cloth) | ISBN 9781487543518
   (paper) | ISBN 9781487543525 (EPUB) | ISBN 9781487543532 (PDF)
Subjects: LCSH: School environment – Canada. | LCSH: Well-being –
   Canada. | LCSH: Education – Social aspects – Canada. | LCSH:
   Students – Canada.
Classification: LCC LC210.8.C2 W45 2024 | DDC 370.15/80971 – dc23

Cover design: Heng Wee Tan
Cover illustration: FatCamera/iStockphoto.com

We wish to acknowledge the land on which the University of Toronto Press operates. This land is the traditional territory of the Wendat, the Anishnaabeg, the Haudenosaunee, the Métis, and the Mississaugas of the Credit First Nation.

This book has been published with the help of a grant from the Federation for the Humanities and Social Sciences, through the Awards to Scholarly Publications Program, using funds provided by the Social Sciences and Humanities Research Council of Canada.

University of Toronto Press acknowledges the financial support of the Government of Canada, the Canada Council for the Arts, and the Ontario Arts Council, an agency of the Government of Ontario, for its publishing activities.

 Canada Council Conseil des Arts
for the Arts du Canada

Contents

1 Introduction: Framing the Work on Well-Being and Well-Becoming Needed in School Education 3
THOMAS FALKENBERG

Part One: Foundational Questions on Well-Being and Well-Becoming in Schools

2 Three Theories of Well-Being and Their Implications for School Education 23
ERIK MAGNUSSON AND HEATHER KREPSKI

3 Three Foundational Questions for Policymakers and Practitioners Concerned with Student Well-Being 41
HEATHER KREPSKI

4 Responding to the Other: The Need for an Ethic of Well-Being 59
REBECA HERINGER AND THOMAS FALKENBERG

Part Two: Conceptualizing Well-Being and Well-Becoming in Schools

5 Well-Being as a Core Focus of School Education: Conceptualizing Indigenous Well-Being 79
FRANK DEER AND JESSICA TRICKEY

6 Meaning in Life: A Core Component of Human and Student Well-Becoming 100
THOMAS FALKENBERG

7 Well-Being of School Counsellors and School Psychologists 120
VIRGINIA M.C. TZE AND STEPHANIE BREKELMANS

Part Three: Contextualizing Well-Being and Well-Becoming in Schools

8 Well-Being in the Context of School Organizations 139
LESLEY EBLIE TRUDEL

9 Well-Being and Well-Becoming in Inner-City Schools: Supporting Students' Wholistic Flourishing in Inner-City Communities 159
JEANNIE KERR

10 Developmental Evaluation as a Tool for Promoting Well-Being in Schools: A Case Study 178
CAMERON HAUSEMAN, THOMAS FALKENBERG, JENNIFER WATT, AND HEATHER KREPSKI

11 A Complex Adaptive Systems Approach to Well-Becoming in Schools 197
THOMAS FALKENBERG, HEATHER KREPSKI, CAMERON HAUSEMAN, AND JENNIFER WATT

Part Four: Curricularizing Well-Being and Well-Becoming in Schools

12 Finding Meaning in Life through School Mathematics 219
THOMAS FALKENBERG

13 Making Meaning of Science Curriculum through Ecojustice and Place-Based Education: Looking through the Lens of Well-Being and Well-Becoming 235
MICHAEL LINK

14 Kitchen Table and Greenbelt Writers: Flourishing Writing in English Language Arts and Beyond 254
JENNIFER WATT

15 Conclusion: Where to Go from Here 271
THOMAS FALKENBERG

Index 281

WELL-BEING AND WELL-BECOMING IN SCHOOLS

1 Introduction: Framing the Work on Well-Being and Well-Becoming Needed in School Education

THOMAS FALKENBERG

What do we wish for our children? What do we wish for our neighbours and our communities? What do we wish for ourselves? Indigenous peoples in Canada, drawing on their traditional teachings, provide their answer: *mino-bimaadiziwin*, meaning "the good life" or "living in a good way."[1] Michael Hart (2002) for instance, has identified five foundational concepts central to *mino-pimatisiwin*: wholeness, balance, harmony, growth, and healing. These concepts are supported by key values, which "support one to reach *mino-pimatisiwin*" (p. 45): sharing, respect, and spirituality. Nicole Bell (2016), drawing on her conversations with Anishinaabe Elders, notes that in traditional Anishinaabe education

> the word *good* [as in *the good life*] should not be taken lightly when considered from an Anishinaabe perspective. *The good way* means fostering the child's development using the seven sacred values of honesty, wisdom, love, respect, bravery, humility, and truth, which result in great things for the person receiving the teachings. (p. 14)

Furthermore, Bell (2016) writes, Anishinaabe education is concerned with the whole child: "the *whole child* is a child who is a person with a heart, a body, a spirit, and a mind" (p. 14).

These traditional Indigenous teachings point to a path of inquiry that the chapter authors of this book collectively pursue, each with a different but complementary perspective. They inquire into the central importance of a purpose of life and of a purpose for our own lives, of a holistic and relational view of what it means to be human and of life more generally, of core values and principles that guide social and individual living, and of the important role that education plays in all of this. This book brings Indigenous and non-Indigenous scholars from Manitoba together to develop the notion that what we wish for our children is their well-being and well-becoming as they live their lives. If, as guardians of our children – and as a society at large – we are concerned with their well-being and well-becoming, we need to ask, What role can school education play – or even what role does it need to play – in light of this concern? This question is the focus of this book, and the different chapters address this question, each doing so from a different perspective, and each contributing to at least one of five scholarly domains in school education. In this introductory chapter, I draw on some of the relevant literature from these five domains to demonstrate how the book in general, and the chapters in particular, fit into the current scholarly discourse and address the questions of what we wish for our children and what role schools can or need to play in making this wish become reality.

Before I get to this scholarly discourse, however, I want to explain the use of the somewhat unusual term of "well-becoming" in the title of this book and in its chapters. In my own work, I have started using this term, first, as a component of the phrase "well-being and well-becoming" (e.g., Falkenberg 2019, 2020) and now as a stand-alone phrase (e.g., chapters 6, 11, and 12 in this volume). While *well-being* has been used in different disciplines as an alternative to the term *flourishing* for some time (e.g., Griffin, 1986; Haworth & Hart, 2007; Kahneman et al., 1999), I have been using the term *well-becoming* to reflect the dynamic character of human living and experiencing as I started understanding human living through a complex adaptive system lens (Falkenberg, 2019; chapter 11, this volume). Through this lens, humans are seen as constantly developing, and by emphasizing that such developing is often directional by intention, the term *becoming* seems to capture this notion quite appropriately, while *well-being* seems to suggest more a state of being rather than a state of becoming. *Becoming: Basic Considerations for a Psychology of Personality*, by Gordon Allport (1955), argues for a developmental perspective on human personality and has influenced my thinking in this regard, including my choice of terminology. As the chapter authors of this book started to meet to discuss the book project, we engaged with each other's work and thinking around flourishing and well-being in the context of education. Some authors picked up the idea of complementing *well-being* with *well-becoming*, while others used the more commonly found term *well-being* only. The title of this book reflects the former, but in the remainder of this introductory chapter I use the phrase *well-being* only to reflect the more common term in the literature.

A View on the Scholarly Discourse

While the research and scholarly literature on well-being in schools is burgeoning, less-travelled paths and even identifiable gaps on the topic remain. The scholarly contribution of the present book lies in travelling such less- travelled paths and bridging such gaps.

What follows is not a systematic or comprehensive review of the research and scholarly literature on well-being in schools. One challenge in attempting such a review is that research on teaching and learning and school education more broadly is always also research on well-being, particularly student well-being. Research on teaching mathematics to middle-year students is about their well-being, if we consider the learning of mathematics an aspect of students' well-being, for instance, because it might be important for their educational and professional future. While this makes the scope of any literature review on well-being in schools enormous, almost insurmountable, one way in which such an enormous task can be supported is by undertaking partial reviews, and reviews with a specific focus and purpose, like the review in this chapter.

The following review is intended to demonstrate how the book project as a whole as well as the individual chapters fit into a thematic structure of the already available research and scholarly literature on well-being in schools. I thus draw on my knowledge of this literature, which I have developed over the last six years and as part of the writing of this introductory chapter, to provide a general sense of a *thematic structure* that addresses how well-being in schools is taken up in the research and scholarly literature. What follows is not intended as a systematic and thorough engagement with the literature on these themes but rather a sharing of my observations of the literature around these themes.

I have structured my thematic overview of the literature on well-being in schools by using categories that derive from a system understanding of school education: purpose, concepts, contexts (school ecology), experiences (teaching and learning), and content (curriculum).

Purpose of School Education and Well-Being

In terms of the purpose of school education in the context of the well-being literature, I make the following four observations. First, there seems to be a clear division of labour among the academic disciplines. The purpose question – What is the purpose of school education? – is most directly addressed in the philosophy of education scholarship, where a number of scholars have argued that human well-being is *the* end of school education, and, accordingly, all other purposes have to be understood as serving this end (e.g., Brighouse, 2006), and that human well-being is one among a number of other ends of school education (e.g., Noddings, 2003).

A second observation is that the philosophical and psychological literature has been centrally focused on the quality of life of the individual human being. This is not to say that philosophers of education and psychologists have denied the relevance of the social context of school education, but rather that the *concern* has been for the quality of life of the individual. Of course, by their very disciplinary natures, sociologically oriented and Indigenous scholarships have been emphasizing the cultural aspect of well-being (e.g., Bell, 2016; Veenhoven, 2008). A focus on the individual human being when considering the purpose of school education emphasizes individual-centred qualities that students should develop, like "a positive attitude toward lifelong physical activity," "critical thinking," and "resilience." On the other hand, when the locus of concern is students as social beings, quality of life for a student is understood as the quality of the relationship between the individual and the other members of the social system that they are embedded in. In this case, the purpose question for school education is concerned with the quality of life *within and as part of* the given school and societal context, and with the quality of the school context as a developmental aim for school education. For instance, for this locus of concern, the quality of the working conditions for staff of a school is part of the purpose question for school education. The working conditions for staff impact the way staff interact with others and, thus, the social system as a whole, which in turn is the system within which students experience their lives as connected to the school. As this example suggests, if the purpose of school education includes concern for students as social beings, the quality of schools as social systems have to be a central focus of the purpose question.

A third observation of the literature on well-being as a central purpose of school education has been the temporal distinction between a concern for students' future lives as adults and students' present lives as students. In terms of the purpose of education, the former has clearly been the most dominant view in countries of the Global North: schools are primarily intended to help children develop knowledge, skills, and attitudes that adult society considers of importance for children to live their lives as adults. On the other hand, more recent scholarly work – for instance, the New Sociology of Childhood, the child well-being literature in applied philosophy, and the child rights movement (on these, see Falkenberg & Krepski, 2020) – has given rise to a greater focus on the learning needs in childhood, not on children's development into adults but rather as human beings living their lives in childhood: "Qvortrup (1999) laid the foundation for considering children's well-being [as children] in claiming that the conventional preoccupation with the next generation is a preoccupation of adults" (Ben-Arieh, 2008, p. 10).

A fourth observation gleaned from the literature is the clear division of that scholarship into two branches, which generally do not overlap, although the implications for the respective other branch have been generally acknowledged. One branch has been focusing on the well-being of students, while the other branch has been focusing on the well-being of teachers and administrators.[2] With regard to the purpose of school education, the scholarly literature is almost exclusively focused on the well-being of students, which is understandable, because schools are by design institutions focused on students and their development. However, when we start out with a concern for well-being for all and understand the importance that work and workplaces have for adult well-being, the consideration of adult well-being when thinking about the purpose of schools – as workplaces for adults – naturally follows. Thus, with a general concern for well-being for all, the purpose of school education (as an institutional endeavour) has to also include the provision of experiences for adults that support their well-being within and through their engagement with the school, be it as an employee, parent, or community member.

Conceptualizing Well-Being in School

Not surprisingly, many conceptions of student well-being have either been adopted or directly derived from more general notions of human well-being, without any further refinement or distinction. In many of the positive psychology approaches to student well-being, for instance, the relevant concepts have been directly drawn from the scholarship around these concepts that were originally developed without any distinction between adults and children, like hope (e.g., Marques et al., 2014) and flow (e.g., Shernoff et al., 2014). Similarly, many approaches to teacher and administrator well-being have drawn on general human well-being frameworks in their inquiries into teacher and administrator well-being (e.g., Cherkowski & Walker, 2018a).

Some conceptions of child well-being have been derived from approaches to well-being that have not distinguished between adult and child well-being, but they themselves developed a distinct concept for child well-being based on an ontological distinction between children and adults by which children are considered beings in their own right and not just "adult-becoming" (Falkenberg & Krepski, 2020). The approach to child well-being developed by Biggeri and his collaborators (Ballet et al., 2011; Biggeri et al., 2006) is one example. Building upon the capabilities approach to well-being developed by Sen (1993/2009a; 2009b) and Nussbaum (2011), Biggeri et al. modified Sen and Nussbaum's capabilities approach to account for the ontological distinction between children and adults mentioned earlier.

A third approach to conceptualizing child or student well-being has taken its starting point not in an already existing approach to well-being, but rather in children's or students' views about what it means *to them* to flourish as children or students (e.g., Simmons et al., 2015; Soutter et al., 2011, 2014). A similar approach has been taken by some scholars who inquire into administrator well-being. Cherkowski and Walker (2016), for instance, conceptualized administrator well-being based on the latter's perspective of what it means to flourish as an administrator. When students were asked what they wish their school would be like (e.g., Rudduck, 2007; Smyth, 2007) or what it meant for them to flourish as a student (e.g., Falkenberg et al., 2021), they generally did not seem to draw on the quality of their experiences in other life domains, but rather stayed focused on the quality of their school experiences. While the subjective perspective of students was centred on the school experiences, researchers found evidence of cross-domain influences. For instance, racial discrimination in a child's social domain impacts their attendance and, thus, well-being at school (e.g., Benner & Graham, 2011), and a child's socio-economic status impacts the quality of their experiences and, thus, well-being at school (e.g., Horgan, 2009). There is ample evidence to support an approach to student well-being that considers also students' well-being in other life domains. One such approach, which has at its very centre the notion that a person's development needs to be understood as responding to disturbances by a structure of interacting life-domains, is Bronfenbrenner's (1979) bio-ecological approach to human development; indeed it has been used in various contexts as the theoretical framework for understanding children's well-being (e.g., Minkkinen, 2013; Newland, 2015).

School Ecology and Well-Being

Drawing on Bronfenbrenner's (1979) bio-ecological systems approach to human development, we can identify three levels of a school's ecology as it impacts students' well-being in schools: the school as an ecological system itself; the other social systems that directly impact the school ecology, like the parental home and the school division as a whole; and the socio-cultural system (which includes the political) into which the other two systems are embedded.

Using this tripartite structure to organize some of the literature on well-being and school ecology, the relevant literature seems to fall predominantly into the first level of school ecology, that is, the school as a system impacting individual well-being. Huebner et al.'s (2014) quote exemplifies this type of literature on schools as sites of well-being:

> Schooling is a primary activity during childhood and adolescence. In light of the amount of time that children and adolescents spend in school, it is perhaps not surprising that the quality of their school experiences appears to be associated with students' SWB [i.e., subjective well-being]. The results reviewed herein suggest the importance of a number of key aspects of the school environment that matter, including the quality of interactions with teachers and peers, parental involvement in schooling, instructional practices in the classroom, students' perceptions of safety, students' perceived and actual academic performance, and opportunities to participate in extracurricular activities. The school context is clearly an important determinant, beyond the family environment, of positive child and adolescent SWB and quality of life. (Huebner et al., 2014, p. 810)

Other examples in which schools are considered as sites of well-being can be found in Cherkowski and Walker (2013), Gray et al. (2011), Huebner et al. (2009), and Morrison and Peterson (2013). Two particular foci of research on schools as sites of well-being are the role of school climate for student well-being (e.g., Aldridge et al., 2016; Bacete et al., 2014; Kutsyuruba et al., 2018) and the importance of student voice for student well-being (e.g., Falkenberg, 2018; Simmons, 2015).

Beyond the school as a social system, there are other social systems within a community or society that interact with the school system in ways that impact students' well-being. Reupert (2020), for instance, distinguished three such systems as "school partnerships" (p. 115): families, community, and professional agencies. Some scholars, like Reupert (2020), analysed the structure of interaction within this level of the school ecology with respect to student well-being, while others looked at the impact of specific system relationships, like the home environment (e.g., Hooja & Shaktawat, 2017) or the relationship with professional agencies, as in the case of children in care (e.g., Janzen et al., 2020). Overall, there seems to be far less research available on this school ecological level than is available on schools as sites of well-being.

There is ample research on the relationship between school systems and the larger socio-cultural system into which school systems are embedded. Inquiry into this relationship is at the heart of the scholarship in the sociology and politics of school education (e.g., Wotherspoon, 2009). However, as far as the scholarship goes that speaks explicitly to well-being in schools, there seems to be very little research on this school ecological level available at this time. It is noteworthy – though not surprising to me – that where such literature can be found, it is often about socio-cultural contexts in which there is an explicit interest in human well-being in general and in schools in particular at the larger social and political level. For instance, Spratt's (2017) study inquired into the political discourse of well-being in schools in Scotland, where student well-being has been an explicit concern for the government (Munn, 2010). Similarly, Noble and McGrath's (2016) discussion of educational policy for student well-being (in the Australian context) was presented in the context of an explicit concern by the Australian government for children's well-being (e.g., Fraillon, 2004, 2005; Hamilton & Redmond, 2010).

Teaching and Learning and Well-Being

As I wrote above, by its very nature school education is concerned with student well-being. This particularly applies to school educational research literature that focuses primarily on teaching and learning in the school context. This research is centrally about student well-being in the widest sense, although not always expressed in the language of flourishing or well-being. For instance, the research literature on the Reggio Emilia approach to early childhood and early years teaching and learning is all about helping students to be able to live a flourishing life as students and adults (e.g., Cuthbert, 2020; Link 2018). Similarly, the research literature on how to create a safe and caring classroom (Alder, 2002; Steele & Cohn-Vargas, 2013), on culturally responsive teaching (e.g., Gay, 2000), and on success for all students in the learning of mathematics (e.g., Warren & Miller, 2016) is about student well-being in school. Again, the language used is different, but in substance, the concern in all these cases is with students' well-being. Thus, the educational research literature with a focus on teaching and learning and student well-being is vast. However, in this literature student well-being is often left undefined, and generally this literature does not take as its starting point a comprehensive understanding of student well-being but is rather focused on a much narrower understanding of teaching and learning within specific learning domains, for instance, as within specific subject areas. On the other hand, the education scholarship that takes as its starting point an understanding of student well-being has generally not yet explicated what such an understanding implies for teaching and learning in schools. One exception is the educational literature in which scholars and practitioners have built on the now quite expansive positive psychology literature on child and student well-being (e.g., Furlong et al., 2014) to develop specific approaches to teaching and learning for student well-being (e.g., White & Murray, 2015).

Curriculum and Well-Being

If we simplistically distinguish between the "how" and the "what" of school education, then the former can be linked to teaching and learning in schools and the latter to the school curriculum. While the field of curriculum studies has long blurred such simplistic distinctions (e.g., Connelly & Clandinin, 1988; Pinar et al., 1995), the categorical separation still has a heuristic purpose for an initial engagement with different aspects of school education.

As was the case for teaching and learning (the "how" of school education), those engaged in the question of "what" to teach in school have always been engaged in the curriculum discourse from a stance of concern for children's well-being in the widest sense. This is the case for those who argued for an externally determined common core curriculum for all students based on traditional subject areas (e.g., Adler, 1982), those who argued for a completely student-chosen curriculum (e.g., Neill, 1960), and those who argued for a holistic curriculum (e.g., Miller, 2007). However, as was the case for teaching and learning, such scholarly work has rarely been grounded in an explicit understanding of student well-being as a core purpose of school education. The only exception that I am aware of is work by the philosopher of education Nel Noddings. In her book *Happiness and Education*, Noddings (2003) suggested a curriculum for "educating for personal life" (p. 94) and "educating for public life" (p. 195) that is grounded in the notion that "happiness should be an aim of education, and a good education should contribute significantly to personal and collective happiness" (p. 1).[3]

Nevertheless, there is a range of scholarly work that is explicitly concerned with human, child, or student well-being and in which the "what" of school education is discussed. It is interesting that these scholars often move away from a framework of traditional subject matters as the primary basis for responding to the "what" question toward a curriculum that is more based on capabilities (e.g., Biggeri & Santi, 2012) or values (e.g., Lovat et al., 2010).

Framing the Discourse on Well-Being in Schools: The Book's Contributions

My reading of the current scholarly and professional discourses on well-being in school education outlined in the previous section suggests that the following is currently missing or insufficiently developed: consideration of the range of disciplinary perspectives on well-being in schools; an integration of these perspectives; and a consideration of scholarship from traditions other than those currently prominent in scholarship on well-being in schools, particularly in educational scholarship. In my view, this book addresses each of these concerns to some degree by bringing together the work from scholars from a range of educational fields of studies under one general heading: well-being in schools.[4] What I find particularly exciting about this book project is that even those chapter authors whose research had not heretofore been focused on well-being in schools were able to demonstrate that direct connections to their work and the core ideas and themes of the book can fruitfully be made. Each chapter stands on its own within the demands and traditions of the scholarship of a particular educational field of study, but each nevertheless contributes different perspectives under the theme of well-being in schools.

To this end, the book is structured into four parts that reflect the different research domains discussed in the previous section: philosophical foundations; conceptualizing well-being; the school and social ecology of and for well-being; and curriculum, teaching, and learning for well-being. The scholars offer perspectives from different areas of educational studies. What follows in the remainder of this introductory chapter is my attempt to link the different chapter contributions within as well as across different parts and thus provide an outline of a general framework for those interested in a more comprehensive approach to well-being in schools. Accordingly, rather than describing the focus of and ideas developed in each of the chapters in turn, I indicate how in my view each of the book chapters contributes to such an integrative framework. I need to point out that what follows is based in this specific rationale and, thus, will leave out other contributions that a chapter makes to the overall purpose of the book.

In table 1.1, I present this integrative framework in the form of statements derived from the work presented in the referenced chapters and that are directed at those who are concerned with the theory and practice of well-being within the school system. The statements are structured by the foci that distinguish the four different parts of this book,

Table 1.1. Integrative framework statements

Foundational Matters

- Making well-being a core focus of school education requires *a conceptual commitment* – a commitment to understanding *well-being* in a particular way – because different conceptions have different implications for programming in schools due to them having different theoretical and practical implications (chapter 2).
- Making well-being a core focus of school education requires *value commitments* in response to the following four questions (chapter 3):
  - Should education for well-being be a goal of school education?
  - If yes, what is the relationship between this goal and other goals of school education?
  - If yes, what are the capabilities ("educational goods"), to be developed through schooling, that are linked to the conception of well-being?
  - How should these educational goods be *distributed*, given limited resources (including time) available in school education to do so?
- Any approaches of conceptualizing well-being for an individual person (individual well-being) need to be complemented by an *ethic of well-being* that connects that concept with the normative perspective of an ethic (chapter 4).

Conceptual Matters

- Conceptualizing human well-being requires a commitment to particular assumptions about humans as living beings. For instance, if humans are meaning-making beings, being able to make meaning in life is a central aspect of human well-being (chapter 6); if humans are relational beings, the quality of these relationships is a central aspect of human well-being (chapters 5 and 8).
- A *general* conceptual framework of understanding well-being can be useful across different cultural contexts (chapter 5).
- A *specific* conception of well-being might need to pertain to a cultural and even communal context. Particularly, conceptions might be distinguished to account for cultural differences between more individualistic and more collective cultures (chapters 5 and 9).
- Conceptualizing human well-being requires developing conceptual details (chapter 6).
- Conceptualizing well-being in schools needs to include the well-being of staff in schools and the school system (chapter 7).
- The well-being of professionals working in schools and school divisions (teachers and other school-based professionals) is particularly challenged due to the nature of their work (chapter 7).

Contextual Matters

- Making well-being a core focus of school education is best approached through a whole-school approach (chapter 8).
- Making well-being a core focus of school education needs to be organizationally supported by linking this focus to legislation, policy, and communal and parental responsibilities (chapter 8).
- The professionals working in a school system that has made well-being a core focus need to be prepared to be able to support this focus (chapters 7 and 8).
- A holistic understanding of well-being in schools considers the need for understanding flourishing communities and flourishing community living, which schools and school life are an integral part of. How we understand flourishing communities and flourishing community living needs to be informed by the community itself and its history and culture (chapter 9).

(*Continued*)

Table 1.1. Integrative framework statements (Continued)

Contextual Matters (cont.)

- At a structural level, schools and school systems are complex adaptive social systems. Understanding well-being in schools requires an understanding of those systems, their interactions, and how they create expectational constraints and agentic possibilities for human living (chapter 10).
- Making well-being the focus of school educational programming, the evaluation of such programming requires an evaluation methodology that is adequate to the understanding of school and school systems as complex adaptive social systems. Thus, if schools and school systems are understood as such, educational program evaluation needs to select methodologies adequate to programming in complex adaptive systems, like developmental evaluation (chapter 11).

Curriculum, Teaching, and Learning Matters

- Well-being requires the development of capabilities, which require organized learning in schools, which in turn requires learning based on a curriculum (chapter 12).
- If the traditional subject-matter teaching stays in place, such learning needs to *systematically and intentionally* be undertaken within the teaching of the subject matter (chapter 15), a goal which is indeed possible (chapters 12–14).
- A conceptual and theoretical framework for well-being in school education is needed to frame the curricular work in the classroom (chapters 12–14).
- Educational concerns for the learning of mathematics can be integrated into/framed by education for well-being (chapter 12).
- Educational concerns in science education, like sustainability and social justice education, can be integrated into/framed by education for well-being (chapter 13).
- Educational concerns in and approaches to teaching creative writing can be integrated into/framed by education for well-being (chapter 14).

---

although some ideas and topics presented in a chapter of one part will overlap with those found in other sections.

The statements in table 1.1, structured into four sections that correspond to the four parts of the book, provide an *integrative framework for well-being in schools*, which can be used as a guide by those concerned with and for a theory and practice of well-being in schools. This framework is *integrative* in the sense that the statements in the different categories integrate the different categories through a meaningful network of statements that interlink philosophical foundations of school education, conceptualization of purpose, ecological contextualization of school education, curricularization of school education, and teaching and learning in schools. Because the statements have been derived from the chapters of this book, we can say that table 1.1 suggests an integrative framework for well-being in schools as it can be cumulatively derived from the chapters in this book.

In the book's concluding chapter (chapter 15), I will revisit this integrative framework and inquire into the direction in which the main ideas presented in table 1.1 can be expanded upon through future research. Accordingly, the concluding chapter will list possible questions for research that builds upon the ideas presented in this book.

Finally, I want to take this opportunity to inform the reader of a project that derived from the authors' joint work on this book and that is to complement the book. While the book provided the contributors with an opportunity to present their ideas on the theme of the book in chapter format, it has not provided us with an opportunity to engage with each other on the same subtheme and to have that engagement also made available to audience. For this reason, the authors of all of the chapters have agreed to participate in a discussion with the other authors whose chapters address the same subtheme, to have these discussions audio-recorded, and then to have these recordings made public as part of a podcast series on the topic of this book. This podcast series, entitled *Well-Being in Schools*, is to complement this book and is to be made available to the public at https://umfm.com/series at the time of the publication of this book.

NOTES

1. There are different spellings and translations for this notion in use. The Cree scholar Michael Hart (2002) uses *mino-pimatisiwin* ("the good life"), while Anishinaabe scholar Nicole Bell uses *mino-bimaadiziwin* ("living life in a good way," "living a good life").
2. Recently, a team of Canadian researchers has not just been making substantial contributions to the second branch (e.g., Cherkowski & Walker, 2018a; Kutsyuruba et al., 2021; Walker et al., 2021), but is also contributing to the scholarship bridging the two branches (e.g., Cherkowski & Walker, 2018b).
3. Noddings (2003) uses the term *happiness* in the sense of well-being and flourishing (p. 10).
4. For a comparable contribution, see the scholarship referenced in note 2.

REFERENCES

Adler, M.J. (1982). *The Paideia Proposal: An educational manifesto*. Collier Macmillan Publishers.

Alder, N. (2002). Interpretations of the meaning of care: Creating caring relationships in urban middle school classrooms. *Urban Education, 37*(2), 241–66. https://doi-org.uml.idm.oclc.org/10.1177/0042085902372005 https://doi.org/10.1177/0042085902372005

Aldridge, J.M., Fraser, B.J., Fozdar, F., Ala'I, K., Earnest, J., & Afari, E. (2016). Students' perceptions of school climate as determinants of well-being, resilience and identity. *Improving Schools, 19*(1), 5–26. https://doi.org/10.1177/1365480215612616

Allport, G.W. (1955). *Becoming: Basic considerations for a psychology of personality.* Yale University Press.

Bacete, F.J.G., Perrin, G.M., Schneider, B.H., & Blanchard, C. (2014). Effects of school on the well-being of children and adolescents. In A. Ben-Arieh, F. Casas, I. Frønes, & J.E. Korbin (Eds.), *Handbook of child well-being: Theories, methods and policies in global perspective* (pp. 1251–305). Springer.

Ballet, J., Biggeri, M., & Comin, F. (2011). Children's agency and the Capabilities Approach: A conceptual framework. In M. Biggeri, J. Ballet, & F. Comin, (Eds.), *Children and the Capabilities Approach* (pp. 22–45). Palgrave Macmillan.

Bell, N., (2016). Mino-bimaadiziwin: Education for the good life. In F. Deer & T. Falkenberg (Eds.), *Indigenous perspective on education for well-being in Canada* (pp.7–20). Education for Sustainable Well-Being Press. https://www.eswb-press.org/publications.html

Ben-Arieh, A. (2008). The child indicators movement: Past, present, and future. *Child Indicators Research, 1*, 3–16. https://doi.org/10.1007/s12187-007-9003-1

Benner, A., & Graham, S. (2011). Latino adolescents' experiences of discrimination across the first 2 years of high school: Correlates and influences on educational outcomes. *Child Development, 28*(2), 508–19. https://doi.org/10.1111/j.1467-8624.2010.01524.x

Biggeri, M., Libanora, R., Mariani, S., & Menchini, L. (2006). Children conceptualizing their capabilities: Results of a survey conducted during the First Children's World Congress on Child Labour. *Journal of Human Development, 7*(1), 59–83. https://doi.org/10.1080/14649880500501179

Biggeri, M., & Santi, M. (2012). The missing dimensions of children's well-being and well-becoming in education systems: Capabilities and philosophy for children. *Journal of Human Development and Capabilities, 13*(3), 373–95. https://doi.org/10.1080/19452829.2012.694858

Brighouse, H. (2006). *On education.* Routledge.

Bronfenbrenner, U. (1979). *The ecology of human development: Experiments by nature and design.* Harvard University Press.

Cherkowski, S., & Walker, K. (2013). Schools as sites of human flourishing: Musings on efforts to foster sustainable learning communities. *Journal of Educational Administration and Foundations, 23*(2), 139–54.

– (2016). Purpose, passion and play: Exploring the construct of flourishing from the perspective of school principals. *Journal of Educational Administration, 54*(4), 378–92. http://dx.doi.org/10.1108/JEA-10-2014-0124

- (2018a). *Teacher wellbeing: Noticing, nurturing, sustaining, and flourishing in schools*. Word & Deed Publishing.
- (Eds.). (2018b). *Perspectives on flourishing schools*. Lexington Books.

Connelly, F.M., & Clandinin, D.J. (1988). *Teachers as curriculum planners: Narratives of experience*. Teachers College Press.

Cuthbert, R. (2020). Sigurbjorg Stefansson Early School: Learning naturally. In C. O'Brien & P. Howard (Eds.), *Living schools: Transforming education* (pp. 67–78). Education for Sustainable Well-Being Press. https://www.eswb-press.org/publications.html

Falkenberg, T. (2018). Assessing student well-being: Providing for student voice. In S. Cherkowski & K. Walker (Eds.), *Perspectives on flourishing in schools* (pp. 111–26). Lexington Books.
- (2019). *Framing human well-being and well-becoming: An integrated systems approach*. www.wellbeinginschools.ca/paper-series
- (2020). An ethic of sustainable well-being and well-becoming: A systems approach to virtue ethics. In H. Bai, D. Chang, & C. Scott. (Eds.). *A book of ecological virtues: Living well in the Anthropocene* (pp. 157–77). University of Regina Press.

Falkenberg, T., & Krepski, H. (2020). On conceptualizing child well-being: Drawing on disciplinary understanding of childhood. *Canadian Journal of Education 43*(4), 891–917. www.cje-rce.ca

Falkenberg, T., Ukasoanya, G., & Krepski, H. (2021). Students' understanding of student well-being: A case study. *McGill Journal of Education*, *56*(2/3), 201–24. https://mje.mcgill.ca/issue/view/575.

Fraillon, J. (2004). *Measuring student well-being in the context of Australian schooling: Discussion paper*. Retrieved from http://research.acer.edu.au/well_being/8
- (2005). *Measuring student well-being in the context of Australian schooling: Discussion paper*. Ministerial Council on Education, Employment, Training and Youth Affairs. Retrieved from http://cmapspublic.ihmc.us/rid=1LHK7QMY7-267PTX2-2R2N/Fraillon.pdf

Furlong, M.J., Gilman, R., Huebner, E.S. (Eds.). (2014). *Handbook of positive psychology in schools* (2nd ed.). Routledge.

Gay, G. (2000). *Culturally responsive teaching: Theory, research, and practice*. Teachers College Press.

Gray, J., Galton, M., McLaughlin, C., Clarke, B., & Symonds, J. (2011). *The supportive school: Wellbeing and the young adolescent*. Cambridge Scholars Publishing.

Griffin, J. (1986). *Well-being: Its meaning, measurement and moral importance*. Clarendon Press.

Hamilton, M., & Redmond, G. (2010). *Conceptualisation of social and emotional wellbeing for children and young people, and policy implications: A research* report for the Australian Research Alliance for Children and Youth and the Australian Institute of Health and Welfare. Retrieved from http://www.australianchildwellbeing.com.au/research-findings

Hart, M.A. (2002). *Seeking mino-pimatisiwin: An Aboriginal approach to helping*. Fernwood Publishing.

Haworth, J., & Hart, G. (Eds.). (2007). *Well-being: Individual, community and social perspectives*. Palgrave Macmillan.

Hooja, H.R., & Shaktawat, P. (2017). The role of home environment and achievement motivation on psychological well-being among school going children. *Indian Journal of Health and Wellbeing, 8*(7), 697–706. http://www.iahrw.com/index.php/home/journal_detail/19#list

Horgan, G. (2009) "That child is smart because he's rich": The impact of poverty on young children's experiences of school. *International Journal of Inclusive Education, 13*(4), 359–76. https://doi.org/10.1080/13603110802707779

Huebner, E.S., Gilman, R., Reschly, A.L., & Hall, R. (2009). Positive schools. In C.R. Snyder & S.J. Lopez (Eds.), *Oxford handbook of positive psychology* (pp. 561–8). Oxford University Press.

Huebner, E.S., Hills, K.J., Jiang, X., Long, R F., Kelly, R., & Lyons, M.D. (2014). Schooling and children's subjective well-being. In A. Ben-Arieh, F. Casas, I. Frønes, & J.E. Korbin (Eds.), *Handbook of child well-being: Theories, methods and policies in global perspective* (pp. 797–819). Springer.

Janzen, M., Levine, K., & Sutherland, D. (2020). Improving educational experiences for children in our care: An ethic of hospitality. *Canadian Journal of Education, 43*(4), 953–75. www.cje-rce.ca

Kahneman, D., Diener, E., & Schwarz, N. (Eds.). (1999). *Well-being: The foundations of hedonic psychology*. Russell Sage Foundation.

Kutsyuruba, B., Cherkowski, S., & Walker, K.D. (Eds.). (2021). *Leadership for flourishing in educational contexts*. Canadian Scholars Press.

Kutsyuruba, B., Klinger, D.A., & Hussain, A. (2018). The impact of positive school climate on student well-being and achievement. In S. Cherkowski & K. Walker (Eds.), *Perspectives on flourishing in schools* (pp. 69–90). Lexington Books.

Link, M. (2018). *Nature, capabilities, and student well-being: An evaluation of an outdoor education approach* [Doctoral dissertation, University of Manitoba]. MSpace. http://hdl.handle.net/1993/33289

Lovat, T., Toomey, R., & Clement, N. (Eds.). (2010). *International handbook on values education and student wellbeing*. Springer.

Marques, S.C., Lopez, S.J., Rose, S., & Robinson, C. (2014). Measuring and promoting hope in schoolchildren. In M.J. Furlong, R. Gilman, & E.S. Huebner (Eds.), *Handbook of positive psychology in schools* (pp. 35–50). Routledge.

Miller, J.P. (2007). *The holistic curriculum* (2nd ed.). University of Toronto Press.

Minkkinen, J. (2013). The structural model of child well-being. *Child Indicator Research, 6*, 547–58. https://doi.org/10.1007/s12187-013-9178-6

Morrison, W., & Peterson, P. (2013). *Schools as a setting for promoting positive mental health: Better practices and perspectives* (2nd ed.). Pan-Canadian Joint Consortium for School Health.

Munn, P. (2010). How schools can contribute to pupils' well-being. In C. McAuley & W. Rose (Eds.), *Child well-being: Understanding children's lives* (pp. 91–110). Jessica Kingsley Publishers.

Neill, A.S. (1960). *Summerhill: A radical approach to child rearing*. Hart Publishing Company.

Newland, L.A. (2015). Family well-being, parenting, and child well-being: Pathways to healthy adjustment. *Clinical Psychologist, 19*, 3–14. https://doi-org.uml.idm.oclc.org/10.1111/cp.12059 https://doi.org/10.1111/cp.12059

Noble, T., & McGrath, H. (2016). *The PROSPER school pathways for student wellbeing: Policy and practices*. Springer.

Noddings, N. (2003). *Happiness and education*. Cambridge University Press.

Nussbaum, M.C. (2011). *Creating capabilities: The human development approach*. Cambridge, MA: Harvard University Press.

Pinar, W.F., Reynolds, W.M., Slattery, P., & Taubman, P.M. (1995). *Understanding curriculum: An introduction to the study of historical and contemporary curriculum discourses*. Peter Lange.

Reupert, A. (2020). *Mental health and academic learning in schools: Approaches to facilitating the wellbeing of children and young people*. Routledge.

Rudduck, J. (2007). Student voice, student engagement, and school reform. In D. Thiessen & A. Cook-Sather (Eds.), *International handbook of student experience in elementary and secondary school* (pp. 587–610). Springer.

Sen, A. (2009a). Capability and well-being. In M.C. Nussbaum & A. Sen (Eds.), *The quality of life* (pp. 30–53). Clarendon Press. (First published 1993)

– (2009b). *The idea of justice*. Harvard University Press.

Shernoff, D.J., Abdi, B., Anderson, B., & Csikszentmihalyi, M. (2014). Flow in schools revisited: Cultivating engaged learners and optimal learning environments. In M.J. Furlong, R. Gilman, & E.S. Huebner (Eds.), *Handbook of positive psychology in schools* (pp. 211–26). Routledge.

Simmons, C., Graham, A., & Thomas, N. (2015). Imagining an ideal school for wellbeing: Locating student voice. *Journal of Educational Change, 16*(2), 129–44. https://doi.org/10.1007/s10833-014-9239-8

Smyth, J. (2007). Toward the pedagogically engaged school: Listening to student voice as a positive response to disengagement and 'dropping out'? In D. Thiessen & A. Cook-Sather (Eds.), *International handbook of student experience in elementary and secondary school* (pp. 635–58). Springer.

Soutter, A.K., Gilmore, A., & O'Steen, B. (2011). How do high school youths' educational experiences relate to well-being? Towards a trans-disciplinary conceptualization. *Journal of Happiness Studies, 12,* 591–631. https://doi.org/10.1007/s10902-010-9219-5

Soutter, A.K., O'Steen, B., & Gilmore, A. (2014). The student well-being model: A conceptual framework for the development of student well-being indicators. *International Journal of Adolescence and Youth, 19*(4), 496–520. https://doi.org/10.1080/02673843.2012.754362

Spratt, J. (2017). *Wellbeing, equity and education: A critical analysis of policy discourses of wellbeing in schools.* Springer.

Steele, D.M., & Cohn-Vargas, B. (2013). *Identity safe classrooms: Places to belong and learn.* Corwin.

Veenhoven, R. (2008). Sociological theories of subjective well-being. In M. Eid & R.J. Larsen (Eds.), *The science of subjective well-being* (pp. 44–61). The Guilford Press.

Walker, K.D., Kutsyuruba, B., & Cherkowski, S. (Eds.). (2021). *Positive leadership for flourishing schools.* Information Age Publishing.

Warren, E., & Miller, J. (2016). *Mathematics at the margin.* Springer.

White, M.A., & Murray, A.S. (Eds.). (2015). *Evidence-based approaches in positive education: Implementing a strategic framework for well-being in schools.* Springer.

Wotherspoon, T. (2009). *The sociology of education in Canada* (3rd ed.). Oxford University Press.

PART ONE

Foundational Questions on Well-Being and Well-Becoming in Schools

2 Three Theories of Well-Being and Their Implications for School Education

ERIK MAGNUSSON AND HEATHER KREPSKI

In Western industrialized societies, school education has traditionally focused on preparing students for adult life by equipping them with the knowledge, skills, and dispositions required to become active citizens and productive economic contributors. On this approach toward school education – call it the *standard preparatory model* – student success has typically been defined in terms of the successful acquisition of curricular content knowledge across a variety of academic disciplines as well as in the development of transferable cognitive skills such as problem solving, critical thinking, and effective communication. Recently, however, some educational researchers have begun to challenge this approach by emphasizing the role of schools in cultivating student well-being (Gilman, Huebner & Furlong, 2009; Noddings, 2003; OECD, 2017; White, 2011). On this alternative approach toward school education – call it the *well-being model* – student success not only (or even primarily) consists in the successful acquisition of curricular content knowledge or transferable cognitive skills, but also in the development of a broader set of skills and dispositions that will enable students to live flourishing lives, both as the children they are and as the adults they will eventually become.

The well-being model represents a more holistic approach toward school education, one that has the potential to radically transform contemporary thinking about the purpose and function of schools. However, developing this model to a point where it can be implemented presents a number of theoretical challenges, not the least of which is articulating the theory of well-being on which it is based. Well-being is a deeply contested concept, and different theories of well-being offer different and sometimes competing accounts of what it means to live a flourishing life. Thus, in order to determine what the well-being model is committed to – as well as how, and to what extent, it diverges from the standard preparatory model – proponents must first settle the question of what, exactly, they mean when they talk about "well-being."

In this chapter, we draw on recent philosophical work on well-being in order to shed light on this question. Our main goal is not to defend a particular theory of well-being to serve as the basis for the well-being model, but rather to offer a framework through which a defensible theory can be arrived at. In a nutshell, we believe that proponents of the well-being model must be guided by two sets of considerations when thinking about the theory of well-being it is based on: (1) the attractiveness and internal coherence of the theory itself (that is, how well it accords with, explains, and systematizes our pre-theoretical intuitions about well-being); and (2) the implications of that theory in the context of school education. In a perfect world, both of these considerations would align, and an independently attractive theory of well-being would lead to palatable practical implications when applied in the context of school education. As we hope to demonstrate, however, this is not always the case: some theories of well-being have attractive implications in the context of school education while facing serious objections at the level of theory, while other theories of well-being are sounder at the level of theory while leading to unattractive implications in the context of school education. This leaves proponents of the well-being model with difficult choices to make as they seek to combine conceptual rigour with practical applicability when developing their model.

The chapter is divided into two parts. In the first part, we introduce the general concept of well-being and outline three leading substantive theories of well-being: *hedonism, desire fulfilment,* and *objective list theories*. In the second part, we explain what each theory of well-being implies in the context of school education and how it may support or diverge from the standard preparatory model.

Three Theories of Well-Being

If we are to propose a model of schooling that takes the cultivation of well-being as a central goal and measure, then we need to define what we mean by well-being. On the one hand, this might seem like a daunting task – after all, philosophers have been debating the concept of well-being for over 2500 years, and much of this debate has been characterized by deep and pervasive disagreement about its nature and constituents. On the other hand, the long-standing debate about well-being has also resulted in a set of sophisticated theories about what well-being is, how it is achieved, and what role it ought to play in our practical reasoning, providing a rich framework in which to gain clarity about how this central concept should be understood. It is not necessary to provide a definitive theory of well-being in order to further the project of developing a model of well-being in schools, though proponents of this model should at least be aware of what type of theory they endorse and how it fits within the broader philosophical landscape, including the types of claims it is committed to and the objections it faces from rival theories.

A useful place to begin in getting a handle on these issues is to distinguish the general concept of well-being from the various theories of well-being that have gained currency among philosophers. In the philosophical literature, the general concept of well-being is normally understood as indicating what is non-instrumentally or ultimately good for a person (Crisp, 2016). On this understanding, well-being is a measure of how well a person's life is going for that person, or from the perspective of their own interests. Things that have a positive effect on a person's well-being are things that are good for that person, or which benefit them or contribute to their interest or advantage, while things that have a negative effect on a person's well-being are things that are bad for that person, or which harm them or detract from their interest or advantage (Campbell, 2015, p. 403).

Different theories of well-being provide different accounts of what is ultimately good for a person and why. For the purposes of this chapter, it is useful to distinguish between two types of theory. *Substantive* or *enumerative* theories seek to provide a list of items that are ultimately good for a person. The question these theories seek to answer is: what kinds of things make a person's life go better for them? *Formal* or *explanatory* theories, by contrast, seek to provide an explanation of *why* these items are good for a person, or offer an account of their good-making features. The question these theories seek to answer is: what makes a particular thing good for a person? (Rodogno, 2016). In this chapter, we limit our focus to providing an overview of substantive theories of well-being that seek to provide a concrete account of the things that make a person's life go well. This, after all, is the most important type of theory for developing a model of well-being in schools: while we can develop such a model without a sophisticated understanding of *why* a particular set of goods makes a person's life go well, we cannot develop such a model without a clear understanding of *what* those goods actually are.

Hedonism

Following a taxonomy originally introduced by Derek Parfit (1984, Appendix I), it is now common for philosophers to distinguish between three main substantive theories of well-being: *hedonistic*, *desire fulfilment*, and *objective list* theories. Hedonistic theories conceive of well-being as the balance of pleasure over pain, where "pleasure" can be understood broadly to include a range of positive feelings and mental states, and "pain" can be understood broadly to include a range of negative feelings and mental states. On the simplest version of this view, often called *simple* or *quantitative* hedonism, a person fares better or worse in their lives according to how much of their total experience is characterized by pleasurable states as opposed to painful states, combined with the intensity of those experiences.

For many philosophers since antiquity, hedonism has seemed quite plausible as a theoretical model of well-being – after all, well-being is a measure of what is non-instrumentally good for a person, and pleasure is a good that is an end in itself, to which many other goods are often just means. Nevertheless, hedonism prompts a number of important objections. First, many critics have questioned the idea that all forms of pleasure are equally valuable. Imagine, for example, there are two people who derive an equal amount of pleasure from two different activities: (1) composing music on the piano, and (2) counting blades of grass on their front lawn. It is plausible that a creative activity like composing music contributes more to a person's well-being than a pointless activity like counting blades of grass, though simple hedonism cannot distinguish between them so long as the pleasure they yield is of equal intensity and duration.

Some philosophers have simply bitten the bullet on this issue and conceded that all forms of pleasure are equally valuable. Jeremy Bentham (1830), for example, famously proclaimed that "Prejudice apart, the game of push-pin[1] is of equal value with the arts and sciences of music or poetry" (p. 206) so long as it yields equal pleasure for those who engage in it. Others, however, have attempted to accommodate this objection by adopting a *qualitative* version of hedonism that distinguishes between pleasures of different kinds. For instance, John Stuart Mill (1859, 1863) argued that we can distinguish between "higher" and "lower" pleasures based on the preferences of people who have experienced both kinds. This type of view is compatible with attributing greater prudential value to the pleasure gained from composing a sonata to the pleasure gained from counting blades of grass, and so is thought by proponents to avoid the counterintuitive implications of treating all pleasures equally.

Whether or not qualitative versions of hedonism can truly avoid these implications is a matter of controversy – some critics have questioned whether they even count as forms of hedonism given that non-hedonic values must be invoked to determine what are considered "higher" and "lower" forms of pleasure (Feldman, 1997). In either case, however, qualitative versions of hedonism still face a second major objection to hedonism generally, which challenges the notion that pleasure is the *only* thing that matters for a person's well-being. While the experience of pleasure must figure prominently in any plausible theory of well-being, we also seem to value a wide range of goods and experiences that have little or no hedonic value. For example, we tend to value having the freedom to choose our own careers or places of residence, even if it can sometimes result in anxiety or indecisiveness. Similarly, we tend to value honesty in our interactions with friends, family, and colleagues, even if their revelations can sometimes hurt us deeply. If we think that a life devoid of these goods is worse than a life that includes them – despite potentially scoring higher on the hedonic index – then we might think that hedonism is incomplete as a theory of well-being.

A proponent of hedonism might respond to this objection by claiming that a life containing goods like freedom and honesty tends to be more pleasurable on balance than a life that is devoid of them, such that these goods can also be justified indirectly on hedonistic grounds. It is of course debatable whether this response provides the best interpretation of why we value goods like freedom or honesty; even if it succeeds, however, hedonism still faces a third major objection, which challenges the assumption that well-being can be wholly determined by a person's mental states. In a famous version of this objection, Robert Nozick (1974) presents the following thought experiment:

> Suppose there was an experience machine that would give you any experience you desired. Super-duper neuropsychologists could stimulate your brain so that you would think and feel you were writing a great novel, or making a friend, or reading an interesting book. All the time you would be floating in a tank, with electrodes attached to your brain. Should you plug into this machine for life, preprogramming your life experiences? (pp. 44–5)

If well-being were wholly determined by our mental states, then we should all plug into the experience machine and guarantee ourselves pleasurable mental states for the rest of our lives. However, most people would not regard this as any kind of flourishing life, which suggests that factors other than pleasurable mental states are important determinants of well-being.

Desire Fulfilment

Desire fulfilment theories are one family of theories that take a more expansive view of well-being. According to these theories, well-being consists in the fulfilment of a person's desires, such that what is ultimately good for a person is getting the things they want, whatever they happen to be. Desire theories may overlap with hedonistic theories insofar as we desire to experience a range of pleasurable mental states, though they can also register prudential value in other types of goods to the extent that those goods form the object of a person's desires. This allows them to sidestep some of the major objections that apply to hedonistic theories. For example, they are able to account for the prudential value of goods and experiences with potentially low hedonic value, like freedom or honesty in one's social interactions, and they would not recommend plugging into the experience machine, where most of our desires would in fact go unfulfilled.

One of the major appeals of desire theories lies in their strongly subjectivist nature. It is plausible that what is ultimately good for a person will have a strong connection to what that person finds to be compelling or attractive; as Peter Railton (1986) claims, "It would be an intolerably alienated conception of someone's good to imagine that it might fail in any way to engage him" (p. 9). This presents a possible advantage over more objectivist theories of well-being, including objective list theories, which attribute prudential value to certain items regardless of a person's attitude toward them.

Despite this appeal, however, desire fulfilment theories also entail a number of challenges. The first challenge is to specify the *type* of desire whose fulfilment contributes to a person's well-being. On the simplest interpretation of the desire theory, the satisfaction of our *actual* desires contributes to our well-being, but this interpretation involves some serious problems. First, due either to weakness of will or ignorance about the facts, we often desire things that are actually bad for us, including foods that are unhealthy, relationships that are toxic, or careers that leave us feeling burnt-out or empty. It seems implausible to suggest that the satisfaction of *these* desires contributes to our well-being. Similarly, some people have desires that are malicious or ignoble, such as desires to harm other people, or for a variety of other injustices to come to fruition. Counting the satisfaction of *these* desires as determinants of well-being might also seem misguided.

On a different interpretation of the desire theory, the satisfaction of *idealized* desires contributes to our well-being. On this interpretation, what is ultimately good for a person is to get what they *would* desire if they were fully informed and acting rationally in pursuit of their good (Rawls, 1971, p. 417). This interpretation may avoid the problem of misinformed and/or malicious desires – we may not want what is bad for ourselves or others if we are fully informed and rational – though it also brings a few problems of its own. First, in associating a person's well-being with the satisfaction of idealized as opposed to actual desires, the idealized interpretation largely abandons the desire theory's subjectivist appeal. Indeed, by focusing on what we *would* want in a hypothetical scenario characterized by full information and rationality, the idealized interpretation looks less like a version of the desire theory and more like a thought experiment for arriving at a defensible list of objective goods. Moreover, unless this interpretation can provide a fairly clear account of the content of idealized desires, it also runs the risk of circularity, suggesting that well-being consists in the satisfaction of the desires that we *would* have if we were fully informed and acting rationally in pursuit of our well-being (Heathwood, 2015, p. 140). But this simply begs the question – it does not give us a clear picture of the kinds of things that contribute to a person's well-being, and therefore fails as a substantive theory.

A second challenge for the desire theory is specifying the *scope* of the desires whose fulfilment contributes to a person's well-being. Many of our desires are desires about our own lives, including things we want to have or the type of people we want to be (e.g., "I want a wife and kids"; "I want to become a doctor"), yet other desires are desires about other people's lives or about general states of affairs (e.g., "I want my friend to be happy"; "I want the Bornean Orangutan to avoid extinction"). It is easy to understand how the satisfaction of the former desires would have prudential value for the desirer, though it is less clear how the satisfaction of the latter desires would. Consider, for example, the following case from Parfit (1984):

> Suppose I meet a stranger who has what is believed to be a fatal disease. My sympathy is aroused, and I strongly want this stranger to be cured. We never meet again. Later, unknown to me, the stranger is cured. (p. 494)

On Parfit's view, it is implausible to suggest that the stranger's being cured could have any effect on his well-being, suggesting that an unrestricted version of the desire theory – that is, one that places no restrictions on the scope of the desires whose fulfilment contributes to a person's well-being – is false.

Parfit's example suggests two possible restrictions on the scope of relevant desires: the first is the requirement that the desire be *self-regarding*, or principally about our own lives, while the second is the requirement that we *experience* the fulfilment of the desire in some tangible way. Either or both of these restrictions could explain why the recovery of the stranger has no effect on Parfit's well-being. For example, the recovery of the stranger could lack prudential value because it is not a self-regarding desire, and/or because it is unknown to Parfit and thus cannot be experienced in any tangible way. However, not everyone agrees that these restrictions are warranted, and there are compelling counter-examples that seem to suggest otherwise. Consider, for example, Julio's desire that Argentina win the World Cup. This desire is not self-regarding – Julio does not himself play for the team – though it seems uncontroversial to claim that the satisfaction of this desire would have significant prudential value for him (indeed, it would be impossible to explain the phenomenon of sports fandom if we did not assume this to be the case). Or consider Brian's desire that his wife remain faithful to him. Even if Brian never experiences the non-fulfilment of this desire – suppose his wife has an affair that is forever concealed from him – it is plausible to claim that his life still goes worse in some way as a result of its non-fulfilment. Examples like these suggest that other-regarding and "unexperienced" desires can also count toward determining well-being, though taking this stance might mean accepting counter-intuitive implications in other types of cases, including the implication that our lives can go better or worse according to the unknown fate of a distant stranger. Proponents of the desire theory will have to resolve these tensions in one way or another.

Objective List Theories

The preceding responses to the problems of misinformed and unexperienced desires suggest that our well-being can be determined by factors other than our own subjective experiences. This is one of the assumptions behind *objective list* theories of well-being, which hold that what is ultimately good for a person is to be in possession of a particular list of objective goods, such as health, love, family, friendship, leisure, knowledge, freedom, fulfilment, and many others. For many people, objective list theories will bear the strongest resemblance to their pre-theoretical intuitions about well-being. For example, if you ask a person at the bus stop "What makes a person's life go well?" chances are they will rattle off a diverse list of items rather than identifying a singular determinant of well-being, such as pleasure or desire-fulfilment. In this sense, objective list theories have a strong intuitive appeal.

Because there is a wide range of items that can be designated as objective goods, objective list theories comprise a wide and varied class of theories; nevertheless, they tend to share two important features (Fletcher, 2015, p. 148).[2] The first feature is *pluralism* about prudential value, meaning that objective list theories tend to identify a range of different items that are ultimately good for a person, while the second feature is *attitude-independence*, meaning that objective list theories attribute prudential value to these items regardless of a person's attitude toward them. Taken together, these features provide a formidable bulwark against some of the major objections that apply to other theories of well-being. For example, because they can include a plurality of goods, objective list theories can account for the value of hedonic experience while avoiding the pitfalls of hedonism – pleasure can simply be listed as one good among many (thus avoiding the implications of claiming that pleasure is the *only* prudential good) and they would not recommend plugging into an experience machine, as this would preclude the enjoyment of other objective goods. Similarly, because they measure well-being according to certain objective criteria, objective list theories can also explain why a person's life goes poorly even when they are subjectively satisfied with their current state of affairs. This can make sense of some important cases. Consider, for example, a woman in a deeply patriarchal society who is happy to live a life of subservience to her husband because she has internalized her society's cultural norms. The desire fulfilment theory might have trouble explaining why this woman's life goes poorly given that she desires to a live a life of subservience to her husband, though objective list theories can provide a different diagnosis due to its absence of goods that are partially constitutive of well-being, including freedom, autonomy, or independence. For many proponents of objective list theories, this counts as a significant advantage (see Nussbaum, 2000; Sen, 1999).

However, while pluralism and attitude-independence supply objective list theories with their greatest strengths, they are also the source of their most notable weaknesses. Consider first the feature of pluralism about prudential value. This feature allows objective list theories to account for a wide range of goods that we intuitively associate with living well, though it also brings with it the problem of *arbitrariness*: what reason do we have for endorsing list a, b, and c over list x, y, and z, other than our own intuitive judgments about well-being? For some critics, objective list theories represent nothing more than an unconnected heap of goods masquerading as a theory of well-being. Moreover, there are some circumstances in which we need to compare the well-being of different individuals, though objective list theories seem ill-equipped to facilitate this given that they cannot provide a single metric of comparison. Suppose, for example, that we endorse an objective list comprising goods x, y, and z. How do we compare the life of person A, who possesses x and y but is deficient in z, with the life of person B, who possesses z and y but is deficient in x? This seems difficult if not impossible in the absence of a complex ranking or weighting of different goods, which is itself vulnerable to the charge of arbitrariness.

Consider next the feature of attitude-independence. This feature allows objective list theories to measure a person's well-being independently of their own subjective attitudes, though it also brings with it the problem of *alienation*: a person could possess many or most of the goods on a particular objective list while being subjectively dissatisfied with their own life (and vice versa). Recall the woman who is happy to live a life of subservience to her husband. Depending on the content of their respective lists, many objective list theorists will claim that this woman's life goes poorly in certain respects due to a lack of objective goods, including freedom, autonomy, or independence. But suppose this woman's endorsement of her role is the product of deep reflection on her religious or cultural commitments and a genuine desire to maintain the social norms that she holds dear. On what basis can objective list theorists claim that this woman would be better off living under a different type of arrangement? This might seem objectionably paternalistic, particularly when the list itself is subject to the worry about arbitrariness. Objective lists theorists might be able to avoid some of these problems by building desire fulfilment and other subjective criteria into their lists of objective goods, though it is doubtful that they can avoid the problem of alienation entirely, given the sheer diversity of opinion about what it means to live well.

Well-Being and School Education

We can see from this brief overview that while each theory of well-being has a number of attractive features, each is also vulnerable to a number of difficult objections. The ability to satisfactorily respond to these objections is one consideration that must factor into the choice of theory that will serve as the basis for the well-being model. However, beyond considering the attractiveness and internal coherence of each theory, we must also consider its implications in the context of school education, for students, practitioners, administrators, and policymakers. After all, a defensible theory will not only be one that is philosophically sound, but one that also has desirable implications when applied in the relevant context.

As each theory of well-being provides a different account of what is ultimately good for a person and why, each carries a different set of implications for programming in schools. Consider first the theory of hedonism. Applied in the context of school education, this theory implies that schools should aim to maximize students' experience of positive mental states and minimize their experience of negative mental states. Placing students' feelings of pleasure as an aim for school education might at first seem strange and in some ways inconsistent with its preparatory mission. As Kristján Kristjánsson (2012) argues, at least a certain amount of displeasure, disruption, and pain seems necessary to achieve important aims of schooling. At the same time, however, parents, classroom teachers, and other school practitioners who work closely with students demonstrate that they *are* concerned with students' sense of happiness and pleasure while they are at school. For example, Gibbons and Silva (2011) shows that parents and teachers are interested to know the extent to which students are experiencing gladness, enjoyment, excitement, and satisfaction at school. A focus on pleasure and experiences of happiness at school can also be found in the play-based, child-centred, and inquiry-based approaches found in curricula across Canada. For instance, the Reggio Emilia approach, popular in early years education programming, holds that "pleasure, aesthetics and play are essential in any act of learning and knowledge-building" (Rinaldi, 2006, p. 64). Another prominent example in education policy and programming that demonstrates concern for pleasurable states of mind is the *positive education* movement, born out of the burgeoning field of positive psychology. When he first wrote about the field, Martin Seligman characterized positive psychology as being concerned with positive subjective experiences, which include "well-being and satisfaction; flow, joy, the sensual pleasures, and happiness, and constructive cognitions about the future – optimism, hope, and faith" (Seligman & Csikszentmihalyi, 2000, p. 4). Correspondingly, positive education is "a blend of evidence-based learning from the science of positive psychology and best practices in learning and teaching" (White, 2016, p. 2), which includes an emphasis on students' subjective experience of happiness and satisfaction.

So there is clearly an important place in school education for the experience of positive mental states. Challenges start to emerge, however, if we take the cultivation of positive mental states to be the guiding aim of school education. As we hinted at above, one of the obvious drawbacks of this approach is that negative mental states can sometimes accompany valuable educational experiences. For example, imagine that a Grade 1 student, Zoya, experiences painful emotions during the process of learning how to read. A strictly hedonistic approach may recommend that Zoya avoid this discomfort in favour of more pleasurable experiences, though this would cause her to miss out on reading skills that will provide her with other opportunities for well-being in the future.

A proponent of hedonism might respond to this objection by noting that the discomfort Zoya experiences in the short term will be offset by the positive mental states she will experience in the long term from learning how to read, such that it too can be justified on hedonistic grounds. On this view, we are not to apply hedonism discretely to individual experiences, but rather broadly to educational programming so that children have the opportunity to achieve the greatest happiness over the course of their lives. This justificatory approach is perhaps a more plausible interpretation of hedonism as applied to school education, though it comes with some challenges of its own. One such challenge is that hedonism actually seems like a poor justification for many of the attitudes and dispositions that we seek to cultivate in children. For example, when we teach children to be non-prejudicial or tolerant of difference, we do so *not* because this will maximize happiness for children, but rather because it is a requirement of exhibiting respect for persons, and hence something that children ought to do irrespective of its impact on their happiness. Moreover, as hedonism is a subjectivist approach toward well-being, it must also contend with the fact that different children will ultimately take pleasure in different things, which may pose challenges for curriculum development and standardization in education. Proponents of hedonism must resolve these challenges in one way or another.

Consider next desire fulfilment theories of well-being. Like the experience of hedonic value, the satisfaction of desires as a guiding principle for school education might initially seem to conflict with many of its preparatory aims. After all, if the adults in schools simply left students to pursue their own goals and desires, schools may collapse into a state of chaos, particularly if you believe that children are not yet rational agents and lack the capacity to make sound judgments based on normative or moral principles (Schapiro, 1999). However, a focus on desire satisfaction and the experience of setting and achieving one's own unique goals at school (and in life) is actually pervasive in pedagogy and assessment approaches across Canada. Differentiated instruction (DI) and universal design learning (UDL) approaches take students' unique interests, skills, backgrounds, and learning goals as a fundamental starting point throughout the learning and teaching process (Tomlinson, 1999). These "open-ended learning experiences are designed to offer students real choices and opportunities to develop their own voice" (Ontario Ministry of Education, 2011, p. 21). UDL and DI provide "opportunities for different kinds of activities and different means of demonstrating learning" (Ontario Ministry of Education, 2011, p. 22). Correspondingly, student involvement and choice in assessment have become the focus of increasing interest in assessment and evaluation research and policy (Tillema, 2014). For several decades, researchers have been advocating for students to assume much greater ownership over their unique assessment goals (Sadler, 1989) and for teachers to guide assessment processes that enable students to "compete against themselves" as they strive to "achieve stable goals" that are not necessarily shared among students (Tomlinson & Moon, 2013, p. 137).

We must note, however, that the desire fulfilment theory also runs into a number of challenges when taken as a guiding aim of school education. One obvious challenge for this theory is that, at least on the terms of the standard preparatory model, one of the central purposes of school education is to *shape* children's preferences, goals, and ambitions. Thus, taking the fulfilment of children's *existing* preferences as a guiding aim of school education might be putting the cart before the horse. For instance, when we send our children to school, we not only (or even primarily) hope they will get what they desire, but also hope that they will come to desire certain things, such as the ability to learn, to work hard, to treat others with respect, and to contribute positively to their communities. Successfully cultivating these desires in children may conflict in certain ways with measures aimed at satisfying their existing desires.

A second and related challenge for the desire theory is that a child's existing desires can sometimes be misinformed, or otherwise in tension with what is considered best for them from the perspective of their educators, families, or communities. Imagine that new Canadian Solomon starts out his Grade 9 school year with the goal of learning to read, write, and speak in forms that he views as the dominant "Canadian" way in order to fit into certain peer groups and prepare for what he views as a job market that might discriminate against his thick accent. Solomon's teachers, parents, and members of his community might reasonably question whether this goal is a good one, as it could further perpetuate unwarranted feelings of shame, redirect his efforts away from other important academic and personal goals, and later cause a disconnect between him and his family, community, and cultural background. A proponent of the desire theory might suggest that this problem can be avoided by adopting an idealized interpretation of the desire theory that focuses on the fulfilment of desires that children *would* have if they were fully informed and rational. This interpretation may avoid the problem of misinformed desires – Solomon may not desire to assimilate if he was fully informed and rational – though it also seems to leave far less room for students' existing desires to inform choices about their education.

A third challenge facing the desire fulfilment theory is that maximizing or optimizing children's current goals and aims can sometimes conflict with their future goals and aims. Recall the case of Zoya, who experiences discomfort during the process of learning how to read. If Zoya's well-being is promoted by fulfilling her existing desires, then this may entail respecting her desire *not* to learn how to read, though this will inevitably frustrate future desires whose fulfilment is dependent on literacy. A proponent of the desire theory might respond to this problem in a similar way to the proponent of hedonism above and suggest that the desire theory can accommodate it by focusing on the fulfilment of a child's global desires. On this view, schools should not focus on satisfying children's present desires, but rather on providing them with the intellectual resources required to satisfy the global desires they will eventually develop about the shape and content of their entire lives. This is an intelligible response to the problem of temporal desire conflicts, though we should note that an approach focused on global desires may depart significantly from existing approaches like UDL or DI, which seem to focus more on children's present desires.

The last of the three theories of well-being is perhaps the most intuitive and most common, particularly at the policy and systems level within education. Objective list approaches are well-suited to ministries and boards of education whose resource allocation is grounded in metrics of reporting and large-scale data collection. Items related to school buildings, staffing, programs, and initiatives can be categorized into well-being domains which can then be followed up through accountability measures and quantitative data sets. Similarly, an objective list approach to well-being in schools can be itemized under selected domains of well-being for schools to carry out and perhaps even report on. We can see the features and advantages of both pluralism and attitude independence when we look at specific examples of provincial-wide frameworks for well-being in schools across Canada. For example, Ontario's well-being strategy defines well-being as made up of the following components: cognitive, emotional, social, and physical (Ontario Ministry of Education, 2016).

The Ontario strategy aims to foster children's development in these four domains, with the implication that, if realized, it will promote children's well-being. Several school divisions across Canada take a similar approach to conceptualizing well-being as a list of items, and frameworks for well-being in schools exist at federal, provincial, divisional, and local levels (e.g., JCSH, 2016).

Despite their intuitive appeal and practical advantages, however, objective list frameworks also face a number of challenges when applied in educational settings. The first and most obvious challenge is the problem of arbitrariness: what rationale can be provided for the particular list of objective goods that a school division or educational authority takes to be constitutive of well-being? This challenge applies to objective list theories generally, but it seems particularly salient in the context of multicultural societies like Canada, where there is often deep and pervasive disagreement about what kinds of things make our lives go well. Even if this problem can be sidestepped in some way by identifying a general list of all-purpose goods that tend to cross cultural boundaries, further challenges arise when attempting to operationalize this list in a practical setting. By way of illustration, imagine that a rural school division in Ontario follows the provincial well-being strategy and conceptualizes well-being in terms of four domains: cognitive, emotional, social, and physical. The school division now faces several definitional, methodological, and empirical questions such as: How will the division practically define each domain? How will they monitor and assess each domain? How will they ensure that each domain fairly addresses the diverse needs and backgrounds of their student population? How will they weigh the importance of each component within and across domains? How will this particular approach compare approaches employed in other (including urban) school divisions to ensure that students are getting equal access to well-being? These are just a few of the difficult questions that must be addressed before employing an objective list framework in an educational setting.

A second set of challenges stems from the more general problem of alienation, which occurs when an agent's subjective assessment of their own well-being does not track a particular list of objective goods. Students may experience alienation if they are told that, according to a particular objective list measure, their lives are going well when in fact they are subjectively dissatisfied with how their school life is going (or vice versa). Suppose that sixth grader Rosa, who lives in a rural school division in Ontario, is told in her tri-conference interview that she is faring poorly in the social domain of well-being due to her consistent desire to read books during recess rather than engage with her peers. As a natural introvert, however, Rosa is perfectly content with her current level of engagement and would feel uncomfortable having to spend more time socializing rather than reading. An objective list theory must now explain why Rosa is mistaken about her own well-being, though this type of explanation might seem implausible in light of strong subjectivist intuitions about well-being. After all, how could Rosa's well-being exist in a certain level of socialization with her peers if this level of socialization fails in any way to engage her?

A final problem for objective list theories relates to the issue of interpersonal comparisons. Like the standard preparatory model, which evaluates and ranks students based on their acquisition of curricular content knowledge and development of transferable cognitive skills, the well-being model will have application as a means of assessment and a guide to resource allocation. However, because they are pluralistic about value, objective list theories cannot provide a single metric of comparison, which can make comparisons *between* students (to inform decision-making and resources allocation) somewhat complicated. For example, how should the rural Ontario school division compare the well-being of Rosa, who scores very low on the social domain of well-being while scoring very high on all the others, with that of Horatio, who scores very high on the social and physical domains of well-being and moderately on the cognitive and emotional domains? This type of comparison seems difficult in the absence of a complex weighting and ranking of different components of well-being, which is of course also vulnerable to the charge of arbitrariness. To be sure, hedonist and desire fulfilment theories also face challenges in terms of measure and comparison – for instance, there may be epistemic challenges associated with measuring mental states or the fulfilment of desires – though they at least provide a single metric by which well-being can be measured (i.e., positive mental states and fulfilled desires).

Conclusion

In this chapter, we have presented three leading substantive theories of well-being and outlined some of the implications they might have if taken as a guiding aim of school education. While each theory of well-being has a number of attractive features, each also presents a number of important theoretical and practical challenges that must ultimately be addressed if taken as the basis for the well-being model. Proponents of the well-being model must take these challenges seriously as they continue to develop and operationalize this model in Canada and beyond.

NOTES

1 Push-pin was a popular children's game in nineteenth-century England, and so in the context of Bentham's quotation is meant to reflect an unsophisticated form of entertainment.
2 Note, however, that these may not be necessary features of objective list theories. Guy Fletcher (2015), for example, argues that only attitude-independence is a necessary feature, and that pluralism is a common but unnecessary feature.

REFERENCES

Bentham, J. (1830). *The rationale of reward*. Robert Heward.

Campbell, S.M. (2015). The concept of well-being. In G. Fletcher (Ed.) *The Routledge handbook of the philosophy of well-being* (pp. 402–13). Routledge.

Crisp, R. (2016). "Well-Being," In N. Zalta (Ed.), *Stanford Encyclopedia of Philosophy* (Fall 2016 ed.) Stanford University. https://plato.stanford.edu/archives/fall2017/entries/well-being/

Feldman, F. (1997). *Utilitarianism, hedonism, and desert: Essays in moral philosophy*. Cambridge University Press.

Fletcher, G. (2015). Objective list theories. In G. Fletcher (Ed.) *The Routledge handbook of the philosophy of well-being* (pp. 148–60). Routledge.

Gibbons, S., & Silva, O. (2011). School quality, child wellbeing and parents' satisfaction. *Economics of Education Review, 30*(2), 312–31. https://doi.org/10.1016/j.econedurev.2010.11.001

Gilman, R., Huebner, E.S., & Furlong, M.J. (2009). *Handbook of positive psychology in schools*. Routledge.

Heathwood, C. (2015). Desire fulfillment theory. In G. Fletcher (Ed.) *The Routledge handbook of the philosophy of well-being* (pp. 135–47). Routledge.

Joint Consortium for School Health [JCSH]. (2016). *What is comprehensive school health?* www.jcsh-cces.ca

Kristjánsson, K. (2012). Positive psychology and positive education: Old wine in new bottles? *Educational Psychologist, 47*(2), 86–105. https://doi.org/10.1080/00461520.2011.610678

Mill, J.S. (1859). *On liberty*. John W. Parker and Son.

– (1863). *Utilitarianism*. Parker, Son, and Bourn.

Noddings, N. (2003). *Happiness and education*. Cambridge University Press.

Nozick, R. (1974). *Anarchy, state, and utopia*. Basic Books.

Nussbaum, M. (2000). *Women and human development: The capabilities approach*. Cambridge University Press.

OECD. (2017). *PISA 2015 Results (Volume III): Students' Well-Being*. OECD Publishing. https://doi.org/10.1787/9789264273856-en

Ontario Ministry of Education. (2011). *Learning for all: A guide to effective assessment and instruction for all students, Kindergarten to Grade 12*. Queen's Printer for Ontario.

– (2016). *Promoting well-being in Ontario's education system: Ontario's well-being strategy for education. Discussion document*. http://www.edu.gov.on.ca/eng/about/WBDiscussionDocument.pdf

Parfit, D. (1984). *Reasons and persons*. Clarendon Press.

Railton, P. (1986). Facts and values. *Philosophical Topics, 14*(2), 5–31. https://doi.org/10.5840/philtopics19861421

Rawls, J. (1971). *A theory of justice*. Harvard University Press.

Rinaldi, C. (2006). *In dialogue with Reggio Emilia: Listening, researching and learning*. Routledge.

Rodogno, R. (2016). Prudential value or well-being. In T. Brosch & D. Sander (Eds.), *Handbook of value: Perspectives from economics, neuroscience, philosophy, psychology and sociology* (pp. 287–312). Oxford University Press.

Sadler, D.R. (1989). Formative assessment and the design of instructional systems. *Instructional Science, 18*(2), 119–44. https://doi.org/10.1007/BF00117714

Schapiro, T. (1999). What is a child? *Ethics, 109*(4), 715–38. https://doi.org/10.1086/233943

Seligman, M.E.P, & Csikszentmihalyi, M. (2000). Positive psychology: An introduction. *The American Psychologist, 55*(1), 5–14. https://doi.org/10.1037/0003-066X.55.1.5

Sen, A. (1999). *Development as freedom*. Knopf.

Tillema, H. (2014). Student involvement in assessment of their learning. In C. Wyatt-Smith, V. Klenowski, & P. Colbert (Eds.), *Designing assessment for quality learning* (pp. 39–53). Springer.

Tomlinson, C.A. (1999). *The differentiated classroom : Responding to the needs of all learners*. Association for Supervision and Curriculum Development.

Tomlinson, C. Ann, & Moon, T.R. (2013). *Assessment and student success in a differentiated classroom*. Association for Supervision & Curriculum Development.

White, J. (2011). *Exploring well-being in schools: A guide to making children's lives more fulfilling*. Routledge.

White, M.A. (2016). Why won't it stick? Positive psychology and positive education. *Psychology of Well-Being 6*, Article 2. https://doi.org/10.1186/s13612-016-0039-1

3 Three Foundational Questions for Policymakers and Practitioners Concerned with Student Well-Being

HEATHER KREPSKI

Student well-being has become an important focus of attention for school education policy and practice across Canada and in many parts of the world (see chapter 1, this volume). In the Canadian context, student well-being is clearly identified as an area of interest by policymakers and educators in the public K-12 system (see chapter 10, this volume). Yet, as we discuss throughout this book, there is still much work to be done to untangle notions of well-being at the reform level and in classrooms. There is also much work to be done to clarify the theoretical foundations that underpin notions of student well-being, as well as to determine how these conceptions might translate into school programming across socio-political and geographic contexts. Both the conceptualization and implementation processes to address student well-being in schools are value-laden measures that involve choices and trade-offs about what to prioritize for students in schools.

In light of the decision-making processes embedded within school policy and practice, this chapter draws attention to three foundational questions for policymakers' and practitioners' consideration with regard to educating for well-being in K-12 schools. First, how does well-being fit into the aims for school education? In other words, what place does – or should – well-being occupy relative to the other traditional goals for school education, and how might they be incompatible? Second, what are the "educational goods" that we link to student well-being? For instance, should the capacity for building and engaging in healthy personal relationships be considered such an educational good? Third, how do we distribute these goods for well-being in schools? This section outlines various distributive principles school policymakers and practitioners (consciously or not) choose between when it comes to opportunities for well-being in an unequal society with vastly unequal outcomes. This chapter considers the moral and political values involved when selecting educational aims and educational goods for students' well-being at both the reform and teacher-practitioner levels.

Purposes and Aims for Public Schooling

Before embarking on a discussion about the goods and their distribution linked to student well-being, it is important to contextualize the well-being movement within the discourse of aims for education, since it is unclear whether or how educating for well-being fits into the schooling agenda(s).

Endorsing well-being as an educational aim raises several important philosophical questions about the purposes of formal public schooling. These include the questions of whether the pursuit of student well-being in and of itself is an acceptable goal for schooling and, if it is, how it compares and competes with other socially valued goals, such as academic achievement, equity, citizenship, economic prosperity, and social cohesion (Chapman, 2014). Not surprisingly, in a pluralist, or what Mignolo and Walsh call pluriversal (2018, p. 3), democratic society there is considerable disagreement on what the aims for public schooling should be. There are numerous, often competing, aims for education across time, contexts, and between stakeholders. This plurality can be viewed as a strength in a democracy, acting as a buffer against more radical changes in school education. However, competing aims can also hinder or slow the development or progress in any one area. Numerous co-existing aims for public schooling also mean there is less time available to spent on any one aim. These educational aims have corresponding programming, pedagogical, and curricular implications. Therefore, when we speak about well-being as an aim for public schooling, we must give consideration to the landscape of educational aims within which it fits, or doesn't fit, into, as well as how different aims impact programming in schools differently.

David Labaree (2010) and Diane Ravitch (2008) offer separate but complementary historical accounts of ideological views and disputes over how school education has been directed and organized over the past two centuries.[1] Schools, they argue, are a product of a complex history of reform, with several competing aims and objectives. During the first part of the nineteenth century, school reform was at first motivated by a desire to establish or solidify national identity, social order, and social cohesion. For example, Noah Webster argued that schooling ought to promote a strong national identity by promoting a common language among children: "form the child, Webster urged, and you will ultimately form the nation, its government, and the character of its civil society" (Ravitch, 2008, p. 44). Webster's endeavour to promote the aim of social cohesion seems to have had success, considering he sold tens of millions of copies of his blue-backed speller (Ravitch, 2008). At roughly the same time Thomas Jefferson advanced the ideal of educating children to protect the state and its citizens, including future citizens, from potential intrusions or threats. Jefferson wanted children to study history and to be informed enough to protect themselves against attacks on their freedoms and on democracy (Ravitch, 2008, p. 45). At the end of the nineteenth century, however, many school reformers wanted to respond more robustly to the needs of an industrialized labour market; many held the view that the highest purpose for a democratic school system was to promote social efficiency and economic development. The thinking at that time – and arguably still today – was that since most children would grow up to occupy specific social roles (e.g., as farmers, labourers, industrial workers, housewives), schools should focus on training them for these roles (Ravitch, 2008). At this time and by the early twentieth century, schools also began to provide cultural capital, or positional goods, to middle-class families (Labaree, 2010), and "the line between public and private schools grew sharper" (Ravitch, 2008, p. 47). Consequently, educational streaming, beginning in middle schools, was introduced in the early twentieth century, with "streams" determined on predictions about a child's future prospects for higher education (Ravitch, 2008).

> School reformers insisted that the academic curriculum was not appropriate for all children, because most children – especially the children of immigrants and of African Americans – lacked the intellectual capacity or the need to study subjects like algebra and chemistry. Some of the efficiency experts, like John Franklin Bobbitt, argued that girls should not study such subjects because, as future housewives, they had no need or use for them. (Ravitch, 2008, p. 48)

This stratification in schools represented a departure from the original idea that all children should receive an equal education, education that was designed to prepare them for citizenship, build a strong national identity, and protect personal freedoms.

The first half of the twentieth century witnessed competing demands from reformers, for instance to improve the quality of pedagogical approaches in classrooms, especially in terms of being more child-centred, while also expanding accountability and access to schooling based on demands from the public (Labaree, 2010). John Dewey led the charge against the vocational preparatory model of social efficiency, claiming that such an approach was "self-defeating because of rapid advancements in technology and labour markets" (Ravitch, 2008, p. 49). Yet the work of creating curriculum streams and assigning students to them was already deeply entrenched. Facilitated by the introduction of standardized IQ testing during World War I, programs were developed by which educational psychologists were hired by the military to determine quickly which recruits were officer material and which were not (programs which directly affected nearly two million men). When the war was over, the psychologists developed group IQ tests for schools (Ravitch, 2008, p. 52). By the early 1920s, intelligence testing was a regular feature in public education, serving the purposes and aims of social efficiency and preparation for the labour market.

More recently, schools have continued along the path of stratification, streaming, and preparation for the labour market. We can still see Webster's aims for social cohesion and socialization. The introduction of the standards movement in the 1980s, which includes PISA (Program for International Student Assessment), the No Child Left Behind policies in the United States, and the Pan-Canadian Assessment Program in Canada, all point to a commitment from educational leaders to evaluate the aims of education through testing and standardization.

Labaree and Ravitch both point out that, historically, two irreconcilable aims for education have operated simultaneously: social goals versus the individual ambitions of parents. School reformers have fought for social cohesion, social efficiency, and the training of productive citizens. Illustrated by the examples of Webster and Jefferson, these social aims can be complementary but they are also distinct and sometimes in tension with one another. On the other hand, parents and guardians who send children to school want to accrue personal gains and educational advantages, and maintain their station and privilege in the social hierarchy (Labaree, 2010). Labaree argues that schools are a bad way to fix social problems but a good way to express (if not realize) personal dreams (p. 6). The problem is that these aspirations are deeply conflicted and thus the school system is conflicted as well. Though parents may wish to include an agenda for well-being in schools, they also want schools to serve the ambitions they have for their children, while also protecting them from the ambitions of parents of other children. It may be argued that current schooling practices and policies try to have it both ways – our society is simply expanding access to higher education, and expanding it upward, while never really changing the educational position in the "race" (Labaree, 2010, p. 7). The school system can only let my child get ahead of yours, and yours stay ahead of mine, by constantly expanding the system upward, which allows for an increase in educational access, to be followed by an increase in educational advantage.

The long-standing history of these educational aims, which includes the sifting and sorting of students into social positions, raises important considerations about the aims of educating for student well-being. While in some cases student well-being may be compatible with some of these historical aims, there are clearly other cases when it is not. For instance, educating for social efficiency may actually expel (quite literally) any student who does not fall into a pre-identified range of social norms and utility, undoubtedly having negative impacts on their well-being. Further, the predictive streaming model is likely to perpetuate social reproduction in denying access to positional goods for large groups of minoritized and marginalized students (Davies & Guppy, 2014). Teaching for national cohesion and identity may leave many, if not the majority, of Canadian students feeling alienated and like objects of colonial, racial, and ethnic oppression. Other aims for public schooling might overlap with the aim for student well-being, for example, as in the case of educating for economic participation. As I will discuss in the next section, preparation for the labour market can be conceived of as a good that contributes positively to students' flourishing. Indeed, students themselves cite economic reasons as one of their goals and reasons for attending school (Türken et al., 2016). This aim, however may entail hidden costs, such as student anxiety and disillusionment about the hoped-for connection between economic success and overall happiness and well-being (Brighouse et al., 2018).

This description of the broad historical context and of the public-versus- private aims illustrates the vast landscape that a well-being-in-schools agenda wants and needs to be part of. Conceptions of well-being underpinning the goals for schooling invite questions about whether well-being in and of itself represents a robust goal for schooling, or if well-being is the means by which we achieve other ends, such as academic outcomes or economic ends (Chapman, 2014). Advocates for well-being in schools face the question of whether student well-being is instrumental toward the aim of public or private aims for education, or whether the public and private aims for education serve the flourishing of individuals and societies. In the former case, the aim of student well-being is to serve either parental hopes and aspirations for their children or the broader social aims of cohesion, efficiency, or improvement (and the list goes on). The latter case, by contrast, dictates that parental goals and social aims are really to serve student well-being. In other words, well-being as an aim for school education is an end in itself. Both school policy and programming decisions are made based on which of these goals the decision-makers agree with and also how much overlap there is between well-being initiatives, traditional preparatory aims, parental aims, and so on. As I show in the next section, these aims can intersect, although not always.

Educational Goods for Well-Being

Another foundational question for the well-being-in-schools movement is, What do we define as the educational goods for well-being in schools? Expanding on the discussion on educational aims, which shines a light on the normative dimensions of school education, this section draws attention to the various goods that can be considered, but are not necessarily agreed upon, to be important educational goods of a well-being agenda in schools. Just as educational goals are not neutral, educational goods for well-being are value-based decisions that beget different actions and outcomes in schools.

It is difficult to precisely define educational goods, but, as a starting point, the term *educational good* may be thought of as signifying that which is valued in the sense that it helps individuals to flourish and to contribute to the flourishing of others, either in the present or future (Brighouse et al., 2018). The adjective in the term *educational good* refers to the fact that the good emerges from an educational process (Brighouse et al., 2018). Educational goods are positives in that "they contribute to valuable outcomes for the individuals possessing them or for others in either the present or future" (p. 20). For example, cognitive skills and social or emotional capacities are educational goods, because they generate value in the present and future (p. 21). Educational goods do not constitute flourishing itself; rather, they can only provide opportunities for flourishing rather than flourishing itself (p. 21). Another way to think about educational goods is by stating what they are not (Brighouse et al, 2018):

- educational goods ≠ flourishing (they provide opportunities to flourish);
- educational goods ≠ consumer goods (consumer goods are ultimately consumed, rather than used in the production of another good); and
- educational goods ≠ tangible goods (educational goods are not objects to be traded, nor are they reliant on availability of resources. Educational goods are not reliant on natural material resources and therefore theoretically anyway, not a zero-sum commodity).

Educational goods, then, are not material or concrete goods. Rather, they are opposite to "bads" and, importantly, are not a zero-sum commodity. There is an important distinction between educating for well-being and educating for other personal goals or for personal aims such as academic achievement or social mobility. Theoretically, every student should be able to access educational goods for well-being since they are not, for the most part, contingent on any material goods.

Educational goods broadly understood are the knowledge, skills, attitudes, and dispositions needed to enable people to flourish and to contribute to the flourishing of others (Brighouse et al., 2016, 2018). Consistent with Martha Nussbaum's (2011) capabilities approach, the fundamental dimension of value is not flourishing itself but opportunities for flourishing (Brighouse et al., 2016, p. 23). The emphasis on opportunity is central, "because the most educational goods can do is equip people with what they need for their lives to go well" (Brighouse et al., 2016, p. 6).

Table 3.1 lists and describes the six educational goods identified by Brighouse and his colleagues (2018, pp. 23–5). For each educational good, I have stated whether that good applies to the capacity for flourishing of children qua child, qua future adult, or both.

Table 3.1. Educational goods (based on Brighouse et al., 2018)

Capacity for … (present and future)	Description	Examples
Economic productivity (human capital) *Mostly qua future adults*	– Ability to participate effectively in the economy – Disposition to work (p. 23)	– Cognitive skills – Literacy skills – Numeracy skills
Personal autonomy *Qua child and qua future adults*	– Ability to make and act on well-informed and well-thought-out judgments. – Engagement in activities and relationships that reflect a person's sense of who they are and what matters to them. – Having sufficient knowledge of the relevant variables, and sufficient self-knowledge and fortitude, to make their own choices (p. 23–4)	– Choosing one's own spiritual or religious beliefs based on knowledge of many religious and non-religious views – Choosing one's own occupation in the face of parental pressure

(Continued)

Table 3.1. Educational goods (Continued)

Capacity for … (present and future)	Description	Examples
Democratic competence *Mostly qua future adults*	– Ability to be effective and morally aware participants in social life and political processes – Knowledge and skills vary and depend on context – Understanding of the history and structures of a society's political institutions – Ability to assess evidence to bear on claims and arguments made by others – Ability to engage (p. 24–5)	– Depends on the context; may include meaningful participation, obedience to the law, breaking the law, or various ways of engaging in the political process – Acquiring ability to engage and the capacity for democratic competence
Healthy personal relationships *Qua child and qua future adults*	– A variety of relationships – Lasting, intimate, positive relationships with others (pp. 25–6) – Development of attributes such as emotional openness, kindness, a willingness to take risks with one's feelings, trust – Families may or may not provide the kind of environment for these qualities to develop, but schools can also facilitate opportunities for these qualities to develop.	– Deriving meaning from close personal relationships with children, parents, close friends, and from more casual ties with personal acquaintances in the neighbourhood or work
Treating others as equals *Qua child and qua future adults*	– Equal respect for the basic dignity of persons underlies the idea that everybody has the same basic human rights regardless of their sex, race, religion, or nationality. – All people have fundamentally equal moral status. – Does not rule out that we care about strangers as much as we do about our family members or ourselves. Nor does it rule out judgments that people are unequal with respect to attributes such as strength, intelligence, or virtue.	– Racism, even without legal discrimination, continues to disadvantage people who are Black and Indigenous. Material effects of legal discrimination are compounded by personal interactions with others who, often unconsciously, assume their superiority. Offences based on racial discrimination – as with those involving discrimination regarding gender, sexuality, or physical or mental abilities – undermine the

Capacity for ... (present and future)	Description	Examples
	– Grounds norms against discrimination in hiring, promotion, and provision of government services. – Develops and exercises the capacity to treat other people as moral equals is important also for one to strike the right balance between pursuing one's own flourishing and discharging one's obligation to contribute to the flourishing of others.	self-respect and self-confidence of the those targeted, making it harder for them to flourish. The impact is worse if internalized feelings of inferiority or accepted harm and insult as a given.
Personal fulfilment *Qua child and qua future adults*	– Complex and satisfying work, school, and recreational activities that engage one's physical, aesthetic, intellectual, and spiritual faculties. – Opportunities to exercise and develop one's talents and meet challenges. – The capacity to find joy and fulfilment from experiences and activities.	– People find great satisfaction in music, literature, the arts, games and sports, mathematics and science, and religious practice. – In school, children's horizons can be broadened. They can be exposed to – and can develop enthusiasm for and competence in – activities that they would never have encountered through familial or communal networks.

Lars Lindblom (2018) critiques this framework as being too narrow an interpretation of values, arguing for a more inclusive account of educational goods and a different understanding of them. What Lindblom points to is the central predicament that any list of educational goods poses: the challenge of weighting of different goods and corresponding values. Such weighting, however, raises an important distinction between professional roles and professional tiers within the education system. At the classroom level, educational aims and goods for well-being may be administered in ways that may not always reflect the espoused policies. The way that educational goods are identified and defined at the administrative levels may depart from or even conflict with the ways in which classroom teachers understand and teach for well-being. Both classroom teachers and education administrators are concerned with providing opportunities for students to progress toward some identified aims. While the intended purpose of the framework for educational goods in table 3.1 is to assist policymakers with their decisions about how to promote flourishing in schools, an argument can be made that this framework works equally well for teachers and their decision-making at the classroom level.

A list such as the one above does not offer a final answer to the question of which educational goods should be promoted. The purpose of listing the above six educational goods here is to demonstrate how there will be side effects, trade-offs, and unintended consequences involved in prioritizing one set of goods for flourishing over others. Therefore, while I do not necessarily advocate for the list in table 3.1 in particular (though it seems like a good place to start), it is a clear representation of how we might agree or disagree on the educational goods for promoting well-being in schools.

In speaking with dozens of teachers on this subject, it is clear to me that each educator has a different understanding of which educational goods for well-being can or should be prioritized in schools. These differences are in part a reflection of the stratified needs of students from different cultures, socio-economic backgrounds, and so on. Education practitioners do their best to respond to the complex well-being needs that students, parents, and communities have identified or expect from their children. In my experience, the educational goods for student well-being that teachers support range from providing for basic security and welfare needs through school initiatives such as breakfast, lunch, or winter coat programs, anti-bullying programs, and mental health and social-emotional supports, to facilitating leadership opportunities, learning enrichment opportunities, and global citizenship opportunities. The challenge for the classroom teacher is which priority to give to which educational good in the face of finite resources (including time). Take as an example the fictitious classroom teacher Ms. Lee, who values preparing her students for the Grade 12 provincial exams. Of course, Ms. Lee wants her students to do well so that they feel good about their accomplishment and achieve the necessary grades for acceptance into a post-secondary program. Ms. Lee, however, may also view her students' achievement on the provincial exams as an accountability measure for her own job performance. But this value may compete with her values in regard to teaching for personal fulfilment, autonomy, and treating her students equitably.

Brighouse and colleagues (2018) propose that there are independent values to be taken into consideration, beyond the educational goods listed in Table 3.1, such as special goods of childhood, parental interests, and democratic protections. Acknowledgment of these other educational goods is where, in many cases, we find the intersection between the public, social, and parental aims listed in the preceding section, and the educational goods that create opportunities for individual flourishing discussed in this section. Put side by side, we see how parental aims might conflict with or constrain both social aims and educational goods for well-being, such as personal freedom and autonomy for students. Another example of aims and goods in tension occurs when democratic equality is severely undermined as schools increasingly operate within a broader, global system of social inequality. In fact, schools are in many ways increasingly and aggressively promoting social inequality (Labaree, 2010). These examples beg the question of how to make decisions about the fair and equitable distribution of educational goods for student well-being.

Distributing Opportunities for Student Well-Being

The third foundational question is, How should we distribute educational goods for well-being within and across schools, or in other words, How should we distribute opportunities for developing capacities for well-being? As mentioned in each of the preceding sections, we live in a world with extreme and pervasive inequalities. Worldwide there are devastatingly high numbers of children whose basic welfare rights are consistently violated. More than 570 million children live in extreme poverty; up to 1 billion children currently experience sexual, physical, or psychological violence; 119,000 children die every week from preventable diseases, such as those caused by unsafe drinking water; and 250 million children lack access to good quality education (UN General Assembly, 2015). This disparity and injustice on a global scale raises many important questions – only one of which is how to mitigate inequality in and across schools.

This section focuses on how much the public education system can feasibly neutralize the effects of inequality on children and the role that methodological approaches to distributive justice have in reproducing or challenging school inequalities. Asking school education to equalize life chances in the absence of other egalitarian social and economic programming is largely futile, since "equality of educational opportunity implies major changes in society at large," including changes in the "distribution of political power between races and among social classes," changes that "cannot be achieved by the efforts of the educational system alone" (Bowles et al., 2009, p. 12). Yet, a well-being in schools agenda must take into account students' abilities to access the goods of education in schools irrespective of their race, sex, ethnicity, or social class (Macleod, 2018).

Several decades ago, Jean Anyon demonstrated in her research the role that socially stratified schools have in reproducing inequality, revealing the hidden curriculum attached to teachers' approaches in their classrooms. For example, school teachers in what was labelled lower-class schools tended to focus on rote memorization, while teachers in elite schools focused not just on understanding content but also on manipulating curricular rules and conventions (Anyon, 1981). Anyon makes the case that, despite similarities in curriculum topics and materials, there are profound differences in pedagogical approaches and curriculum-in-use in different socio-economic school cultures. School knowledge in working-class schools is about technical drills and rote learning rather than understanding and critical thinking. According to Anyon (1981), working-class children are not offered what for them would be cultural capital, namely knowledge of and skills for manipulating ideas and symbols, , that is, "historical knowledge and analysis that legitimates their dissent and furthers their own class in society and in social transformation" (Anyon, 1981, p. 34). In the same vein, Annette Lareau (2011) depicts how upper-class parents and families bolster their private aims for education with an approach she calls concerted cultivation. By contrast, lower SES families demonstrate more of a hands-off approach to their children's education outside of school hours. Through a combination of social forces and hidden curricula in schools, we do not have to look far to see the resulting inequitable outcomes for students, affecting in particular racialized and lower-class students, who are already oppressed. Thus we see inequities in educational outcomes persist over time and across generations. Gillborn (2008) puts it bluntly: "Conspiracy is not only a useful metaphor for how the education system operates, but it also accurately describes the nature of the problem and the scale of the task facing anti-racists" (p. 233). The well-being-in-schools agenda cannot avoid the pressing distribution questions that accompany such persistent challenges in schools. It is imperative to consider the principle of distribution that should be operative for students to access opportunities and outcomes for well-being.

Equality of opportunity has been among the most enduring and broadly embraced political ideals in the twentieth century (Gordon, 2017). Christopher Jencks (1988) points out that no one argues that educational opportunity should not be equal or defends unequal opportunity. However, because there is disagreement about what a good, successful, and fair society looks like, there is disagreement about the meaning and implementation of educational opportunity. This is seen in the many arguments that have explored what equality of opportunity can and should look like in schools (see, for instance, Meyer, 2014).

Brighouse et al. (2018) argue that education decision-makers should consider at least three different notions of distribution: sufficiency, adequacy, and helping the least advantaged. These distributive values refer to educational goods as a whole and not to each individual good. Furthermore, "decision makers cannot directly distribute educational goods or prospects for flourishing" (Brighouse et al., 2018, p. 31), since luck and choice are both at play.

The first principle of adequacy (sometimes referred to as sufficiency) dictates that all schools ensure that all students have adequate educational goods to enable them to attain a reasonable level of overall flourishing (Anderson, 2007; Brighouse et al., 2018; Frankfurt, 1987; Raz, 1978; Satz, 2007). The second principle of equality can be considered as supplementary to the adequacy principle. As Annette Lareau (2011) observed, we live in a society with substantial economic and social inequalities, whereby some children benefit from private investments of educational goods (what Lareau calls the principle of concerted cultivation) and therefore positional goods. Equalizing educational goods would require extremely unequal investments in children (Ben-Shahar, 2016; Brighouse, 2000; Brighouse & Swift, 2014), while the result of a more equal distribution of educational goods (i.e., opportunities for flourishing) would not necessarily ensure egalitarianism or equality of flourishing. The third principle of distribution is benefits the least advantaged. Somewhat self-explanatory, this principle requires value-based decisions about what constitutes advantages as well as predictions about opportunities for flourishing in the future. Predicting future opportunities for success based on current investments is tricky, and it is one thing to "distribute educational goods (or the resources to produce them) in such a way as to increase the educational goods possessed by the worse off members of society but it is another thing to distribute educational resources in ways that do the most for their overall prospects for flourishing" (Brighouse et al., 2018, p. 35).

While Brighouse and his colleagues focus their distribution concerns on the policymaking level, Christopher Jencks (1988) offers a way to consider questions of inequality of opportunity in schools at the classroom level and in how teachers' approach resource allocation in schools, particularly when schools inherit broader social problems. The central problem, for Jencks, resides in decisions about the distribution of the main educational resources, for instance, teacher time, energy, and attention, since "classroom teachers decide how to allocate

Table 3.2. Principles of distribution of resources by a classroom teacher (based on Jencks, 1988, pp. 519–20)

Distribution principle	Description
Democratic equality	Everyone gets equal time and attention, regardless of their ability, effort, access to resources, home situation, aspiration, or how much they or others will benefit.
Moralistic justice	Rewards virtue and punishes vice. Virtue involves effort, and this view involves rewarding those who make the most effort to learn. The class is bound by a contract of "I'll do my best if you'll do yours." This system should focus on effort, but oftentimes it is only actual achievement that is assessed (which depends not only on effort but also on ability, prior knowledge, and environmental protective factors).
Weak humane justice	Compensate those students who have gotten less than their proportionate share of advantages by giving them more than their proportionate share of attention. The "weak" variant only requires that teachers compensate those who have been short-changed at home or in early schooling (and not genetically). All children have an equal claim on *educational resources* (including home and institutional resources).
Strong humane justice	Requires that teachers compensate those who have been short-changed in any way in the past, including genetically. This involves giving the most attention to the struggling students, regardless of their reasons for struggle. This position holds equality of outcomes as its goal.
Utilitarianism	Suggests that every activity is a race for unequal rewards. Races are open to all, run on a level playing field, and are judged solely on the basis of performance. The prizes should go to the best.

their time, energy, and attention within the classroom and to what end" (Brighouse et al., 2018, p. 31). Jencks delineates five possible options to address inequality in the classroom (see table 3.2).

Considering the five principles in table 3.2, it is unclear what justice and fair equality of opportunity in the classroom should look like. It is possible that resource distribution in the classroom is not just about teachers distributing extra time and help but also about teachers forming close and influential relationships with students. It is plausible that teachers will form closer relationships with some individual students than with others. Further, it is plausible that in some cases the potential a teacher sees in a student (based on merit: the utilitarianism model) may dictate the closeness of the relationship. While students who are identified as having low literacy skills or to be low achievers may get additional supports from the system as a whole, for instance through a resource teacher, consultant, or clinician, it is not a given that an influential caring relationship is formed with those students (as is often the case with teachers and students, who have more frequent contact and a more essential bond).

When I teach Jencks's framework of five distributive principles for social equity in the classroom to teacher candidates, I take a poll to see which of the five they think they will adopt as teachers. The highest number of votes often will go to weak humane justice, and the lowest to utilitarianism. However, the margins are quite small; among bachelor of education students in my classes, I observe an almost equal distribution across all five options. These informal polls confirm the importance of the third foundational question discussed in this section. While everyone can agree that fair equality of opportunity for well-being is good, educators do not agree on how to achieve such fairness. Invariably, a teacher candidate will ask why they cannot just use a combination of the five different distribution principles at different times. This eclectic approach has its own implications, and requires the same rigour in terms of justification and acknowledgment of trade-offs as those based on a single principle of distribution.

Something to keep in mind with the list of equality principles of distribution (table 3.2) is that while some teachers may be willing to equalize access to educational goods to counter the effects of background inequalities, schools operate within a society and polis that is willing to tolerate sizable inequalities. So, it may be challenging for educators to mitigate differences in how children respond to opportunities provided in schools. Decision-makers at both the policy and classroom levels face dilemmas about the need to engage in trade-offs between different distributive values as well as the need to weigh different educational goods and educational aims against one another.

What also needs to be kept in mind is that how one defines the aim of school education fundamentally impacts which principle of resource distribution one sees as appropriate. For instance, if someone promotes an aim of school education that justifies the form of stratification of the student population described in the first section of this chapter, "equalizing access to educational goods" is not even on the agenda.

The purpose of this section was to demonstrate how impactful the distribution question is that accompanies any identified school educational aim or educational good for student well-being in schools. How one answers the third foundational question discussed in this section will determine the kinds of efforts that are made, and how groups of children are identified to receive the goods that will improve their opportunities for developing capacities for well-being.

Conclusion

This chapter posed three foundational questions to decision-makers at the policy and classroom level within the context of a concern for student well-being: (1) How does well-being fit into the aims of school education? (2) What do we define as the educational goods for well-being in schools? (3) How should we distribute these goods in schools? Posing these questions to those who promote the student well-being agenda demands greater clarity and efficacy for that very agenda. Once the issues raised through these questions are clarified at the policy level, there is still work to be done on how those policies are to be implemented at the school and classroom levels.

Most people who enter the teaching profession do so because they care about the well-being of students. The teachers that I know and have worked with prioritize building good relationships with their students and spend the bulk of their time and energy trying to figure out ways to support their students in the best ways possible. But teachers face system-wide expectations and competing responsibilities that directly result from the issues raised by the three foundational questions posed in this chapter. For instance, how can teachers be both responsive to an individual student's needs and attentive to general educational standards? How should teachers choose the educational goods to confer to students? How should teachers think about the distribution of educational goods in their classrooms? Teachers operate in a setting that is largely centred on developing personal relationships with students, families and communities, and each year they must adapt to context-specific features of their classroom makeup. Administrators and policymakers, on the other hand, focus on what is universal across classrooms. Their focus is on broad political and social aims that are measurable and can be publicly accounted for. These two broadly defined groups are positioned differently, as shown throughout this chapter, and their different positions need to be kept in mind when trying to answer the three foundational questions posed in this chapter.

NOTE

1 The discussion in this section draws on select US sources and perspectives.

REFERENCES

Anderson, E. (2007). Fair opportunity in education: A democratic equality perspective. *Ethics, 117*(4), 595–622. https://doi.org/10.1086/518806

Anyon, J. (1981). Social class and school knowledge. *Curriculum Inquiry, 11*(1), 3–42. https://doi.org/10.1080/03626784.1981.11075236

Ben-Shahar, T.H. (2016). Equality in education: Why we must go all the way. *Ethical Theory and Moral Practice, 19*(1), 83–100. https://doi.org/10.1007/s10677-015-9587-3

Bowles, S., Gintis, H., & Groves, M.O. (2009). Introduction. In S. Bowles, H. Gintis, & M. O. Groves (Eds.), *Unequal chances: Family background and economic success* (pp. 1–22). Princeton University Press.

Brighouse, H. (2000). *School choice and school justice*. Oxford: Oxford University Press.

Brighouse, H., Ladd, H., Loeb, S., & Swift, A. (2016). Educational goods and values: A framework for decision makers. *Theory and Research in Education, 14*(1), 3–25. https://doi.org/10.1177/1477878515620887

– (2018). *Educational goods: Values, evidence and decision-making*. University of Chicago Press.

Brighouse, H., & Swift, A. (2014). The place of educational equality in educational justice. In K. Meyer (Ed.), *Education, justice and the human good* (pp. 14–33). Routledge.

Chapman, A. (2014). Wellbeing and schools: Exploring the normative dimensions. In K. Wright & J. McLeod (Eds.), *Rethinking youth wellbeing: Critical perspectives* (pp. 143–59). Springer.

Davies, S., & Guppy, N. (2014). *The schooled society: An introduction to the sociology of education* (3rd ed.). Oxford University Press.

Frankfurt, H. (1987). Equality as a moral ideal. *Ethics, 98*(1), 21–43. https://doi.org/10.1086/292913

Gillborn, D. (2008). Coincidence or conspiracy? Whiteness, policy and the persistence of the Black/White achievement gap. *Educational Review, 60*(3), 229–48. https://doi.org/10.1080/00131910802195745

Gordon, L. (2017). If opportunity is not enough: Coleman and his critics in the era of equality of results. *History of Education Quarterly, 57*(4), 601–15. https://doi.org/10.1017/heq.2017.35

Jencks, C. (1988). Whom must we treat equally for educational opportunity to be equal? *Ethics, 98*(3), 518–33. https://doi.org/10.1086/292969

Labaree, D. (2010). *Someone has to fail: The zero-sum game of public schooling*. Harvard University Press.

Lareau, A. (2011). *Unequal childhoods: Class, race, and family life* (2nd ed.). University of California Press.

Lindblom, L. (2018). Goods, principles, and values in the Brighouse, Ladd, Loeb and Swift framework for educational policy-making. *Studies in Philosophy and Education, 37*(6), 631–45. https://doi.org/10.1007/s11217-018-9619-2

Macleod, C. (2018). Just schools and good childhoods: Non-preparatory dimensions of educational justice. *Journal of Applied Philosophy, 35*(S1), 60–75. https://doi.org/10.1111/japp.12227

Meyer, K. (2014). *Education, justice and the human good: Fairness and equality in the education system.* Routledge.

Mignolo, W., & Walsh, C. (2018). *On decoloniality: Concepts, analytics, praxis.* Duke University Press.

Nussbaum, M. (2011). *Creating capabilities: The human development approach.* Belknap Press of Harvard University Press.

Ravitch, D. (2008). Education and democracy: The United States of America as a historical case study. In D. Coulter & J. Wiens (Eds.), *Why do we educate? Renewing the conversation* (pp. 43–57). John Wiley & Sons.

Raz, J. (1978). Principles of equality. *Mind, 87*(3), 321–42. https://doi.org/10.1093/mind/LXXXVII.3.321

Satz, D. (2007). Equality, adequacy, and education for citizenship. *Ethics, 117*(4), 623–48. https://doi.org/10.1086/518805

Türken, S., Nafstad, H., Phelps, J., & Blakar, R. (2016). Youth's future orientation and well-being: Materialism and concerns with education and career among Turkish and Norwegian youth. *International Journal of Child, Youth & Family Studies, 7*(3/4), 472–97. https://doi.org/10.18357/ijcyfs73-4201616175

UN General Assembly. (2015). *Transforming our world: The 2030 Agenda for Sustainable Development.* http://www.refworld.org/docid/57b6e3e44.html

4 Responding to the Other: The Need for an Ethic of Well-Being

REBECA HERINGER AND THOMAS FALKENBERG

There are different conceptions of what human well-being means (for a structural overview of Western approaches to conceptualizing well-being and flourishing, see Falkenberg, 2014; Ryan & Deci, 2001). For instance, Keyes (2006a, 2007) emphasizes the role of mental health, while other scholars stress the correlation between well-being and one's personality, environmental mastery (Larson, 1989; Ryff, 1989), and academic achievement (Howell, 2009). The question of what role the well-being of others plays in a person's own well-being is another distinct area that has attracted scholarly attention.

Two general types of responses to this question are discussed in the literature. The first builds on the idea that a person's well-being is about quality of life as experienced by that person, what we call *individual well-being*. In this case, the well-being of others is *conceptually* not considered relevant – although seeing someone else suffer could impact one's well-being. In subjective well-being approaches in psychology (e.g., Diener et al., 1999; Keyes, 2006b; Ryff, 1989) and in subjective theories of well-being in philosophy (e.g., Sumner, 1996), a person's well-being is thus conceptually independent of the well-being of others.

The second type of response integrates the well-being of others into the conception of human well-being. For instance, this is done in some objective list approaches to well-being in philosophy (e.g., Nussbaum, 2011), and in some character and virtue-based approaches to well-being in the field of positive psychology (e.g., Peterson & Park, 2004), depending on the kinds of values or virtues postulated. As an example of the latter, Peterson (2006) lists strengths of character and values as positive individual traits, which form one of the three pillars of positive psychology – the other two are positive subjective experiences and positive institutions, such as families, schools, and communities. These three pillars come together in the following way in human well-being:

"Positive institutions facilitate the development and display of positive traits, which in turn facilitate positive subjective experiences" (Peterson, 2006, p. 20). The "Values in Action" classification system of strengths of character (Peterson & Seligman, 2004) identifies 24 such strengths of character, among which are kindness, love, fairness, and forgiveness/mercy. These strengths of character are all linked to positive subjective experiences of others. Thus, this version of a defining human well-being conceptually integrates the well-being of others into an understanding of what it means for a person to live a flourishing life.

At the conceptual level, the two responses described above are incompatible with each other. But can we still hold on to the first type of approach and understand human well-being as *individual well-being* without having to give up the concern for the well-being of others as an aspect of what it means to live a flourishing life?

To address this question, we proceed as follows. First, we deconstruct the shortcomings of an *individual well-being* approach. Second, we argue that we should conceptually distinguish between individual well-being and human flourishing and consider the former a building block of the latter. Third, we inquire whether a particular ethic, namely an ethic of hospitality, can serve as such an ethic of well-being. We conclude the chapter by discussing some implications of an ethic of well-being for school education.

Individual Well-Being and the Idea of and the Need for an Ethic of Well-Being

The first type of approach to human well-being described above does not *conceptually* include a concern for the well-being of others. However, the approach might still include the possibility that the social context of a person's life plays a role in understanding that person's well-being. For instance, the approach taken by the Organization for Economic Cooperation and Development (OECD, 2017) defines student well-being as "the result of interactions among four distinct but closely related domains: psychological, social, cognitive and physical" (p. 62), whereby "the *social dimension* [emphasis added] of students' well-being refers to the quality of their social lives" (p. 63). Although the social lives of students are conceptually part of this understanding of student well-being, it is the impact of that social life on the life experiences of a student that is considered here, not the quality of life of other students per se. In other words, the impact of others (and thus indirectly of their lives) on a person's well-being can conceptually be part of the first approach to conceptualizing human well-being without the concept itself making reference to the well-being of others. Subjective and hedonistic approaches to well-being in psychology (e.g., Diener et al., 1999; Kahneman et al., 1999) provide additional examples of conceptualization of human well-being that give consideration to others, but only as the lives of these others impact the quality of life of the person whose well-being is under consideration.

Why are individual well-being approaches insufficient as guides for one's own life and for educational and social interventions, which are the main purposes of any theory of well-being? If we choose an individual well-being approach to understanding what it means for humans to live a flourishing life, we can have a situation where we conceptually can speak of some living a flourishing life without much concern for the well-being of others, or, in other words, we could have situations where we have to accept that someone's life is flourishing while everyone else around them is in distress or pain. We find this conceptually problematic. Indigenous scholars also raise concerns about the philosophy of individualism that dominates countries of the Global North, which fails to value the interconnectedness of all forms of life, thus having tragic consequences for individuals, for the land, and for the planet as a whole (Archibald, 2014; Friesen, 2000; Moore, 2017; Stonechild, 2020).

Drawing on Falkenberg (2020), we argue that we can hold on to an individualistic notion of well-being, but that we also need to introduce the notion of an ethic of well-being to arrive at an adequate approach to human flourishing, one that we can conceptually use for self-formation and educational and social interventions for others: living a flourishing life is to live in accordance with an ethic of well-being, whereby *well-being* itself is understood in the sense of individual well-being. This idea is in line with an understanding of *ethics*, for instance, found in Appiah (2008), which "follow[s] Aristotle in using 'ethics' to refer to questions about human flourishing, about what it means for a life to be well lived" (p. 37).

Conceptually individual well-being does not include a concern for others; therefore there is a *need* for an ethic of well-being to conceptually bridge individual well-being and flourishing. This need, however, arises because of our conceptual distinction between well-being and flourishing, raising the question why we make that distinction in the first place. We provide three reasons in response.

First, in the larger socio-political and economic context of the Global North, which is the context we are writing within, human beings are considered from an individualizing perspective. This perspective is probably most explicitly expressed in human rights codes that are, ultimately, built upon the Universal Declaration of Human Rights (UN,

1948). These are rights that *individual* citizens can claim against societal demands. Second, the cultural context from which we are writing ascribes agency to human beings (e.g., Bowden & Mummery, 2009; Martin et al., 2003). From this perspective, human beings are understood as having *individual* life trajectories that they can actively direct and pursue. Third, humans' perceptual systems work such that humans cannot help but see themselves as separate individual physical entities, even if they simultaneously also see the individual as a member of a certain class of individuals.

All three perspectives lead us to a conceptual framework that takes into account states of being of an individual, for instance their state of well-being. From this perspective, however, the need for an ethic of well-being arises, as argued above. To explore the notion of an ethic of well-being for human flourishing further, we suggest how a particular ethic – the ethic of hospitality – might serve us well as an ethic of well-being in the sense just introduced.

An Ethic of Hospitality

Based on philosophical and psychoanalytical theories, we begin this section by exploring how *ethics* is here understood. Then, we resort to the hospitality metaphor to demonstrate the challenges and complexities of relating to the Other in an ethical way.

Ethics: Relating to the Other

Levinas proposed a reconceptualization of ethics *as relation* rather than as a set of moral values. For Levinas (1972, 1982, 1995), the proximity of the Other (which he often referred to as "the face")[1] indicated both its uniqueness and irreducibility as well as its vulnerability. This shift, in turn, calls for a reconceptualization of difference and the implications that come with it. Thus understood, ethics "becomes an attentiveness to and the preservation of this alterity of the Other" (Todd, 2003, p. 3), and one's responsibility is, thus, the welcoming of the difference in its wholeness.

But Levinas makes it clear that the Other is not simply an alter ego, another "I," but a complete Other, whose necessary otherness makes it infinitely unknown. The Other is absolutely unknowable, so any knowledge (*connaissance*) is ultimately self-centred assimilation; any attempt of categorizing the Other is an attempt to reduce the Other to what one's own self can comprehend and grasp, which makes such attempts acts of violence against the uniqueness of the Other. Following

Levinas, Derrida observed that "the other is the other only if his alterity is absolutely irreducible, that is, infinitely irreducible; and the infinitely Other can only be Infinity" (Derrida, 1978, p. 104). In other words, what makes alterity possible is exactly its otherness, without which the Other cannot exist.

Conversely, as observed by Levinas and Derrida throughout the years, Western philosophy tends to follow a totality-driven mindset, a metaphysical gesture that "includes a *hierarchical axiology* in which the origin is designated as pure, simple, normal, standard, self-sufficient, and self-identical, in order to *then* think in terms of derivation, complication, deterioration, accident, etcetera" (Peters & Biesta, 2009, p. 21). This myth of the origin leads the self to try to understand or define the Other in understandable terms, being thus an attempt of possessing the Other, reducing the Other to what the self can comprehend and hence attacking the alterity of the Other (Fagan, 2013; Todd, 2003; Trifonas, 2001).

Supporting these perspectives, psychoanalytical theories point out that there is in the self a natural resistance to difference, for it interrupts the self, causing discomfort in one's psyche (Freud, 1923/2018; Todd, 2003). Drawing on earlier philosophers such as Kant, Arendt, Levinas, and Derrida, Todd (2003, 2009) argues that any ethical possibility of engaging with the Other in a non-violent way challenges our understanding of humanity itself. However, these encounters with discomfort are inevitable in society, requiring self-negotiations, the id becoming an ego through social institutions "that furnish the subject with meaning, that impose limitations upon the subject's desire and drives" (Todd, 2003, p. 19). Such an understanding harmonizes with that of Levinas, who argues that there is not a moment of solitude of the self, rather the self is always in relation with the Other – and in fact desires the Other (Levinas, 1972). As Fagan (2013) summarizes, "Levinas places the relation with the Other as prior to, and constitutive of, the self or ego" (p. 51). However, it must be observed that, in our tendency to avoid resistance, it is not uncommon for the self to search for and expect commonalities with the Other while suppressing alterity.

To the extent that one's response to the Other is based on a conception of humanity shaped by one's own, even apparent "benevolent" acts will not be a responsible response to the uniqueness of the Other. Todd (2003) argues that in the face of human suffering, acts of empathy or feelings such as guilt are not ethically moved, because they are ultimately self-centred and limited movements. Todd observes that empathy takes place either through projection or identification. In the first case, an ethical response would happen by putting oneself "in the

Other's shoes" (p. 53). However, drawing on Freudian works, Todd stresses that it is not only impossible to feel what the Other feels, but that this imaginary reconstruction is both an attempt to recognize oneself in the Other (hence maintaining the centralization of the self to the detriment of the uniqueness of the Other) and an attempt to limit the Other. As she explains, "the effect of putting oneself in place of the Other means that one has, in some profound way, defined that Other in terms of the limits or expansiveness of one's imagination, and in terms of one's own psychical material" (Todd, 2003, pp. 56–7). Todd (2003) sees the second scenario – empathy that takes place through identification – as an attempt to bring the Other to the realm of the self, for example by imitation. However, she observes that in this approach, responsibility "remains within the purview of consciousness as opposed to sensibility" (p. 59). That is, the self-Other relation remains dictated by the identification of differences and commonalities rather than by the immediate openness to the Other. Conversely, any ethical possibility requires the surprise that can only happen when the otherness of the Other remains absolutely and unconditionally distinct from the self, for only then will responsibility be possible. As Fagan (2013) summarizes, "rather than concern for the Other arising from the commonality between us, Levinas sees it as arising precisely out of the lack of commonality" (p. 49). In other words, it is through alterity itself that ethical togetherness can take place.

Hospitality and the Ethical Im-possibility

For Levinas, responsibility comes before reason. Responsibility is immediate, unlimited, and not reciprocal. I, and only I, am immediately and unlimitedly responsible to the Other, and no one can be responsible for the Other but me, and I am responsible for the Other without expecting anything in return. Following Levinas, Derrida illustrates the ethical responsibility through the metaphor of the hospitality gesture, considered a universal right since Kant (Derrida, 2000b; Kant, 1795/2007). Genuine hospitality, as an event, means it is necessarily unpredictable and unforeseen (Derrida, 2007). Derrida argues that true hospitality is not expressed with the arrival of the habitual, pleasant guest; it is through the arrival of the unknown at an unexpected time that the host's hospitality can be genuinely evidenced. Ruitenberg (2011, 2016) adds that in true hospitality, the guest has agency to make changes to the environment, which will inevitably interfere in the host's quietude, customs, and habits. Genuine hospitality is thus necessarily uncomfortable, unpredictable, and unconditional (Derrida, 1998, 2000a, 2007).

Genuine hospitality is given to the one I do not even know the name of, from whom I do not expect anything in return, not even the "reward" of having been hospitable, for it is only for the guest to know whether hospitality has taken place or not. Hospitality is asymmetrical and infinite, not guided by universal rules but by ethical spontaneity.

However, genuine hospitality also brings with it several challenges. For instance, to say "welcome" to the Other is already to demarcate the threshold of one's property. To say "make yourself at home" is already telling the Other that this is not their home. But as Derrida (2000a, 2007) argues, it is in this seeming impossibility of hospitality that its possibility lies. The fine line between hospitality and hostility (Derrida, 2000b) is what keeps the host always alert, constantly deferring their response to the Other so as not to respond irresponsibly, an act which Derrida (1982) called an act of *différance*, a peaceful response in resistance to our totalizing tendency.

Hospitality is not about surrendering mastery either by making one's home guest-centred or making it anarchical. In order for hospitality to take place, there must be a host who holds mastery. After all, "to hang out a sign saying 'Come right in; there is no one at home' is not the equivalent of hospitality" (Dewey, 1916/2011, p. 98). Notwithstanding, in true hospitality the host is decentralized and the guest empowered with agency, creating an ongoing tension that is constantly negotiated in the peaceful response to "what turns up" (Derrida, 2000a).

The aporia of hospitality is also evidenced when considering the existence of another Other (the *Third*, as Levinas says). But the impossibility of being unconditionally responsible for the Other and for the Third, rather than destroying any ethical attempt, is actually where the hope of justice lies. For both Levinas and Derrida, justice is not defined a priori; it erupts as a response to the uniqueness of the Other. For that reason, there is no justice in universalizations. Being constructed a priori, rules and guidelines (or the law, for Derrida) not only nullify the self's responsibility to the Other by attributing it to others but are also destructible; that is, it is possible to break the rules. However, Peters and Biesta (2009) observe that it is exactly the possibility of breaking the rules that opens up the possibility of responsibility. As they point out, "Derrida argues that ethics and politics *begin* only with this undecidability, which makes the decision at the very same time 'necessary and impossible'" (p. 33). Thus, ethics as relation can take place only in response to the uniqueness of the Other.

What these philosophical and psychoanalytical observations point to is that any attempt to respond to the Other in a just and ethical way must necessarily be led by the uniqueness of the subject. Todd (2009) argued that "justice is about securing the other's freedom to be" (p. 63), focusing on how one is to respond to the *suffering* of the Other. In the context of well-being, however, we contend that the concept of suffering by itself is an insufficient standard to lead one to responsively respond to the Other. Rather, what is at stake here is the Other's "being (un)well" that we need to responsively respond to.

Being well must not be predetermined as a right but as part of a tactful responsiveness to the uniqueness of the Other. As Todd (2009) argues, "where justice lies is not in the rights themselves but in defending the inalienable freedom of the Other to be, which at times requires acting beyond the letter of the law" (p. 63). Universal human rights, for example, however helpful, are not sufficient in themselves to allow the Other to be well, because "humanity is ... not an ideal, but an orientation (a responsibility) that responds to human difference; it is here that dignity resides" (Todd, 2009, p. 21).

The mere act of opening the door to a guest is not hospitality. Genuine hospitality implies being "a hostage" to the unknown Other (Derrida, 2000b), because it necessarily involves openness to unpredictable outcomes. In order for the Other to be well, well-being must not be predetermined by the host's standards. Levinas argues that "rights do not begin with myself but that they are rooted in a sense of an original right that has no origin, but lies in the proximity between a self and absolutely other" (Todd, 2009, p. 63).

As the aporia of hospitality, justice for the Other's well-being lies in the hiatus between the possibility and impossibility of responsibility. The *im-possibility* of responsibility (Fagan, 2013) is a constant reminder that giving the same gift to two unique "Others" is not an ethical response to each one's uniqueness. The law, as a set of boundaries defining the threshold of the home, should not be disregarded, but it should not be taken as defining one's response to the Other. Deconstruction, an act which Derrida constantly speaks of, is about looking at the openness of what is given: "deconstruction shows how we are always already vulnerable and exposed to, and in relation with, the Other" (Fagan, 2013, p. 95). Deconstruction constitutes an ethical exigency, however intractable (Derrida & Ewald, 2001), for it is in the moments where conventions are suspended that hospitality erupts. Therefore, rather than trying to escape or limit the emergence of alterity, the ethical response to the Other is about responding to their ungraspable uniqueness without totalizing it. That does not mean responding, when I perceive the Other suffering or being unwell, by trying to determine what is good for the Other, but rather welcoming a possible transgression of the boundaries of the law as a genuine openness to the Other.

An Ethic of Hospitality as an Ethic of Well-Being

The ethic of hospitality, in its response to the uniqueness of the Other, appears to be a sustainable approach to a responsive concern for the well-being of the Other. However, because the host is decentralized from the concern within an ethic of hospitality, does such an ethic not put the host's own well-being in jeopardy? Ruitenberg (2016) herself acknowledges the challenge for educators who take up an ethic of hospitality, given the "often deeply inhospitable conditions in which teachers do their work" (p. 111). Indeed, at first glance, an ethic of hospitality appears to necessarily exclude individual well-being, which can be evidenced, for example, by the fact that a subjective approach to well-being envisions environmental mastery and control (Larson, 1989; Ryff, 1989), while an ethic of hospitality aims at decentralizing the host's control and empowering the guest.

But the complementarity of individual well-being and an ethic of hospitality becomes clear when we understand that the question is not just how I relate to myself or how I relate to the Other, but what role the Other plays in my flourishing and vice versa, and how I can ethically encounter the Other in a way that also supports my flourishing. What individual well-being and an ethic of hospitality have in common is that both are necessarily situational, contextual, and relational: "Students' individual well-being is a result of their interaction with their environment, the material resources they have access to, and students' responses to external opportunities and stress factors" (OECD, 2017, p. 64). Both one's own well-being and the well-being of the Other cannot be pre-determined, for they erupt and evolve in response to contexts and relations.

In that way, individual well-being and the ethic of hospitality are not only compatible, but in fact inform and complement each other in the pursuit of a flourishing life. An ethic of hospitality serves as a suitable ethic for individual well-being, because an ethic of hospitality is so absolutely concerned with the Other, while the notion of individual well-being is so absolutely concerned with the self. An ethic of hospitality as an ethic of well-being, thus, actually brings those two apparently contradictory concerns together in perfect *dis-harmony* for a flourishing life. Living one's life in such perfect dis-harmony means living with the concern for one's individual well-being *by* orienting one's life through an ethic of hospitality.

We offer an anecdote based on the metaphor of hospitality to illustrate how this apparent paradox could be evidenced. Let us imagine that the owner of a house goes to bed at 10 p.m. every night. One day, however, the owner hears someone unexpectedly knocking on the door at 8 p.m.. Informed of their need of shelter and food, the host receives the guest with clean linen, dinner, and conversation. By 11:30 p.m., the host informs the guest that he would go to bed, but that the guest could make themselves comfortable in the house, watch TV if they so choose, and eat anything they want. Evidently, the host's routine was not the same after the arrival of the unexpected guest. The guest altered the space and transformed the course of the evening that would have taken place in that house had they not arrived. The host embraced the uncomfortable arrival of the unpredicted guest, while at the same time they did not neglect their own well-being. The host welcomed the guest and the new context (both spatial and temporal) that was created through the arrival of the guest, while at the same time they were attentive to their own needs, feelings, and sensations. The potential initial discomfort associated with the arrival of the guest – both for disturbing the host's routine and space as well as for tending to the needs of the guest (e.g., hunger, tiredness) – was directed in a way that contributed to the well-being of both the guest and the host. The ethical response in that case, then, was not in the host insisting on their right of ownership by refraining from receiving the guest, or in the host enacting cultural rules of politeness and resisting going to bed before the guest, but in providing opportunities that could work for the guest's *and* the host's well-being.

As it seems, an ethic of hospitality, although almost (if not entirely) solely concerned with the Other, still can be in alignment with the well-being of the host. A "cranky" host will most likely not be able to welcome the guest in a hospitable way. Well-being, as both a requisite and outcome of a flourishing life, is contingent upon the relations with which an individual is involved – including those between teachers and students.

The Role of an Ethic of Well-Being for School Education

So, what does it mean to pursue an ethic of well-being in education? Using the ethic of hospitality as an example, in this section we explore the role of an ethic of well-being for school education that is concerned with flourishing lives for both teachers and students. While there are many possible ways of defining the purpose of education, Biesta (2009) outlines three main functions: socialization, qualification, and subjectification. The qualification function (for example, the acquisition of specific skills deemed necessary for the workforce) and the socialization function ("the many ways in which, through education, we become members of and part of particular social, cultural and political 'orders'" (p. 40)) are usually explicit and valued, while the subjectification function is often implicit and neglected. As Biesta observes, subjectification is "precisely *not* about the insertion of 'newcomers' into existing orders, but about ways of being that hint at independence from such orders; ways of being in which the individual is not simply a 'specimen' of a more encompassing order" (p. 40). Although Biesta does not focus on well-being, it seems that the subjectification function of education is inexorably connected to students' well-being. While socialization and qualification are prominent functions of school education, they still require students' subjectification, that is, students becoming subjects of their own life, which in turn demands that the teacher as the host in the classroom resists the tendency toward resisting the uniqueness of the students as the Others and rather welcomes and cherishes the well-being of each student as the Other in their wholeness and uniqueness, as these emerge in the classroom.

Being guided by an ethic of hospitality in the realm of school education is certainly easier said than done. The unforeseen arrival of the student-guest might be greatly uncomfortable for the teacher-host, who has thoughtfully and in detail developed a lesson plan, seeks to be in control of the class, and intends to teach. Being called to respond in a non-totalizing way is thus an ongoing challenge that is evidenced in extraordinary and unpredicted ways. The context created by the COVID-19 pandemic may serve as a good example for what we are discussing here (see Heringer, 2021). In a time of mandatory physical distancing and rapid transmission of the virus, unforeseen accommodations have had to be made in response to students' needs and changing contexts. Aware of a student's struggles, a teacher may go above and beyond their professional responsibilities and respond to the student in a responsible way, that is, "unlocking the world" (Ruitenberg, 2016) of and for the student in a way that fosters the student's *response-ability* (Oliver, 2001, 2015), allowing the student to be an active subject with agency (Ruitenberg, 2016).

However, constantly attending to students' well-being, educators run the risk of not being attentive to their own well-being, thus experiencing burnout and distress, not uncommon phenomena (Hauseman, 2020; Hinds et al., 2015; Manuel, Carter, & Dutton, 2018; Newhook, 2010). An ethic of well-being honours the teacher's role as an authority (but not as an authoritarian). Despite advances in technology and online education, the teacher-host is necessary and fundamental for hospitality: the presence and the well-being of the teacher are of utmost importance for education, in whichever setting it might take place.

Hence, while it might be obvious that the teacher's individual well-being is not enough to foster students' well-being, there must also be more than an ethics of hospitality so that the teacher, for example, does not feel that they are not fulfilling their professional responsibilities if they choose to respond to a student in a particular way, if they feel the need to take a day off, or choose not to spend extra hours contacting parents or directing extracurricular activities.

If, as Oliver (2015) observes, "I am responsible not only for my own response but also for that of the other" (p. 486), it is necessary to go beyond the dichotomy of self and Other, which creates an either-or situation; that is, either the host is well or the guest is well. Because a flourishing life must necessarily consider both self and Other, and because well-being does not have a universal expression but is rather in constant flux, the host's responsibility lies in fostering relations that invite students' agency. This does not mean accepting all demands from students, but rather a working-through[2] "what turns up" (Derrida, 2000a) with a disposition of vigilant undecidability.

Within an ethic of well-being, teachers are not to approach students with a rigid and immovable idea of what well-being looks like (for students and for teachers themselves) but, resisting any tendency to define, they are to seek to hear and respond to students' unique feelings, thoughts, and identities. Through this dynamic, teachers foster their own well-being. In this context, teachers are called to respond unconditionally and without expecting anything in return, while at the same time being attentive to their own well-being.

An ethic of well-being in schools implies, on the one hand, a pedagogy of discomfort (Boler & Zembylas, 2003), resisting closures, embracing vulnerability, and hesitating before making decisions (Edgoose, 2001). It also requires being cognizant and attentive to one's feelings, emotions, and health in order not to neglect one's own well-being. It is in this sense that we want to say that a central role of an ethic of well-being for teachers, in its interplay with a teacher's concern for their individual well-being, is that of a *professional* ethics in the sense proposed by Higgins (2003). Higgins (2003) suggests that the ethos of service in education should be guided by self-cultivation rather than self-sacrifice: "It makes good sense to ask what teachers as individuals in search of a good life want, need, and derive from their practice, and to view such questions as ethical in nature" (p. 137). In line with the ideas presented in this chapter, what Higgins suggests is that the teacher's individual well-being is intimately linked to an ethic of well-being, which should serve as a professional ethics that guides the teacher's engagement with their students as the Other. Individual well-being and an ethic of hospitality thus complement and inform each other in the pursuit of an ethic of well-being that can lead to both teachers and students living flourishing lives.

Conclusion

In this chapter, we have argued that the pursuit of a flourishing life requires an ethic of well-being that brings together both individual well-being and the concern for the well-being of others. Moreover, we demonstrated that an ethical response cannot be defined a priori. Therefore, although well-being is uniquely experienced by each individual, well-being (flourishing) is not individualistic but always contextual and informed by the self's relations with the Other. Preconceptualized or decontextualized definitions of well-being thus impinge on the Other's flourishing and inevitably on one's own. An ethic of hospitality can complement and inform individual well-being in a sustainable way – that is, through a sensitive and tactful host who welcomes the unknown Other unconditionally while not neglecting their own well-being.

It is the responsibility of educators to be attentive to their own needs and feelings when unforeseen (as every encounter with alterity is) encounters happen; it is also incumbent upon educators to resist any kind of projection of what students' well-being should look like and to make room for students' emerging responses. The apparent aporia and inexactitude of this ethic may be discouraging to the standards-driven mindset so common in school education and to those who fear embracing the discomfort of the unknown. It is, however, in the unpredictability of the encounter of the self and the Other where its strength lies: the promise of a flourishing life.

NOTES

1 Following Levinas (1972, 1982, 1995) and Derrida (1998) (cf. also Galetti, 2015), we use the capital "O" to emphasize the absolute alterity of an *other*.
2 A term used by Freud and discussed by Oliver (2001).

REFERENCES

Appiah, K.A. (2008). *Experiments in ethics*. Harvard University Press.
Archibald, J. (2014). *Indigenous storywork: Educating the heart, mind, body, and spirit*. UBC Press.

Biesta, G. (2009). Good education in an age of measurement: On the need to reconnect with the question of purpose in education. *Educational Assessment, Evaluation and Accountability (formerly: Journal of Personnel Evaluation in Education)*, 21(1), 33–46. https://doi.org/10.1007/s11092-008-9064-9

Boler, M., & Zembylas, M. (2003). Discomforting truths: The emotional terrain of understanding difference. In P. Trifonas (Ed.), *Pedagogies of difference: Rethinking education for social change* (pp. 110–36). RoutledgeFalmer.

Bowden, P., & Mummery, J. (2009). *Understanding feminism*. Acumen.

Derrida, J. (1978). *Writing and difference*. Routledge.

– (1982). *Margins of philosophy*. University of Chicago Press.

– (1998). From adieu a Emmanuel Levinas. *Research in Phenomenology, 28*, 20–36.

– (2000a). *Of hospitality*. Stanford University Press.

– (2000b). Hostipitality. *Angelaki: Journal of Theoretical Humanities*, 5(3), 3–18. https://doi.org/10.1080/09697250020034706

– (2007). A certain impossible possibility of saying the event. *Critical Inquiry*, 33(2), 441–61. https://doi.org/10.1086/511506

Derrida, J., & Ewald, F. (2001). "A certain 'madness' must watch over thinking": Refusing to build a philosophical system, Derrida privileges experience and writes out of "compulsion." A dialogue around traces and deconstructions. In G. Biesta & D. Egéa-Kuehne (Eds.), *Derrida & education* (pp. 55–76). Routledge.

Dewey, J. (2011). *Democracy and education*. Simon & Brown.

Diener, E., Suh, E., Lucas, R., & Smith, H. (1999). Subjective well-being: Three decades of progress. *Psychological Bulletin*, 125(2), 276–302. https://doi.org/10.1037/0033-2909.125.2.276

Edgoose, J. (2001). Just decide! Derrida and the ethical aporias of education. In G. Biesta & D. Egéa-Kuehne (Eds.), *Derrida & education* (pp. 119–33). Routledge.

Fagan, M. (2013). *Ethics and politics after poststructuralism: Levinas, Derrida and Nancy*. Edinburgh University Press.

Falkenberg, T. (2014). Making sense of Western approaches to well-being for an educational context. In F. Deer, T. Falkenberg, B. McMillan, & L. Sims (Eds.), *Sustainable well-being: Concepts, issues, and educational practices* (pp. 77–94). Education for Sustainable Well-Being Press. www.ESWB-Press.org

– (2019). *Framing human well-being and well-becoming: An integrated systems approach*. www.wellbeinginschools.ca/paper-series

– (2020). The ethic of sustainable well-being and well-becoming. In H. Bai, D. Chang, & C. Scott (Eds.), *A book of ecological virtues: Living well in the Anthropocene* (pp. 157–77). University of Regina Press.

Freud, S. (2018). *The ego and the id*. Dover.

Friesen, J. (2000). *Aboriginal spirituality and biblical theology: Closer than you think*. Detselig.

Galetti, D. (2015). The grammar of Levinas' other, Other, autrui, Autrui: Addressing translation conventions and interpretation in English-language Levinas studies. *South African Journal of Philosophy, 34*(2), 199–213. https://doi.org/10.1080/02580136.2015.1023136

Hauseman, C. (2020). How workload influences the emotional aspects of principals' work. *Educational Leadership in Action, 6*(2), 1–30. https://www.lindenwood.edu/academics/beyond-the-classroom/publications/journal-of-educational-leadership-in-action/all-issues/volume-6-issue-2/how-workload-influences-the-emotional-aspects-of-principals-work/

Heringer, R. (2021). Teaching online as an ethics of hospitality: Lessons from a pandemic. *Studies in Philosophy and Education.* Advanced online publication. https://doi.org/10.1007/s11217-021-09791-8

Higgins, C. (2003). Teaching and the good life: A critique of the ascetic ideal in education. *Educational Theory, 53*(2), 131–54. https://doi.org/10.1111/j.1741-5446.2003.00131.x

Hinds, E., Jones, L., Gau, J., Forrester, K., & Biglan, A. (2015). Teacher distress and the role of experiential avoidance. *Psychology in the Schools, 52*(3), 284–97. https://doi.org/10.1002/pits.21821

Howell, A. (2009) Flourishing: Achievement-related correlates of students' well-being. *The Journal of Positive Psychology, 4*(1), 1–13. https://doi.org/10.1080/17439760802043459

Kahneman, D., Diener, E., & Schwarz, N. (Eds.). (1999). *Well-being: The foundations of hedonistic psychology.* Russell Sage Foundation.

Kant, I. (2007). *Perpetual peace.* Filiquarian Publishing, LLC.

Keyes, C. (1998). Social well-being. *Social Psychology Quarterly, 61*(2), 121–40. https://doi.org/10.2307/2787065

— (2006a). Mental health in adolescence: Is America's youth flourishing? *American Journal of Orthopsychiatry, 76*(3), 395–402. https://doi.org/10.1037/0002-9432.76.3.395

— (2006b). Subjective well-being in mental health and human development research worldwide: An introduction. *Social Indicators Research, 77*(1), 1–10. https://doi.org/10.1007/s11205-005-5550-3

— (2007). Promoting and protecting mental health as flourishing: A complementary strategy for improving national mental health. *American Psychologist, 62*(2), 95–108. https://doi.org/10.1037/0003-066X.62.2.95

Keyes, C., & Annas, J. (2009). Feeling good and functioning well: Distinctive concepts in ancient philosophy and contemporary science. *Journal of Positive Psychology, 4*(3), 197–201. https://doi.org/10.1080/17439760902844228

Larson, R. (1989). Is feeling "in control" related to happiness in daily life? *Psychological Reports, 64*(3), 775–84. https://doi.org/10.2466/pr0.1989.64.3.775

Levinas, E. (1972). *Humanisme de l'autre homme.* Le Livre de Poche.

– (1982). *Éthique et infini*. Le Livre de Poche.
– (1995). *Altérité et transcendence*. Le Livre de Poche.
Manuel, J., Carter, D., & Dutton, J. (2018). "As much as I love being in the classroom …" : Understanding secondary English teachers' workload. *English in Australia, 53*(3), 5–22.
Martin, J., Sugarman, J., & Thompson, J. (2003). *Psychology and the question of agency*. State University of New York Press.
Moore, S. (2017). *Trickster chases the tale of education*. McGill-Queen's University Press.
Newhook, J. (2010). Teaching "in town" or "around the bay": Comparing rural and urban primary/elementary teachers' workload concerns in Newfoundland and Labrador, Canada. *Policy and Practice in Health and Safety, 8*(1), 77–94. https://doi.org/10.1080/14774003.2010.11667743
Nussbaum, M.C. (2011). *Creating capabilities: The human development approach*. Balknap Press of Harvard University Press.
OECD. (2017). *PISA 2015 results: Students' well-being*. OECD Publishing. http://dx.doi.org/10.1787/9789264273856-en
Oliver, K. (2001). *Witnessing: Beyond recognition*. University of Minnesota Press.
– (2015). Witnessing, recognition, and response ethics. *Philosophy & Rhetoric, 48*(4), 473–93. https://doi.org/10.5325/philrhet.48.4.0473
Peters, M., & Biesta, G. (2009). *Derrida, deconstruction, and the politics of pedagogy*. Peter Lang.
Peterson, C. (2006). *A primer in positive psychology*. Oxford University Press.
Peterson, C., & Park, N. (2004). Classification and measurement of character strengths: Implications for practice. In P.A. Linley & S. Joseph (Eds.), *Positive psychology in practice* (pp. 433–46). John Wiley & Sons.
Peterson, C., & Seligman, M. (2004). *Character strengths and virtues: A handbook and classification*. Oxford University Press/American Psychological Association.
Ruitenberg, C. (2011). Hospitality and subjectification: On seeing children and youth as respondents. *Jeunesse: Young people, texts, cultures, 3*(2), 133–40. https://doi.org/10.1353/jeu.2011.0012
– (2016). *Unlocking the world: Education in an ethic of hospitality*. Routledge.
Ryan, R.M., & Deci, E.L. (2001). On happiness and human potential: A review of research on hedonic and eudaimonic well-being. *Annual Review of Psychology, 52*(1), 141–66. https://doi-org.uml.idm.oclc.org/10.1146/annurev.psych.52.1.141 https://doi.org/10.1146/annurev.psych.52.1.141
Ryff, C. (1989). Happiness is everything, or is it? Explorations on the meaning of psychological well-being. *Journal of Personality and Social Psychology, 57*, 1069–81. https://doi.org/10.1037/0022-3514.57.6.1069
Stonechild, B. (2020). *Loss of Indigenous Eden and the fall of spirituality*. University of Regina Press.

Sumner, L.W. (1996). *Welfare, happiness, and ethics*. Oxford University Press.
Todd, S. (2003). *Learning from the Other: Levinas, psychoanalysis, and ethical possibilities in education*. State University of New York Press.
– (2009). *Toward an imperfect education: Facing humanity, rethinking cosmopolitanism*. Paradigm Publishers.
Trifonas, P. (2001). Teaching the Other II: Ethics, writing, community. In G. Biesta & D. Egéa-Kuehne (Eds.), *Derrida & education* (pp. 98–118). Routledge.
United Nations. (1948). *Universal Declaration of Human Rights*. https://www.un.org/sites/un2.un.org/files/udhr.pdf

PART TWO

Conceptualizing Well-Being and Well-Becoming in Schools

PART TWO

Conceptualizing Well-Being and Well-Becoming in School

5 Well-Being as a Core Focus of School Education: Conceptualizing Indigenous Well-Being

FRANK DEER AND JESSICA TRICKEY

When considering how well-being may be conceptualized in the context of Indigenous peoples, the topics of both health and well-being merit attention (Wilk et al., 2017). In describing the state of well-being for Indigenous peoples in Canada, it is important to note the considerable inequalities between Indigenous and non-Indigenous people (Hadjipavlou et al., 2018). First Nations people in Canada are six times more likely to die as a result of complications from alcohol use, three times more likely to die from substance use aside from alcohol, and twice as likely to die from suicide (TRC, 2015). There is no doubt that the well-being of many Indigenous people in Canada is a pressing issue, not only for the individuals for whom such risks and harms are prevalent but also for the larger society.

Central to any discussion of Indigenous well-being are the contexts in which many Indigenous people find themselves, namely their dire socio-economic circumstances, their lack of opportunities, and their legacy of historical injustices. Such contexts have been the focus of numerous explorations of Indigenous peoples' experiences in Canada. One of the Truth and Reconciliation Commission of Canada's 94 Calls to Action is an appeal for government to fund centres that promote Indigenous healing in a culturally relevant way (TRC, 2015). Indigenous understandings of well-being (as the focus of the healing) are quite different from Western conceptions of well-being and the two may seem difficult to reconcile. However, the journey toward well-being and the good life in our world should be regarded as encompassing all humanity regardless of nation, creed, or ancestry (Deer & Falkenberg, 2016a, pp. 1–5). In order to explore how Indigenous and non-Indigenous perspectives of well-being converge into a unified discussion, one that is responsive to the reconciliatory project, an understanding of how well-being is understood by Indigenous peoples is required, and must take into account the unique manifestations of relevant knowledges, heritage, consciousness, and traditions. Falkenberg (2019) apprehends the WB2-Framework as one that "should ... have potential supporting some of the non-Western perspectives on well-being" (p. 9). In this chapter, we will consider how Falkenberg's framework provides a point of entry into understanding Indigenous well-being.

The WB2-Framework

In our exploration of Indigenous well-being, we employ Falkenberg's (2019) WB2-Framework (2019), a systematic, integrated approach to well-being.[1] Falkenberg (2019) specified five components to well-being and well-becoming within this framework:

1. Agency
2. Situational Opportunities for Agency
3. Enjoyment of Life
4. Meaningfulness in Life, and
5. Social Connections

The use of the WB2-Framework as a means of coming to understand Indigenous well-being emerges from a collaboration between Falkenberg and Deer in the development of a volume that explored Indigenous well-being (Deer & Falkenberg, 2016b). In this work, Falkenberg asserted that "Indigenous perspectives on (education for) well-being can, and should, be intentionally integrated into what is currently [the] mainstream ... discourse on (education for) well-being" (p. 187). Addressing Indigenous well-being in this way may benefit from a conceptualization of Indigenous well-being that is appropriately economical, delineated, and expansive. The WB2-Framework is a fitting point of entry for an exploration of how Indigenous perspectives relate to well-being. In order to begin this exploration, each of the constituent components of the WB2-Framework will be briefly described, followed by a survey of Indigenous perspectives associated with this particular component. The ways in which Indigenous peoples have described their own journeys toward well-being appear to have some relevance to each of the components of the WB2-Framework. In using this framework as a starting point from which Indigenous well-being may be conceptualized, it is important to acknowledge that the components of the framework do not exist independently but influence one another concurrently; the well-being of Indigenous peoples may thus be understood appropriately within aa holistic context(Rountree & Smith, 2016).

It is not the goal of the authors to articulate new or additional components to the WB2-Framework; rather, it is our goal to discuss how Indigenous knowledge, heritage, consciousness, and experience may be understood as an outworking of this framework.

Agentic Capabilities

The first component of the WB2-Framework is that of agency. Agency may be regarded as the fundamental need for control. People develop knowledge of themselves and their environment using descriptive (knowing that), experiential (knowing based on experience), procedural (knowing how), and causal knowledge (knowing why) (Falkenberg, 2019). These forms of knowledge can then guide them toward particular motivations and decisions – thus leading to control over their own endeavours. Within Indigenous cultures, agency is important for both the individual and the community.

Individual

On the individual level, agency is fostered in Indigenous children when they are born. For example, Briggs (2001) compared autonomy among Inuit people with that of *Qallunaat* (non-Inuit/Western) people. Both groups in the study claimed that their community had agency and that the other did not. Their reasoning differed: While the *Qallunaat* stated that the Inuit were constrained by parents' wishes and traditions, Inuit people referred to the strict rules and regulations *Qallunaat* people must follow. Western society typically maintains strict hierarchies between children and adults. Adults represent authority, as in the case of parents and teachers. Authority figures impose rules onto children at a young age and these rules are not necessarily based on an intuitive understanding of child development. For instance, in school, children learn they must listen, take notes, and acquire information – often without an understanding of how the information may benefit them. This can be confusing for Inuit children, who are often taught to be critical of information presented to them. Traditionally Inuit children learn and acquire knowledge from community Elders with whom they have relationships built on respect and trust. On the other hand, Western societies usually do not bring children into important discussions and decisions (Lines & Jardine, 2019). Western youth may frequently be in situations in which they are given little power over their circumstances. By contrast, Indigenous cultures typically call on youth to offer their opinions and provide input on decision-making (Lines & Jardine, 2019).

Autonomy is essential for the Inuit (Briggs, 2001). As infants, Inuit children are given the space to develop their own sleeping, eating, and playing schedules. Instead of receiving criticism from parents and Elders for "bad" or inappropriate behaviour, they are told to experiment with their environment and form their own answers to difficult questions. Elders only provide guidance when children request it. It has been observed that Inuit children do, at times, receive too much affectionate attention from caregivers and may retract or withdraw from parental support (Wexler, 2009). This differs from *Qallunaat* children, who often rebel against parents' strict authority. Inuit children may feel lonely or disconnected in having to solve many of their own problems. *Qallunaat* children, by contrast, may not develop the appropriate skills and knowledge to carry them through life as they rely on help from others in dealing with problems. Ultimately, children learn best when teachings follow from cultural values (Wexler, 2009). Inuit children's sense of autonomy and competence is fulfilled when they acquire the ability to deal with problems themselves. This relates to Erikson's concept of ego strength, which refers to the developmental stages people undergo as they move through life (Gfellner, 2016). Having robust ego strength and opportunities for development through these stages is associated with achievement and well-being for Indigenous youth, particularly when they are connected with their Indigenous identities.

In order to have agency, Indigenous children need to learn their cultures' knowledges. Having knowledge of their world and why things happen fosters well-being (Falkenberg, 2019). Learning cultural knowledge from Elders, including hunting, camping, toolmaking, stories, and beliefs is an important contributor to happiness and well-being (Kral et al., 2011; Rountree & Smith, 2016). Indigenous youth believe they have an important responsibility to learn and know their cultural traditions in order to carry on their culture (Lines & Jardine, 2019).

To understand health in an Indigenous context, it is important not to generalize from Western conceptions of health. Health may not be easily definable in Indigenous contexts (Carey, 2013). Unlike Western cultures, which divide health into categories of heart health, lung health, and so on, Indigenous cultures are more concerned with overall quality of life. This includes connection between the body, the mind, the land, the community, and the spirits. Central to well-being is control and autonomy. Indigenous peoples need to have control over their safety, security, bodily systems, hormone levels, mental states, emotions, and environment (Carey, 2013).

Community

On a broader community level, Indigenous peoples must have the ability to determine their own futures (Murphy, 2014). Currently, though they can vote in civic elections, Indigenous peoples often have little influence in civic affairs and are under-represented in government bodies such as federal and provincial legislatures. Political under-representation and lack of agency in general are associated with poor psychological health, substance use, suicide, and violence. Research shows that in Indigenous communities greater self-determination is correlated with better health outcomes (Murphy, 2014). Indigenous communities need to have the power to make political and economic decisions that benefit their s needs and that reflect their values. This requires autonomy and control over their respective territories (Kant et al., 2013). Kant et al. (2013) conducted focus groups with First Nations communities to determine indicators of well-being. The most important determinant of communities' well-being was control over land use and cultural activities. In addressing well-being and health among Indigenous peoples, it has become frequently asserted that the federal government should ensure that it is not overstepping boundaries by imposing regulations on land and cultures.[2]

Indigenous communities may greatly benefit by creating their own measures for well-being. In an era in which greater and more deliberate participation by Indigenous communities to explore and conceptualize their own well-being has become a norm in many quarters, their active participation in research and development is essential. Peters, Peterson, and the Dakota Wicohan Community (2019) created a strength-based measure assessing well-being among Dakota people. This measure promotes agency among the respondents by asking them how they perceive physical, mental, and spiritual health, and whether they believe they meet standards in these areas. Respondents are also asked how important these aspects of health are to their lives. Unlike Western measures that focus on singular definitions of bodily and mental health, and determine how individuals fit into categories of "healthy" or "unhealthy," Peters and Peterson's measure focuses on subjective knowledge of health and how people experience their own health from a holistic perspective. Their measure demonstrated reliability and convergent validity, making it a good metric when attempting to understand the well-being of the Dakota people with whom they worked. The Dakota Wicohan Community developed another measure of well-being that assessed how people remember, reclaim, and reconnect with their Indigenous cultures. The two measures were correlated and shown to effectively gauge well-being. As principles of adequate collaboration and employment of such concepts as ownership, control, access, and possession (OCAP; National Aboriginal Health Organization, 2007) have become more accepted, the manner in which researchers and other leads facilitate such collaboration has become more deliberate. Studies such as these support the notion that agency is an important component of well-being – particularly in regard to how Indigenous people govern such work. Having control in their daily lives, their cultures, and perceptions of their cultures contributes to better psychological health and lower stress (Murphy, 2014). As many have said of the importance of Indigenous peoples' contributions to various areas of human endeavour: *Nothing about us without us.*

Situational Opportunities for Agency

Beyond the need for agency, the WB2-Framework focuses upon opportunities to express agency (Falkenberg, 2019). This requires seeing and utilizing situations to act on choices. Unfortunately, due to structural and institutional barriers, many Indigenous peoples lack opportunities that would support their well-being.

Lavoie et al. (2010) studied First Nations' well-being in Manitoba to determine how self-determination and barriers to it may impact health. Primarily, the researchers examined how First Nations' access to nursing stations and community control over health services affected the number of hospital visits. The relationship between First Nations communities and government-provided health care is based on three models: health transfer, integrated community-based care, and non-transferred/non-integrated care. With the health transfer approach, First Nations take full control over resources, programs, and services, and can determine how these respond to community needs. In an integrated community-based approach, First Nations communities design the health care programs but the government is responsible for delivering resources for these programs. In the non-transferred/non-integrated approach, First Nations have full control over a few programs while the government is involved in funding arrangements for each program. Lavoie et al.'s (2010) results showed that greater access to nursing stations and health transfer resources resulted in fewer hospital visits, suggesting that when First Nations have full autonomy over their health services, their communities have better health outcomes, and that governments ought to do more to provide the space and opportunity for Indigenous communities' autonomy.

Self-determination is crucial as communities look to improve well-being and to reduce suicide rates in Indigenous communities. King (2014) explored common metrics for understanding health in Canada, involving statistics that show rates of suicide and substance use. When looking at suicide rates in Canada, First Nations youth have a risk five times greater than that of non-Indigenous youth (King, 2014). The issue with such statistics is that they cluster all First Nations into one category. The statistic is then skewed for certain nations. For instance, in British Columbia, some First Nations reserves show a suicide rate 100 times the national average while other reserves show a suicide rate of zero (King, 2014). The stark difference relates to communities' capacity for self-determination. First Nations that have greater ability to self-determine and more freedom to engage in cultural traditions have a decreased risk of suicide in their communities. This self-determination includes control over policing, social services, education, council, and policies concerning equity and other matters. Providing opportunities for self-determination is, therefore, a life-or-death matter for Indigenous cultures.

It has been asserted that self-determination is crucial to Indigenous well-being. Among the Anishinaabe, the ability to participate in cultural activities and the ability to go about their lives in culturally relevant ways have been important components of self-determination – components that were often denied or inaccessible (Madjedi & Daya, 2016). Access to community Elders and spaces to learn are important to develop agency based on knowledge. In many parts of Canada, well-being is understood to be an ambitious individual and societal goal, especially in contexts in which ongoing hardship, as evidenced in high suicide rates, is central to the collective consciousness. Kral (2019) explores well-being in contexts such as these among the Inuit peoples. One of Kral's central theses is that appropriate communal, cultural, and historical understandings and approaches are necessary to address the well-being of the Inuit and to develop strategies for suicide prevention. A recurrent concept in the discussions on Inuit well-being is *Quajimajatuqangit* – understood to mean *Inuit traditional knowledge* (Government of Nunavut, 2013). *Quajimajatuqangit* has taken on central importance in community initiatives and government activities in regions such as Nunavut in the quest to establish appropriate situational opportunities for agency that address such things as self-harm and the ongoing need to improve well-being (Lévesque, 2014).

Governments worldwide have failed in providing these situational opportunities for agency and self-determination. In Australia, for instance, the government has created a largely unsuccessful program to "close the gap" between Indigenous and non-Indigenous people in terms of health, employment, and income (Carey, 2013). The initiative uses the capability approach, consisting of three components: freedom, agency, and pluralism (Klein, 2016). Agency, in this approach, refers to having the opportunities and means to accomplish that which is valued and desired. Pluralism indicates there is no singular political approach that will be appropriate for all Indigenous cultures in all contexts. Though the Australian government is using this approach to inform policy, Klein (2016) argues that they are applying it incorrectly. First, the Australian government situated the approach through a deficit lens, implying that Indigenous people lacked agency and that government policies would help them develop it. Second, the government assumed that Indigenous people have, until now, relied on welfare. Underlying this idea is the government's belief that Indigenous people should take responsibility to achieve self-determination. This belief ignores the structural barriers that still exist. Additionally, as Klein argues, the idea that welfare is a necessity for autonomy misunderstands *autonomy*. Autonomy is a choice rather than a necessity, and it should be achieved regardless of economic concerns. Finally, the Australian government instituted "basic necessities" such as minimum welfare cheques. This policy, however, is in conflict with the idea of pluralism. Pluralism states that there is no "one-size-fits-all" approach that will apply effectively to all Indigenous people. Assuming there is a minimum welfare amount that will meet all needs is an oversimplification.

Ultimately, when implementing strategies to facilitate self-determination for Indigenous communities, governments have as of now failed to provide a solution. As control is integral to Indigenous well-being (Carey, 2013), it is necessary that the governments step back when evaluating the health of Indigenous people. Listening to Indigenous people and their needs, and providing resources based on their needs, will be an important step forward to ensure communities can self-determine. For instance, many First Nations people do not have access to health care, financial security, or safety in their communities (Graham & Stamler, 2013; Rountree & Smith, 2016). As Indigenous communities have changed over time, there is more unemployment and economic uncertainty (Kral et al., 2011). These structural issues limit one's life choices, adversely affecting one's ability to exercise agency. In supporting the development of agency in Indigenous communities, governments need to listen and be more responsive to Indigenous concerns and provide the resources as necessary.

Enjoyment

A third component of the WB2-Framework is related to the experience of enjoyment of life (Falkenberg, 2019). People need to do activities in which they take pleasure and experience excitement. Though people can enjoy everyday events, and these contribute to their overall enjoyment, this component of well-being refers to a general feeling of happiness in life. Related to this, Indigenous peoples need to have the opportunities to engage in cultural traditions and activities that they enjoy. One example of these activities is artwork.

Research has demonstrated that art can be used as a therapy; it aids self-expression and contributes to positive mental health (Muirhead & Leeuw, 2013). For Indigenous people, artwork may be especially effective as a healing treatment. Therapy typically situates the client in front of a therapist, verbally explaining their personal issues; this creates a power dynamic, with the therapist having authority over the client, determining the client's health problems, and prescribing treatment. This dynamic is not in line with traditional Indigenous worldviews, where learning is frequently communal and reciprocal between the patient and the healer. By contrast, artwork offers a joyful activity for Indigenous people from which many draw meaning (more on meaningfulness in the following section). Engaging in artwork in any form, such as painting, performing, writing, sewing, building, can be fun and empowering. Additionally, artwork provides a medium for expression of feelings and thoughts that may be difficult to communicate verbally. This method of healing promotes self-confidence and self-esteem (Muirhead & Leeuw, 2013) and allows for control over the healing process. In addition to the personal benefits derived from the engaging in art, people can connect with their community through performances and exhibitions, and connect with their identity through culturally specific forms of art.

Feeling joy through pride in their traditions and identity can give Indigenous peoples hope that their culture is thriving. This joy may also be felt through experiences in which the sense of belonging within their community emerge, as well as through the feeling of pride in their identity. These are clearly important factors for well-being among Indigenous people (Rountree & Smith, 2016). Part of well-being involves enjoying one's cultural traditions and appreciating one's cultural community.

Meaningfulness

One of the most important motivations in a person's life is the search for meaning (Falkenberg, 2019). What constitutes meaning cannot be explained through a single definition, as it varies based on culture. How Indigenous people find meaning will vary between communities, but most of their paths will differ substantially from those found in Western societies, particularly in the context of health and well-being. Importantly, while Western cultures use a health paradigm that identifies a problem with a single part of the body, formulates a cause for the problem, and attempts to treat the problem, Indigenous cultures are often holistic in their approach to well-being. The lack of holism and spirituality in treatment facilities can prevent Indigenous people from seeking help for mental health issues (Stewart, 2008). Though Indigenous people have the highest rates of mental illness in Canada, they are the least likely to have access to mental health facilities (Stewart, 2008). Stewart (2008) conducted interviews with Indigenous counsellors in Canada and asked how they incorporate traditional Indigenous perspectives into their practices and how this affects clients. From the interviews, Stewart identified four main facets of well-being: community, cultural identity, holism, and interdependence. All counsellors expressed that healing within the community is important to well-being, including having open relationships with family members, counsellors, community members, and Elders. Further, counsellors reported that their clients felt strength and empowerment in their Indigenous identity; activities that can bolster this identity include participating in cultural activities, speaking Indigenous languages, engaging in dances and celebrations, and following rituals. Finally, counsellors indicated that using a holistic approach was necessary for well-being; using the body, mind, land, and spirit puts the person in balance. This may involve bringing food into the counselling session or taking clients outdoors to experience nature. Research in the United States showed that connection to Indigenous culture and identity was correlated with psychological well-being (Wexler, 2009). Specifically, understanding how historical circumstances shape their positions and finding meaning through cultural values fosters resilience in Indigenous people (Wexler, 2009). This research demonstrates that providing more opportunities for Indigenous people to celebrate and feel pride in their culture can improve health outcomes.

Research in Australia also finds a strong association between connection to culture and well-being. Dockery (2012) created a measure of enculturation, assessing whether people participate in their cultures, identify with their cultures, speak their traditional languages, and engage in traditional activities. Results showed that participating in culture and engaging in cultural activities had the strongest association with well-being and happiness. Speaking traditional languages was associated with better health and lower rates of substance abuse. Dockery observed a nonlinear relationship in regard to identification with culture: Those with a moderate degree of cultural identity had higher rates of psychological stress. Dockery concluded that this may be due to feelings of ambiguity resulting from participation in two cultures (Western and Indigenous). Those having a stronger cultural identity and living in remote areas experienced lower psychological stress, while those in non-remote areas experienced greater stress and discrimination. Dockery determined that those in non-remote areas more frequently interact with Western culture and, therefore, experience greater negativity from others and greater ambiguity. Strengthening cultural identity, then, is integral for well-being.

Traditional Indigenous worldviews and practices must be incorporated into existing health care programs in order for Indigenous people, especially those living in urban areas, to find meaning in their cultural identities. For example, Seeking Safety is a program in Ontario, Canada, that helps those suffering from intergenerational trauma, PTSD, and substance use (Marsh et al., 2015). This program is beginning to incorporate traditional Indigenous practices through a two-eyed seeing approach, combining Western and Indigenous knowledges of healing. While Western well-being uses a treatment model that is quantifiable and context-independent, Indigenous science is usually dependent on the context in which it is learned and it relies on global connection between the earth, the spirits, and the people. This connection is applied in sweat lodges at the Seeking Safety program. Elders are invited to the lodges to use their skills and knowledge to connect positively with people and bring their lives into harmony. The program uses traditional songs, smudging, drumming, and sacred bundles to aid people in the recovery process. Marsh et al. (2015) examined how sacred teachings can be easily mapped onto teachings already a part of the Seeking Safety program. For example, the traditional teaching of carrying a sacred bundle to help a person climb a mountain can be linked to ideas surrounding the burden of substance addiction, control, and recovery. Another example is the way anger can be compared to a sacred fire that must be managed so as not to be destructive. This two-eyed seeing approach can foster greater healing for Indigenous and non-Indigenous people by connecting them with meaning in their lives. Other Indigenous health practices that are useful to incorporate are rituals that use the four sacred medicines: sage, sweetgrass, cedar, and tobacco (Solomon & Wane, 2005). Using a spiritual bath or a shake-tent lodge can be another option in treatment centres (Solomon & Wane, 2005). These holistic practices are meaningful to Indigenous people and help them bring their lives into balance and harmony.

Social Connections

The final component of the WB2-Framework is that of social connections. In this component, the intention is to "capture the idea that humans are social (communal) beings with a need for social connections ... the communal (social) connections have to be subjectively experienced by the person whose well-being is under consideration rather than just being seen by others" (Falkenberg, 2019, p. 22). This component of well-being is important because when people feel isolated and disconnected from others, their well-being suffers. In an Indigenous context, this includes not only friends and family, but also connections with the broader community, the land, and the spirits.

An important aspect of achieving balance and harmony in a holistic approach to well-being is connection with the community, the land, and the spirits – a notion that is central to this final component of the WB2-Framework, in which spirituality is resident (Falkenberg, 2019).

Family

In the context of northern Canada, Kral et al. (2011) identified factors that Inuit communities felt were important to health and well-being. The most commonly cited factor was family. Engaging in cultural activities with family members (e.g., fishing and hunting), communicating negative feelings with family members, and visiting family frequently were crucial to overall happiness in life. Similarly, the most common reasons for unhappiness were feelings of distance or hostility within the family. Many also reported that talking with one another about topics such as negative feelings, daily life, and past experiences was an important part of healing. Among Anishinaabe people, disconnect from families and communities was considered a barrier to health (Madjedi & Daya, 2016). Indeed, relationships and connections are frequently found to be important for Indigenous well-being (Rountree & Smith, 2016). In another study, Kral et al. (2011) asked participants how the communities had changed over time. Many felt that youth were not visiting family members as often and parents were not as responsive and caring. Additionally, many indicated that children were learning from teachers at schools more often than Elders and family members. Children then experienced a "double life" as they learn Western and traditional teachings. Finally, romantic relationships had reportedly changed. Many Inuit felt that they were moving away from traditional conceptions of relationships, such as arranged marriages, and moving toward Western conceptions of love. Overall, however, family and community connections, especially with older knowledge keepers, were considered important for happiness and well-being (Lafleur, 2016).

Community

Feeling like they belong in their community and feeling connections with their community members are important to Indigenous people's well-being (Kant et al., 2013). How they connect with their community and its values is important as well. Research shows that youth prosper when they share community values, particularly values that transcend their own selves and time, continuing through generations (Wexler, 2009). Native Hawaiians' conceptions of individual health depend on their connections with their communities and nature (McCubbin & Marsella, 2009). In contrast to Western beliefs that behaviours result from the processing of stimuli through a series of neurological networks, Native Hawaiians see behaviour as resulting from harmony with all things. Harmful behaviours result from one being out of balance with the land and the community. Losing personal harmony can affect societal harmony, resulting in mental health issues for the individual. For example, behaviours such as bragging, breaking promises, or stealing can damage the society (McCubbin & Marsella, 2009), and bring imbalance for the person. Prosocial behaviours, such as helpfulness and humility, can restore harmony and improve well-being.

In addition to sharing community values, participating in community activities is important for Indigenous well-being. Having Indigenous role models, contributing to the community and relationships, and participating in the community affect well-being (Rountree & Smith, 2016).

Land

One important connection for well-being among Indigenous peoples is the connection with the land (Bell, 2016). Lines and Jardine (2019) asked Dene youth in Yellowknife (aged 13–18) how they perceive and experience health. The overall consensus was that a connection to the land was a necessary component of health. The youth appreciated living off the land, which included learning from Elders, preparing traditional food, and learning skills on the land (e.g., hunting and fishing). They also appreciated the principle of reciprocity: giving back to the land what is taken. The youth felt that they had a big responsibility to maintain the Dene way of life and that the adults could not uphold traditions and cultures alone. Proximity to and closeness with nature are also important for Anishinaabe people (Madjedi & Daya, 2016).

Native Hawaiians believe that the land is important for harmony and, consequently, health. Resisting Western conceptualizations of land as a commodity to be owned and sold, Native Hawaiians believe that the land has a physical aspect (providing a homeland and source of nourishment for people), a psychological aspect (affecting positive and negative thinking), and a spiritual aspect (connecting Hawaiians to the spirits; McCubbin & Marsella, 2009).

Spirituality

Spirituality may be regarded, fundamentally, as subjective experiences through which one engages in, among other things, metaphysical questions as a means of understanding the self and that which is external to the self (Harris, 2014). In Indigenous contexts, spirituality frequently involves relations with ancestors; these relations are cited as important parts of Indigenous worldviews and are connected to well-being. Though spirituality is sometimes not cited in studies as an important component of well-being (Rountree & Smith, 2016), it is nonetheless crucial as it involves connection to cultural traditions. Some studies find that spiritual practice, knowledge, and ceremony (Rountree & Smith, 2016), as well as understanding traditions and languages and experiencing spiritual growth (Graham & Stamler, 2013), are significant for well-being. For instance, mental health among Native Hawaiians involves a balance between the self, the family, the land, and the gods (McCubbin & Marsella, 2009).

Using the Medicine Wheel (a holistic approach to health connecting the body, community, land, and spirits), Indigenous people experience relationships with all parts of the universe, including the sky, the sun, the water, the rain, and the animals (Solomon & Wane, 2005). These relationships are spiritual in nature and connect Indigenous people with their ancestors. They receive guidance from the Creator, who gave life and peace, and from Mother Earth, who gave spirit, truth, and culture (Solomon & Wane, 2005).

We have situated spirituality within the WB2-Framework's component on social connections because these connections are central to communal life for many Indigenous peoples. Such connections, as we have attempted to demonstrate here, are not only resident in a physical human-to-human form but encompass many other parts of our world. Overall, understanding health and well-being among Indigenous communities involves knowing how their social network involves connections with family, community, land, and spirits. Understanding the way Indigenous people feel connected and in harmony requires listening and learning from each community's perceptions of well-being.

Discussion: An Indigenous Perspective on Well-Being

A survey of perspectives on Indigenous well-being that is organized through the WB2-Framework, introduced by Falkenberg (2019), offers a useful starting point for coming to understand how Indigenous well-being may be conceptualized, one that can be applied to particular populations and contexts. What the use of the WB2-Framework for this purpose reveals is that the dimensions of well-being for Indigenous peoples – however straightforward to generally identify and explore – are difficult to delineate for the purposes of conceptualization and intellectual investigation.

From the preceding discussion it becomes clear that various aspects of Indigenous well-being in each of the five WB2-Framework components influence one another (e.g., living a meaningful life involves understanding the community's collective meanings; Wexler, 2009). Understanding the state of well-being as reflected in a particular person or population may be difficult. On the evidence laid out here and elsewhere, the use of any approach to understanding well-being needs to be mindful of the unique manifestations of Indigenous knowledge, heritage, consciousness, and tradition (Deer & Falkenberg, 2016b), including any holistic and spiritual dimensions.

The current discussion of how First Nations, Métis, and Inuit peoples have voiced, represented, and conceptualized their own perspectives of well-being supports the notion that the components of the WB2-Framework – those of agency, opportunities to act on agency, enjoyment of life, meaningfulness in cultures, and social connections – are present within the perspectives of the Indigenous peoples of Canada. We are stating this notion deliberately and in a way that diverges somewhat from the statement above that "Indigenous perspectives on (education for) well-being can, and should, be intentionally integrated into what is currently the mainstream … discourse on (education for) well-being" (Falkenberg, 2016, p. 188). Although Falkenberg goes on to substantiate his intentions with his thesis on Indigenous well-being, we would like to suggest as a trajectory for further study a slightly different perspective, on stemming from the confluence between mainstream ideas on well-being (in this discussion framed by the WB2-Framework) and those related to the perspectives of Indigenous peoples. Reconciliation would be a central lens of such a study. According to definitions provided by the Truth and Reconciliation Commission of Canada, reconciliation may be regarded as the movement of improving relationships between Indigenous and non-Indigenous peoples, while maintaining an understanding of how past events have adversely affected these relationships (Truth and Reconciliation Commission of Canada, 2015). Just as this spirit of reconciliation can lead to understanding between Indigenous and non-Indigenous peoples, so too can it serve as an inspiration for understanding, sharing, and collaborating between various camps in the well-being debate. In this area of confluence, integration would manifest in a different way. Rather than yielding to the possibility that differences in power/authority may adversely affect how one or both perspectives on well-being are understood – as in any integrationist model – what we might embrace is the application of the nation-to-nation principles of *Kashwenta* (the two-row wampum treaty of the Haudenausaunee). Deer (2015) describes the nation-to-nation potential of Kashwenta:

> Established in 1613 ... Kashwentha codifies sovereignty and nationhood in an assertive manner that avoids the concession of lands or the responsibilities of stewardship. With the use of imagery, narrative and trans-generational consistency of interpretation, Kashwentha provides an illustration of an international accord where the quality of relationships are of principal focus as opposed to transactions involving the ownership/control of territories (Alfred, 2009). It is for this reason that Kashwentha is sometimes boldly affirmed as a treaty that codifies the sovereignty of the Indigenous peoples in question. Kashwentha as a coherent whole represents, in principle, an accord of sharing represented by the two rows of dark wampum against a background of white. These two rows represent the separate, and perhaps unique and distinct, paths that the Onkwehonwe and non-Indigenous settlers of this region occupy (Rice, 2013). The two paths are separate, do not interfere with one another, and do not have pre-established/planned destinies. The significance of this representation is to codify not just sovereignty, but agency as well. Essential to this accord are the principles of peace, respect, and responsibility for our own actions. (pp. 4–5)

As Widdowson and Howard (2013) note, there may be two ways of approaching how the Indigenous peoples' experience may be addressed in educational contexts – an *integrationist* approach and a *parallelist* approach. In the integrationist approach, (as the term suggests) the perspectives and contexts of Indigenous peoples are taken and included in another, usually larger, conceptual ethos (in this case, the WB2-Framework). This may be useful as a means of situating Indigenous perspectives into a non-Indigenous framework so as to understand Indigenous perspectives better, as we have ventured to do in this chapter. However, at the confluence of reconciliatory interfaces, at which these different understandings are shared and frequently aggregated, understandings of these Indigenous perspectives on well-being may become diminished among the more dominant non-Indigenous ethos. A parallelist approach would be a departure from the process of integration through which the perspectives of (in this case) well-being are understood, not principally through how they may be situated within a pre-existing non-Indigenous framework but rather through the perspectives themselves. This would involve experiential processes through which the uninitiated approach learning with perspectives that are offered through appropriate Indigenous contexts. In this approach, reductionism is avoided, culture and language are appropriately employed, and commitment to the necessarily lengthy process of coming to understand are essential. The thesis being adduced here is that the process through which fair and just collaboration in a nation-to-nation manner – that which is central to Kashwentha – may better serve to condition the convergence where perspectives become manifest and harmonious with one another.

A final point for consideration. Among the two prevailing and admittedly reductionist and oversimplified positions on well-being reflected in this piece, those of *Indigenous* and *non-Indigenous* positions reflect rather different areas of human concern: individual sovereignty (associated with non-Indigenous perspectives on well-being) and collective consciousness (associated with Indigenous perspectives on well-being). It seems to us that any conversation on Indigenous well-being and its potential connections with non-Indigenous frames such as that of the WB2-Framework must reconcile this issue. The framework does reflect elements of these potentially competing concerns. However, in many areas of human endeavour (especially those for which identity politics and tribalism are resident), the ways in which we minister to these aspects of well-being may become difficult to navigate; there are instances in which Indigenous communities' defence of the communal perspective is offered quite vigorously, just as there are instances in which individuals of a conservative orientation aggressively argue for individualism. The question is, Are these two orientations reconcilable?

NOTES

1 See also the discussions of the WB2-Framework in Chapters 6, 13, and 14 (this volume).
2 The inclusion of self-determination, specifically regarding control of territory, may appear to be out of place in the "agency" component. This potential observation is not lost on the authors, who, in developing this particular section, were compelled to include a communal dimension of Indigenous agency.

REFERENCES

Alfred, T. (2009). *Peace, power, righteousness: An Indigenous manifesto* (2nd ed.). Oxford University Press.

Bell, N. (2016). Mino-bimaadiziwin: Education for the good life. In F. Deer & T. Falkenberg (Eds.), *Indigenous perspectives on education for well-being in Canada* (pp. 7–20). Education for Sustainable Well-Being Press. www.ESWB-Press.org

Briggs, J.L. (2001). Qallunaat run on rails: Inuit do what they want to do. "Autonomies" in camp and town. *Etudes Inuit Studies, 25*, 229–47.

Carey, T.A. (2013). Defining Australian Indigenous wellbeing: Do we really want the answer? Implications for policy and practice. *Psychotherapy and Politics International, 11*(3), 182–94. https://doi.org/10.1002/ppi.1305

Deer, F. (2015). *Skannen ko'wa: Attributing principles of Kashwenta to Manitoba's treaty relationships*. Manitoba Education Research Network. http://www.frankdeer.net/uploads/2/2/6/1/22612190/occ-2.pdf

Deer, F., & Falkenberg, T. (2016a). Introduction. In F. Deer & T. Falkenberg (Eds.), *Indigenous perspectives on education for well-being in Canada* (pp. 1–5). Education for Sustainable Well-Being Press. www.ESWB-Press.org

– (Eds.). (2016b). *Indigenous perspectives on education for well-being in Canada*. Education for Sustainable Well-Being Press. www.ESWB-Press.org

Dockery, A.M. (2012). Do traditional culture and identity promote the wellbeing of Indigenous Australians? Evidence from the 2008 NATSISS. In A.M. Dockery, B. Hunter, & N. Biddle (Eds.), *Survey analysis for Indigenous policy in Australia: Social sciences perspectives* (pp. 281–306). Australian National University Press.

Falkenberg, T. (2016). Conclusion: Learning from Indigenous perspectives. In F. Deer & T. Falkenberg (Eds.), *Indigenous perspectives on education for well-being in Canada* (pp. 187–94). Education for Sustainable Well-Being Press. www.ESWB-Press.org

– (2019). *Framing human well-being and well-becoming: An integrated systems approach.* http://wellbeinginschools.ca/paper-series/

Gfellner, B.M. (2016). Ego strengths, racial/ethnic identity, and well-being among North American Indian/First Nations adolescents. *American Indian and Alaska Native Mental Health Research: The Journal of the National Center, 23*(3), 87–116. https://doi.org/10.5820/aian.2303.2016.87

Government of Nunavut. (2013). Incorporating Inuit societal values. Author.

Graham, H., & Stamler, L.L. (2013). Contemporary perceptions of health from an Indigenous (Plains Cree) perspective. *International Journal of Indigenous Health, 6*(1), 6–17. https://doi.org/10.18357/ijih61201012341

Hadjipavlou, G., Varcoe, C., Tu, D., Dehoney, J., Price, R. & Browne, A.J. (2018). "All my relations": Experiences and perceptions of Indigenous patients connecting with Indigenous elders in an inner city primary care partnership for mental health and well-being. *Canadian Medical Association Journal, 190*(20), E608-E615. https://doi.org/10.1503/cmaj.171390

Harris, S. (2014). *Waking up: A guide to spirituality without religion.* Simon & Schuster.

Kant, S., Vertinsky, I., Zheng, B., & Smith, P.M. (2013). Social, cultural, and land use determinants of the health and well-being of Aboriginal peoples of Canada: A path analysis. *Journal of Public Health Policy, 34*(3), 462–76. https://doi.org/10.1057/jphp.2013.27

King, M. (2014). Addressing the disparities in Aboriginal health through social determinants research. In F. Trovato & A. Romaniuk (Eds.), *Aboriginal populations: Social, demographic, and epidemiological perspectives* (pp. 197–209). University of Alberta Press.

Klein, E. (2016). The curious case of using the capability approach in Australian Indigenous policy. *Journal of Human Development and Capabilities, 17*(2), 245–59. https://doi.org/10.1080/19452829.2016.1145199

Kral, M,J. (2019). *The return of the sun: Suicide and reclamation among Inuit of arctic Canada.* New York: Oxford University Press.

Kral, M.J., Idlout, L., Minore, J.B., Dyck, R.J., & Kirmayer, L.J. (2011). Unikkaartuit: Meanings of well-being, unhappiness, health, and community change among Inuit in Nunavut, Canada. *American Journal of Community Psychology, 48*(3), 426–38. https://doi.org/10.1007/s10464-011-9431-4

Lafleur, G.S. (2016). Ojibwe elders' experiences of our peace as worldview demonstrated: To teach our well-being with earth. In F. Deer & T. Falkenberg (Eds.), *Indigenous perspectives on education for well-being in Canada* (pp. 157–71). Education for Sustainable Well-Being Press. www.ESWB-Press.org

Lavoie, J.G., Forget, E.L., Prakash, T., Dahl, M., Martens, P., & O'Neil, J.D. (2010). Have investments in on-reserve health services and initiatives promoting community control improved First Nations' health in Manitoba?

Social Science and Medicine, 71(4), 717–24. https://doi.org/10.1016/j.socscimed.2010.04.037

Lévesque, F. (2014). Revisiting Inuit Qaujimajatuqangit: Inuit knowledge, culture, language, and values in Nunavut institutions since 1999. *Inuit Studies*, 38(1/2), 115–36.

Lines, L.-A., & Jardine, C.G. (2019). Connection to the land as a youth-identified social determinant of Indigenous peoples' health. *BMC Public Health*, 19(1), 1–13. https://doi.org/10.1186/s12889-018-6383-8

Madjedi, K.M., & Daya, R. (2016). The meanings, barriers, and facilitators of Anishinaabe health: Implications for culturally-safe health care. *University of British Columbia Medical Journal*, 7(2), 17–18. https://ubcmj.med.ubc.ca/the-meanings-barriers-and-facilitators-anishinaabe-health-implications-for-culturallysafe-health-care/

Marsh, T.N., Coholic, D., Cote-Meek, S., & Najavits, L.M. (2015). Blending Aboriginal and Western healing methods to treat intergenerational trauma with substance use disorder in Aboriginal peoples who live in Northeastern Ontario, Canada. *Harm Reduction Journal*, 12(1), 1–12. https://doi.org/10.1186/s12954-015-0046-1

McCubbin, L.D., & Marsella, A. (2009). Native Hawaiians and psychology: The cultural and historical context of Indigenous ways of knowing. *Cultural Diversity and Ethnic Minority Psychology*, 15(4), 374–87. https://doi.org/10.1037/a0016774

Muirhead, A., & Leeuw, S. De. (2013). *Art and wellness: The importance of art for Aboriginal peoples' health and healing*. https://artshealthnetwork.ca/sites/default/files/art_wellness_en_web.pdf

Murphy, M. (2014). Self-determination as a collective capability: The case of Indigenous Peoples. *Journal of Human Development and Capabilities*, 15(4), 320–34. https://doi.org/10.1080/19452829.2013.878320

National Aboriginal Health Organization. (2007). *OCAP: Ownership, Control, Access, and Possession*.

Peters, H., Peterson, T., & Dakota Wicohan Community. (2019). Developing an Indigenous measure of overall health and well-being: The Wicozani instrument. *American Indian and Alaska Native Mental Health Research*, 26(2), 96–122. https://doi.org/10.5820/aian.2602.2019.96

Rice, B. (2013). *The Rotinonshonni: A traditional Iroquoian history through the eyes of Teharonhia:wako and Sawiskera*. Syracuse University Press.

Rountree, J., & Smith, A. (2016). Strength-based well-being indicators for Indigenous children and families: A literature review of Indigenous communities' identified well-being indicators. *American Indian and Alaska Native Mental Health Research*, 23(3), 206–20. https://doi.org/10.5820/aian.2303.2016.206

Solomon, A., & Wane, N.N. (2005). Indigenous healers and healing in a modern world. In R. Moodley & W. West (Eds.), *Integrating Traditional Healing Practices into Counseling and Psychotherapy* (pp. 52–60). Sage Publications.

Stewart, S.L. (2008). Promoting Indigenous mental health: Cultural perspectives on healing from Native counsellors in Canada. *International Journal of Health Promotion and Education, 46*(2), 49–56. https://doi.org/10.1080/14635240.2008.10708129

Truth and Reconciliation Commission of Canada. (2015). *Honouring the truth, reconciling for the future*. National Centre for Truth and Reconciliation. http://nctr.ca/assets/reports/Final%20Reports/Executive_Summary_English_Web.pdf

Wexler, L. (2009). The importance of identity, history, and culture in the wellbeing of Indigenous youth. *The Journal of the History of Childhood and Youth, 2*(2), 267–76. https://doi.org/10.1353/hcy.0.0055

Widdowson, F., & Howard, A. (2013). *Approaches to Aboriginal education in Canada: Searching for solutions*. Brush Education.

Wilk, P., Maltby, A., & Cooke, M. (2017). Residential schools and the effects on Indigenous health and well-being in Canada: A scoping review. *Public Health Reviews, 38*(8). https://doi.org/10.1186/s40985-017-0055-6

6 Meaning in Life: A Core Component of Human and Student Well-Becoming

THOMAS FALKENBERG

The "cognitive revolution" in psychology in the 1950s was "an all-out effort to establish meaning as the central concept of psychology – not stimuli and responses, not overtly observable behavior, not biological drives and their transformation, but meaning" (Bruner, 1990, p. 2). Giving this centrality of meaning in human life, culture-oriented psychology (e.g., Bruner, 1990; Cohen & Kitayama, 2019) and interpretive-oriented philosophy (e.g., Hiley et al., 1991) built their scholarship on the notion that human living is shaped by intentional states (e.g., Searle, 1983) and human agency (e.g., Taylor, 1985), both of which require the utilization of cultural systems of meanings, which, in turn, are reinforced and changed over time by the very utilization of those cultural systems.

As humans, we not only have the potential for meaning-making, we actually have a need for meaning-making in the sense that we experience distress if we encounter "cognitive dissonance" (Festinger, 1957; Harmon-Jones, 2019), that is, "discrepancies among beliefs, behavior, and expectations [that] generate distress and intense motivation to reduce this discrepancy" (Park, 2010, p. 259).

As sense-making beings, we also have the potential and need to make sense of our own life – past, present, and future. The existential psychiatrist and psychotherapist Irvin Yalom postulates meaninglessness as one of four ultimate concerns for humans (Yalom, 1980, p. 8): "The human being seems to require meaning. To live without meaning, goals, values, or ideals seems to provoke, as we have seen, considerable distress. In severe form it may lead to the decision to end one's life" (p. 422). Another existentialistic psychotherapist, Viktor Frankl, proposes that "[humans'] search for meaning is the primary motivation in [their] life and not a 'secondary rationalization' of instinctual drives. This meaning is unique and specific in that it must and can be fulfilled by [them] alone; only then does it achieve a significance which will satisfy [their] own *will* to meaning" (Frankl, 1946/2006, p. 99).

With meaning in life playing such a crucial role in human living, it is not surprising that scholars working on the topic connect the finding and experiencing of meaning in life with living a flourishing life (well-being). Two fundamentally different approaches to this relationship have been used. One is to conceptually separate meaning in life from well-being and then investigate their empirical relationship. For instance, studies by Debats (1996) and Zika and Chamberlain (1992) found a positive correlation between the two concepts.

The second approach to relating meaning in life and human well-being is to incorporate the former into the conceptualization of the latter. In this case, what it conceptually means to live a flourishing life includes finding and experiencing meaning in life. One example of this is Seligman's (2011) approach in which having meaning in life is one of five conceptual components of his concept of human well-being.

In this chapter, I develop the meaning-in-life component of a framework for conceptualizing human well-being and well-becoming (Falkenberg, 2019), which is another example of the second approach to relating meaning in life and human well-being. As such, the chapter contributes to the task of conceptualizing human well-being and well-becoming. To this end, the chapter is structured as follows. In the next section, I outline the conceptual structure of *meaning in life* by drawing on relevant research and scholarly work. Then, I use this conceptual structure to develop the meaning component of a specific framework for conceptualizing human well-becoming. Finally, this meaning component is used to outline implications for school education.

Meaning in Life: A Literature-Based Outline

Drawing on relevant literature, I start off by developing an outline of a conceptual structure of *meaning-in-life* and then identify sources for such meaning. Both tasks serve the subsequent section, in which I conceptualize the meaning-in-life component of a framework for conceptualizing human well-becoming.

Conceptual Structure of Meaning-in-Life

In the research and scholarly literature on meaning in life, a series of conceptual distinctions can be found that allow for an analysis of the conceptual structure of what we might mean by *meaning-in-life* (e.g.,

Baumeister, 1991; Wong, 2012). This section characterizes these distinctions in a way that is suitable to the overall purpose of this chapter.

MEANING OF LIFE VERSUS MEANING IN LIFE

Yalom (1980; pp. 423–4) makes the conceptual distinction between *cosmic meaning* and *terrestrial (personal) meaning*. The former is concerned with the meaning of life more generally, while the latter is concerned with the meaning for a person's ("my") life. Auhagen (2000) suggests that Viktor Frankl, like Yalom, distinguishes "between 'cosmic' and 'worldly, personal' meaning" (p. 38). Following Frankl (as quoted in Auhagen, 2000, p. 37), I use the term *meaning of life* for what Yalom calls *cosmic meaning* and the term *meaning in life* for what he calls terrestrial meaning. *Meaning of life* is the response to the question "What is the meaning of (human) life?," while *meaning in life* is the response to the question, "What is the meaning of *my* life?" The answers to these two questions, however, while different in type, may in some cases be linked to each other. Meaning *of* life can provide the basis for a person's meaning *in* life. For instance, if someone believes in a universe that follows a divine order (meaning *of* life), then the person might derive personal meaning (meaning *in* life) from this divine order by living in accordance with its principles. Indeed, not having belief in a universal meaning of life can contribute to not having personal meaning in life. This is what Yalom (1980, pp. 426–7) suggests has been happening in Western societies over the last three hundred years: an erosion of cosmic religious beliefs has resulted in a loss in individuals' ability to find personal meaning in life.

LEVELS OF MEANING

One common distinction found in the meaning in life literature is that between different "levels of meaning" (e.g., Baumeister, 1991; Frankl, 1946/2006; Park & Folkman, 1997, Wong, 2012). While using the same language, different authors mean often different things by the term *levels of meaning*. The first distinction is between different levels of "life units" that get meaning assigned. We experience life through situations and episodes, and we can reflect on our life in different life units, that is, situations, episodes, life phases (like our high school years), as well as on our lives as a whole up to the present time. We can attach meaning to or find meaning in each of these life units through patterning, that is, by linking life units together to make sense of them as elements of a larger meaning pattern. While some scholars distinguish only two such levels of meaning, for example, situational and ultimate/global life meaning (e.g., Auhagen, 2000; Frankl, 1946/2006; Wong, 2012), others describe a continuum or multi-layering of life units (e.g., Baumeister, 1991), where situations are patterned together within episodes, and episodes within life phases, and life phases within one's whole life to date. The meanings assigned to these different life units are then structurally connected (e.g., Baumeister, 1991, p. 20), much as word meanings are structurally connected to give meaning to sentences.

The second distinction between different levels of meaning captures the distinction between different types of meaning that can be assigned to the same situation. For instance, a woman's neighbour suggests to her that she could go back to university for another degree in response to the woman telling her neighbour that she had just lost her job. The meaning attached to this concrete utterance might have the meaning at that very moment in the woman's life of someone showing concern for her situation. At a more intermediate and more abstract level, this utterance might have the meaning in the woman's life of giving her an idea leading to her studying engineering. At a long-term and very abstract level, the utterance at that moment in the life of the woman might have the meaning of providing her with the opportunity of meeting her future life partner, another engineer.

SUBJECTIVE VERSUS OBJECTIVE MEANING

The literature also suggests what could be called an *epistemological* distinction between *subjective* meaning in life and *objective* meaning in life. This distinction is linked to the adjudication of how meaningful a person's life is and in what sense. On one hand it is the individuals themselves who adjudicate their life in terms of its meaning, with all their biases and subjectivity (epistemologically subjective meaning in life). *Subjective meaning in life* in this distinction refers to the meaning that a person ascribes to their life. It is subjective in the sense that it is the "subject" themselves who is trying to understand their own life's meaning. On the other hand are the research approaches of inquiring into meaning in life more generally and into a person's meaning in life in particular, which some call "objective" meaning (e.g., Wong, 2012, p. xxviii). *Objective meaning in life* in this distinction refers to the "scientific-based" analysis of that person's meaning in life. It is "objective" in the sense that it is the object of a subject-external inquiry.

UNDERSTANDING VERSUS PURPOSE

In his analysis of different approaches to meaning in life, Steger (2009, 2012) suggests two different "dimensions" of life meaning referenced in the literature:

> The first dimension is comprehension, which is the ability to make sense of and understand one's life, including one's self, the external world, and how one fits with and operates within the world. In essence, comprehension

refers to an interconnected network of schemas crafted into a meaning framework for life. The second dimension is purpose, which is one or more overarching, long-term life aspirations that are self-concordant and motivate relevant activity. (Steger, 2012, 382)[1]

In other words, *having meaning in life* can refer to my understanding of my life in the context of my experiences in the world (*meaning in life* as understanding), or it can refer to my being motivated by goals in my life (*meaning in life* as purpose).

HAVING VERSUS SEEKING MEANING

There is a distinction between what Wong (2012, p. xxix) calls "content of meaning" and "process of meaning." What is distinguished here are the conceptions of "having meaning in life" (content) and "seeking meaning in life" (process). While both are important to the understanding of *meaning in life*, the process aspect is particularly of importance to approaches to human well-being which consider humans in their constitution as constantly changing and "becoming," as, for instance, the WB2-Framework does.

Sources of Meaning in Life

In the meaning-in-life literature, the concern for "sources of meaning in life" is focused on two different things. First, there is the understanding of "sources" as the human domain of experiences on which humans draw for their meaning in life. For instance, religion, intimacy, and relationships provide cross-cultural sources of meaning in the life of many people (e.g., Emmons, 1999; Wong, 1998).

In a second sense, *sources of meaning in life* refers to the reasons *why* a human being feels the need to find, have, and sustain meaning in their life. Here, "the sources" are linked to the motivational functioning of human beings. For instance, drawing on people's intuitive understanding of life meaning, Wong (1998, 2012) has identified the following cross-cultural sources of meaning in life in this second sense: happiness, achievement, self-transcendence, self-acceptance, and fairness. In other words, his work suggests that the drive (need) to feel happy, to achieve certain goals, and so on motivates us to find, have, and sustain meaning in life.

Baumeister and his collaborators provide a different but partially overlapping list of sources of meaning in this second sense: "the quest for a meaningful life can be understood in terms of four main sources of meaning. These constitute four patterns of motivation that guide how people try to make sense of their lives" (Baumeister & Vohs, 2002, p. 610). Baumeister identifies the following four sources of meaning in life: the need for purpose, the need for values (justification), the need for efficacy, and the need for self-worth (Baumeister, 1991). As motivational patterns, Baumeister's (1991) four sources of life meaning play a central role in the next section, suggesting the need for some elaboration on each of these sources of life meaning.

About *the need for purpose*, Baumeister and Vohs (2002) write:

> The essence of this need is that present events draw meaning from their connection with future events. The future events lend direction to the present so that the present is seen as leading toward those eventual purposes. Purposes can be sorted into two main types. One is simply goals: an objective outcome or state that is desired but not yet real, and so the person's present activities take meaning as a way of translating the current situation into the desired (future) one. The other form is fulfillments, which are subjective rather than objective. Life can be oriented toward some anticipated state of future fulfillment, such as living happily ever after, being in love, or going to heaven. (p. 610)

The authors explain *the need for values (justification)* as follows:

> The second need is for values, which can lend a sense of goodness or positivity to life and can justify certain courses of action. Values enable people to decide whether certain acts are right or wrong, and, if people shape their actions by these values, they can remain secure in the belief that they have done the right things, thereby minimizing guilt, anxiety, regret, and other forms of moral distress. (p. 610)

The need for efficacy consists in

> a belief that one can make a difference. A life that had purposes and values but no efficacy would be tragic: The person might know what was desirable but could not do anything with that knowledge. (p. 610)

Finally, *the need for self-worth* is explained as follows:[2]

> Most people seek reasons for believing that they are good, worthy persons. Self-worth can be pursued individually, such as by finding ways of regarding oneself as superior to others ... It also can be pursued collectively, such as when people draw meaningful self-esteem from belonging to some group or category of people that they regard as worthy. (pp. 610–11)

Meaning-in-Life in the WB2-Framework

In this section I briefly introduce the WB2-Framework for conceptualizing human well-being (for details, see Falkenberg, 2019) and then extensively develop the *living-a-meaningful-life* component of the WB2-Framework.[3]

The WB2-Framework for Conceptualizing Human Well-Being and Well-Becoming[4]

The WB2-Framework is a framework for conceptualizing human well-being and well-becoming. As the framework has been developed so far (Falkenberg, 2019), it has two main building blocks: (a) five meta-criteria that the framework as a whole is to meet, which in turn are the five meta-characteristics of this particular approach to human well-being and well-becoming, and (b) five components of any conception developed within the framework.

META-CHARACTERISTICS

The following five characteristics of the WB2-Framework are *meta*-characteristics because they are characteristics of a *framework for* conceptualizing well-being and well-becoming rather than characteristics of a specific conceptualization. This distinction should become clearer with the explanation of the second group of meta-characteristics.

First, the WB2-Framework is a systems approach to human well-being and well-becoming, which means that "a systems perspective is used to understand the functioning of humans as bio-psychic systems and as social actors of social and ecological systems" (Falkenberg, 2019, p. 4). This means that well-being and well-becoming are considered a feature of a system that is embedded within other systems.

Second, the WB2-Framework is, as the name suggests, a framework approach to conceptualizing well-being and well-becoming. The WB2-Framework does not offer a specific conception of well-being and well-becoming but rather a *framework for context-specific conceptualizations* of what it might mean for a human being embedded in a specific cultural context to flourish. This meta-characteristic accounts for the critique on some approaches to human flourishing which claim to conceptualize what it means for a human being to flourish regardless of the person's socio-cultural embeddedness. (For such a critique, see for instance Christopher, 1999, p. 149.)

Third, the WB2-Framework is an integrated approach to human flourishing in the sense that it integrates approaches to human flourishing that, for different reasons, have traditionally been kept distinct, including for the reason that they have been developed in different academic disciplines. (For details, see Falkenberg, 2019, pp. 8–11.)

Fourth, the WB2-Framework is grounded in the notion that at the core of what it means to flourish is having one's fundamental human needs addressed. As already explained, for the purpose of this chapter I draw on the notion that it is the concept of human needs that can help us understand what the human need for meaning in life means. This approach to meaning in life is directly connected with the overall approach to human flourishing in the WB2-Framework.

The fifth and final meta-characteristic of the WB2-Framework is that it is a *dynamic* approach, which is grounded in the following dynamic systems view of human functioning:

> As humans we are always becoming. Such becoming is an integral aspect of our interaction with our systems environment and of the enacting of our agency. This dynamic systems view of human *beings* suggests that even as we assess our own or someone else's state of being at a given time, there is a dynamic element in that being, namely the potential of the system to develop in certain ways rather than in others and to be attentive to certain ways of system disturbances by the environment rather than to other ways ...
>
> It is this potential for becoming in the being that the WB2-Framework gives consideration to what it means for humans to flourish. (Falkenberg, 2019, pp. 13–14)

To reflect this dynamic view of human flourishing, this chapter uses in its title, and from here on, the phrase *well-becoming* only, omitting the phrase *well-being*, considering the latter integrated into the understanding of the former in the following sense: "In this integrative sense one can say that *well-becoming* expresses the dynamic aspect of well-being and *well-being* expresses the momentary state of well-becoming" (Falkenberg, 2019, p. 14).

FIVE CONCEPTUAL COMPONENTS

The second core feature of the WB2-Framework is that well-becoming has five general conceptual components:

- having agentic capabilities linked to human needs;
- experiencing situational opportunities to engage one's agentic capabilities in relevant life domains;
- enjoying life;

- living a meaningful life;
- experiencing personal and communal connections that contribute to one's well-becoming.

In the next section I develop the fourth component in detail.

An Integrated Meaning-in-Life Concept: Meaning-in-Life$_{WB2}$

To develop the meaning-in-life concept in the WB2-Framework (Meaning-in-Life$_{WB2}$ = MIL$_{WB2}$), I draw on Baumeister's (1991) four sources of meaning as the basic building block for the development of MIL$_{WB2}$. Baumeister's approach to meaning in life fits well with the WB2-Framework for two reasons. First, it is a needs-based approach to meaning in life and, thus, aligns with the needs-based approach to well-becoming of the WB2-Framework. Second, Baumeister's needs are grounded in human motivational functioning rather than in life domains, which aligns with the type of well-becoming components in the WB2-Framework.

In this section I develop MIL$_{WB2}$ in a three-step integration process. In the first step, I integrate Baumeister's (1991) four needs for meaning themselves. Then I integrate the four needs for meaning with the conceptual distinctions generally made within the scholarship on meaning in life and described above. Finally, I integrate the outcome of the second integration with the other components and the five meta-criteria of the WB2-Framework to arrive at MIL$_{WB2}$.

FIRST LEVEL OF INTEGRATION: MEANING-IN-LIFE$_{WB2i}$

Integrating the four "sources of meaning" leads to the *initial* criteria for Meaning-in-Life$_{WB2i}$ (MIL$_{WB2i}$) presented in table 6.1. These criteria are integrated in the sense that the values aspect of MIL$_{WB2i}$ integrates the purpose aspect, that the efficacy aspect integrated both the values and the purpose aspect, and third, the self-worth aspect integrates the other three aspects. It needs to be noted that Baumeister (1991) does not suggest such an integration of his four sources of meaning. Henceforth, I will call the four sources of meaning, as defined in table 6.1, *the MIL$_{WB2}$ needs*.

Table 6.1.

If I have MIL$_{WB2i}$, ...

---

purpose	... I have a sense of purpose (goals and fulfilment) in my life toward which I do and aim to direct the course of my life.
values	... I can justify this purpose and the way I live my life through my actions toward that purpose by drawing on a value system that I subscribe to.

efficacy ... I have a sense of efficacy to direct the course of my life toward my life's purpose and in accordance with the values that justify directing my life toward that purpose.

self-worth... I have a sense of self-worth that is grounded in my finding meaning through purpose, which is justified by a value system I subscribe to and made possible for me to actually pursue by my efficacy. In turn, my sense of self-worth affirms the purpose and the value system justifying this purpose.

... and if I have all four, I have MIL_{WB2i}.

SECOND LEVEL OF INTEGRATION: MEANING-IN-LIFE$_{WB2}$

At this second level, I integrate MIL_{WB2i} (table 6.1) with the core conceptual distinctions from the meaning-in-life literature introduced above to conceptualize MIL_{WB2}.

Meaning *of* Life versus Meaning *in* Life. MIL_{WB2} is about meaning *in* life, not about meaning *of* life. However, a philosophy of meaning of life can impact a person's subjective understanding of their MIL_{WB2} as well as an "observer's" sense of a person's MIL_{WB2}. But this relationship lies outside of this inquiry into a conceptualization of meaning in life within the WB2-Framework.

Motivation versus Understanding. The categorical distinction between an understanding and a motivational aspect of MIL_{WB2} integrated with the four sources of meaning by Baumeister (1991) leads to the eight criteria for MIL_{WB2} that are described in table 6.2.

Levels of Meaning. To illustrate the idea of a refinement by levels of meaning, let us consider two possible levels of life units: my life experiences of starting a garden in the backyard of my house (more situational), and my life experiences of being a father (more longer-term). Furthermore, let us pick the criterion for MIL_{WB2} as understanding for the need for purpose (top-left criterion table 6.2). The chosen two levels of life would refine this criterion by creating two sub-criteria for MIL_{WB2} for *me* with respect to the specific examples of levels of life units as follows (see table 6.3).

Similarly, each of the eight criteria in table 6.2 are refined along the lines of the example provided in table 6.3 for different levels of life units. table 6.3 only reflects two levels of meaning, but more need to be taken into account, for instance a mid-term level of life unit.

Subjective versus Objective Meaning. Integrating the distinction between subjective and objective life meaning into the criteria listed in table 6.2 with its refinement exemplified in table 6.3 leads to the

Table 6.2.

If I have MIL_{WB2}, ...

	MIL_{WB2} as understanding	MIL_{WB2} as motivational
purpose	... I understand how my present life experiences are linked to my past life experiences and how they provide me with specific options of living my life in the immediate and long-term future.	... I am motivated to live my life along specific immediate, mid- and long-term future life options available to me.
values	... I understand what values I subscribe to and how they guide and justify how I live my life in pursuit of my life's purpose.	... I am motivated to live my life in accordance with the values I subscribe to in pursuit of my life's purpose.
efficacy	... I understand what capabilities are required to live my life toward its purpose in accordance with the value system I subscribe to.	... I am motivated to develop, engage, and get better with capabilities required to live my life toward its purpose in accordance with the value system I subscribe to.
self-worth	... I understand that and how my finding meaning through purpose, justified by a value system I subscribe to and made possible for me to actually pursue by my efficacy, provides me with a sense of self-worth.	... I am motivated through a sense of self-worth to live my life toward its purpose in accordance with the value system I subscribe to.

... and if all eight criteria apply to me, I have MIL_{WB2}.

Table 6.3.

As part of having MIL_{WB2} ...

	MIL_{WB2} as understanding	
	more situational level of life unit	more long-term level of life unit
purpose	... I understand how my experiences as a gardener are linked to my past life experiences (for instance, I might understand how my having grown up as a child spending a lot of time in the outdoors has developed in me a deeper connection to the land and to nature) and how my experiences as a gardener provide me with specific ways of living my life in the present (for instance, living more sustainably).	... I understand how my life as a father to my daughter over the last thirty-odd years is linked to other positive experiences in my life (for instance, it has led to long-lasting friendships with parents of her childhood friends) and how my life as a father to my daughter will now provide me with opportunities to experience life as a grandfather.

Table 6.4.

As part of having MIL_{WB2} ...

	MIL_{WB2} as motivational	
	more situational level of life unit	more long-term level of life unit
efficacy (having)	... I *am motivated, and sustain and adjust as needed*, that motivation to develop, engage, and get better with capabilities required to be a gardener as part of my (more situational) life purpose and in accordance with the value system I subscribe to (for instance, to engage in organic gardening).	... I *am motivated, and sustain and adjust as needed*, that motivation to develop, engage, and get better with capabilities required for me to be father to my daughter, which is part of my (more long-term) life purpose and that is in accordance with the value system I subscribe to (for instance, to advise her on, but not try to direct, her life).
efficacy (seeking)	... I *am seeking to* be motivated, and sustain and expand, that motivation to develop, engage, and get better with capabilities required to be a gardener as part of my (more situational) life purpose and in accordance with the value system I subscribe to (for instance, to engage in organic gardening).	... I *am seeking to* be motivated, and sustain, and expand that motivation to develop, engage, and get better with, capabilities required for me to be father to my daughter, which is part of my (more long-term) life purpose and that is in accordance with the value system I subscribe to (for instance, to advise her on, but not try to direct, her life).

following expansion: in terms of an *adjudication* of someone's MIL_{WB2}, these criteria can be used by the person whose MIL_{WB2} is under investigation (subjective MIL_{WB2}) as well as by third parties who more formally inquire into MIL_{WB2} more generally, or into the particular person's MIL_{WB2}. This distinction is not reflected in the conceptual framework of MIL_{WB2}, but rather comes to bear at the level of an adjudication of someone's MIL_{WB2}.

Having versus Seeking Meaning. Integrating this distinction into the criteria listed in table 6.2 with its refinement exemplified in table 6.3 leads to the following expansion: MIL_{WB2} is as much concerned with finding/experiencing meaning-in-life as it is with seeking/searching for meaning-in-life. The criteria in table 6.2 and the examples in table 6.3 reflect the former. table 6.4 below reflects the latter using the example from table 6.3.

Table 6.5.

If I have MIL$_{WB2}$, ...

		MIL$_{WB2}$ as understanding			MIL$_{WB2}$ as motivational		
		at the situational level	at the mid-term level	at the long-term level	at the situational level	at the mid-term level	at the long-term level
purpose	having						
	seeking						
values	having						
	seeking						
efficacy	having						
	seeking						
self-worth	having						
	seeking						

The integrating of *seeking* MIL$_{WB2}$ into the understanding of meaning-in-life in the WB2-Framework reflects the notion that in the WB2-Framework well-*becoming* (as a process) is an integral part of our conceptual understanding of human flourishing. Meaning-in-life is a process of becoming, not in the sense of a trajectory toward a goal, but rather as a journey where the path influences what the goal for the next part of the journey will be. This notion suggests that meaning-in-life within the WB2-Framework is a constant process of becoming. It is not a destiny of one's life journey; rather it is something that is constructed or found anew, sometimes from one day to another, sometimes over a long period of time.

MIL$_{WB2}$ after the Second Integration. The 48 criteria in the 8 × 6 matrix in table 6.5 are necessary and sufficient criteria for having meaning-in-life$_{WB2}$. While this conceptual approach commits us to being able to say that someone has MIL$_{WB2}$ only if *all* 48 criteria are satisfied, this very requirement forces us to consider aspects of a rich meaning-in-life concept for human beings that might otherwise have been overlooked.

THIRD LEVEL OF INTEGRATION

The third integration step is concerned with the integration of what has been gained through the second integration with the two sets of core features of the WB2-Framework, namely the five meta-criteria and the other four components of well-becoming. Such integration provides additional characteristics of MIL_{WB2}.

A Framework Approach to MIL_{WB2}. As the WB2-Framework is a *framework for conceptualizing* well-becoming so does MIL_{WB2} as developed in this chapter provide a *framework* for an actual conceptualizing of meaning-in-life rather than a conceptualization itself.

A Systems and Dynamic Approach to MIL_{WB2}. In the WB2-Framework, human well-becoming is a quality of complex adaptive psychic systems. Having MIL_{WB2} is thus also a quality of human beings as complex adaptive psychic systems. Within the WB2-Framework, a human's well-becoming is a phenomenon of the complex adaptive psychic system of that human being that emerges from the interaction of the biophysical ecosystem within which the human being is embedded, and the social systems within which the human being is a social actor. As an adaptive complex system, a human's psychic system responds to "disturbances" from its environment. Through the biophysical systems lens, such disturbances come from the interaction of a human being's psychic system with the human's biophysical system. Through the social systems lens, such disturbances come from the interaction of a human being's psychic system with the social systems into which the human being as a social actor is embedded. Finally, through the bio-ecological lens, such disturbances come from the interaction of the psychic system with the bio-ecological system. This is a system-theoretical way of accounting for the impact that a person's bodily functioning, the culture within which the person is embedded, and the natural environment have on the formation, maintenance, and renewal of that person's MIL_{WB2}. Since these systems disturbances are ongoing, a person's MIL_{WB2} as an emergent phenomenon of systems interaction is constantly changing (it is constantly becoming).

The Integrated Nature of MIL_{WB2}. As the steps in which MIL_{WB2} has been developed in this chapter demonstrate, the framework for conceptualizing meaning-in-life provided in this chapter resulted from an integration of different approaches to meaning-in-life, including an integration with a particular approach to conceptualizing well-becoming, that is, the WB2-Framework. Drawing on Allport's (1964) systemic eclecticism argument, such an integrative approach provides for a richer conceptualization of what it means to have, construct, and experience meaning in one's life, and accordingly the way in which MIL_{WB2} was built on the notion that integrating different approaches to meaning-in-life for MIL_{WB2} makes MIL_{WB2} a richer conceptual framework, one that exalts human beings by making generous assumptions about, and thus elevate, human nature (p. 36).

A Needs-Based Approach to MIL_{WB2}. The basic building blocks of MIL_{WB2} are Baumeister's (1991) four needs for meaning. Integrating MIL_{WB2} and the notion that the WB2-Framework is a needs-based approach make these four needs of meaning needs for well-becoming. Thus, the four needs of meaning have to be considered in understanding another component in the WB2-Framework, namely the component of having agentic capabilities linked to human needs. (More on capabilities in the context of MIL_{WB2} below.)

The Actual and Potential Aspects of MIL_{WB2}. The structure of the five WB2 components in the WB2-Framework identifies the component of "having meaning in life" (MIL_{WB2}) as being about "life-results/ achievement" (Falkenberg, 2019, p. 23). That means that in order for someone to live a flourishing life in the context of the WB2-Framework, that person would need to actually have meaning in their life. Seeking MIL_{WB2} is not good enough. However, the way MIL_{WB2} is conceptually framed, there is what could be called a potential aspect of MIL_{WB2}, which links the MIL_{WB2} component with the two agentic capabilities components as follows. MIL_{WB2} is built upon four needs for meaning, namely the needs for purpose, values, efficacy, and self-worth. Within the WB2-Framework, these needs are considered to be such that the two agentic capabilities components of the WB2-Framework ("having agentic capabilities linked to human needs" and "experiencing situational opportunities to engage one's agentic capabilities") apply to them. In other words, in order to live a flourishing life, as understood within the WB2-Framework, one has to have agentic capabilities and has to experience situational opportunities to engage the capabilities linked to these four needs for meaning in order to address these needs. These two life-chances/freedom components of the WB2-Framework provide what could be called a *potential aspect* of MIL_{WB2}: In order to live a flourishing life, I not only have to live a meaningful life, but also have to have the potential, that is, the relevant capabilities, to choose, find, or construct the MIL_{WB2} that allows me to live the life I wish to pursue. Similarly, with reference to the second agentic capabilities component, in order to live a flourishing life, I also need to experience situational opportunities to engage these capabilities linked to the four MIL_{WB2} needs.

Personal and Communal Connections That Contribute to MIL_{WB2}. The connections component in the WB2-Framework is recursive, because it considers personal and communal connections relevant to a person's well-becoming – but only if those connections contribute to one's well-becoming. In a similar vein, personal and communal connections are relevant to one's MIL_{WB2}, but only those connections that contribute to one's MIL_{WB2}. This is not tautological but rather recursive in the sense that for MIL_{WB2} we need personal and communal connections, but only those that contribute to MIL_{WB2}. The need for personal and communal connections for MIL_{WB2} is a reflection of the notion from the meaning-in-life literature that we can only develop or construct meaning-in-life in response to the cultural values and practices we have been enculturated into. Within the MIL_{WB2}-Framework, this means that the four needs of meaning (Baumeister, 1991) that build the foundation for MIL_{WB2} can only be addressed in response to (and sometimes in opposition to) the cultural contexts one is embedded in.

Developing and Experiencing Meaning-in-Life$_{WB2}$ in and through Going to School

The structural features of MIL_{WB2} represented in table 6.5 suggest the following for how going to school can support the development and experience of MIL_{WB2}. School experiences contribute to the development and experience of MIL_{WB2} if they do one or more of the following:

(1) (a) help students develop the four types of understandings of their life as described in table 6.2;
    (b) help students develop these four types of understandings along the level continuum illustrated in table 6.3;
    (c) help students develop the motivation and agentic capabilities needed to seek out these four types of understandings along the level continuum as illustrated in table 6.4;

(2) (a) help students develop the four types of motivation for living their lives in ways described in table 6.2;
    (b) help students develop these four types of motivation for living their lives in these ways along the level continuum as illustrated in table 6.4;
    (c) help students develop the motivation and agentic capabilities needed to seek theses four types of motivation for living their lives in these ways along the level continuum as illustrated in table 6.4.

The framework approach to MIL_{WB2} suggests that socio-cultural differences in values and practices result in differences in which the four MIL_{WB2} needs (needs for purpose, values, efficacy, and self-worth) manifest in people. Accordingly, school experiences contribute to the development and experience of MIL_{WB2} if they

(3) are sensitive to how the four MIL_{WB2} needs manifest differently in students and adults from various cultures and, accordingly, how the understandings and motivations referenced in table 6.5 might vary.

The systems and dynamic approach to MIL_{WB2} involves consideration of human beings as complex adaptive psychic systems. This calls for some further qualification. First, any assessment of MIL_{WB2} for a person would need to inquire into the quality of that person's psychic system. Generally, any assessment of a person's inner life would need to rely heavily – although not exclusively – on that person's self-assessment of their inner life. Second, as a quality of a complex adaptive psychic system, MIL_{WB2} is the outcome of a process of adaptive interaction with the environment of the psychic system. This environment of a psychic system is made up of three interacting systems: the person's biophysical system (the bodily systems including the sensory system), the social system (the norms and values within a society), and the biophysical ecosystem (the natural and physical environment). As an outcome of an ongoing process of adaptive interaction, MIL_{WB2} is (a) impacted by the behaviour of the other three systems (second notion) and (b) constantly changing, whereby those changes are often (generally most of the time) on the periphery and sometimes at the core of the structure of a person's MIL_{WB2} (third notion). These three notions suggest that school experiences contribute to the development and experience of MIL_{WB2} if they do one or more of the following:

(4) help students develop agentic capabilities that facilitate self-assessment of their inner life;
(5) (a) help students develop agentic capabilities to understand and influence how the three environmental systems impact MIL_{WB2} in general and their MIL_{WB2} in particular;
    (b) help students develop agentic capabilities to direct the development of their MIL_{WB2}.

The conceptual framework of MIL_{WB2} suggests three levels of integration. The first integration links the four MIL_{WB2} needs to each other, as suggested in table 6.1. That means that any educational work to address a MIL_{WB2} need requires addressing the other three needs as well and in the integrated way described in table 6.1. The school educational implications from the first integration are already considered in implications (1a) and (2a). The second integration interlinks the four MIL_{WB2} needs with the core conceptual distinctions from the meaning-in-life literature, resulting in the integrated conceptual framework represented in table 6.5, which suggests that MIL_{WB2} (at the level of the second integration) has 48 aspects that all should be of concern to oneself and those concerned with others' MIL_{WB2}. The school educational implications from the second integration are already considered in implications (1a) to (2c). The school educational implications of the third integration are considered in implications (3), (4), (5a), (5b), and (6) below.

The needs-based approach to MIL_{WB2} puts the need for meaning-in-life as defined in table 6.1 at the core of the MIL_{WB2} framework. The school educational implications of the needs-based approach to MIL_{WB2} are considered in implications (1a) and (2a).

The actual and potential aspects of MIL_{WB2} suggest that (a) MIL_{WB2} requires agentic capabilities to develop the understandings and motivation described in table 6.5 *and* situational opportunities to engage these agentic capabilities. The school educational implications of the former requirement are reflected in implications (4), (5a), and (5b). The school educational implications of the latter requirement are reflected in implication (6), below. School experiences contribute to the development and experience of MIL_{WB2} if they do the following:

(6) provide students with situational opportunities to engage the agentic capabilities characterized in implications (4), (5a), and (5b).

Finally, the criterion that we need personal and communal connections that contribute to MIL_{WB2} reflects that we can only develop meaning in our life in response to the cultural values and practices we have been enculturated into and that the four MIL_{WB2} needs can only be addressed in response to (and that sometimes means in opposition to) the cultural contexts one is embedded in. School experiences contribute to the development and experience of MIL_{WB2} if they do one or both of the following:

(7) help students build and maintain personal and communal connections that contribute to their MIL_{WB2};
(8) help students develop agentic capabilities that help them interrogate the cultural values and practices they are and have been enculturated into.

Learning experiences that align with one or more of the listed eight characteristics will go a long way in supporting school education that enhances students' developing and experiencing meaning-in-life.

Conclusion

Having a sense of living a meaningful life has often been identified as a core aspect of what it means for humans to live a flourishing life. The WB2Framework (Falkenberg, 2019) has living of a meaningful life as one of its five conceptual components, and the present chapter has developed in some detail this particular conceptual component.

Students' well-becoming as students and future adults is of growing concern to education systems (see chapters 1 and 8, this volume). Thus, helping students develop a sense of meaning in their lives is also, or needs to, be an important concern. This chapter provides a conceptual framework for education for meaning in life that is integrated into a larger conceptual framework for education for well-becoming, and, as such, allows education systems to address both concerns in an integrated way.

NOTES

1 A similar distinction is made by Yalom (1980, pp. 423–4).
2 For a discussion of values (justification) and self-worth as two different types of needs for life meaning, see Baumeister and Newman (1994, p. 686).
3 WB2 is used in honour of the former executive director of the Manitoba Association of Superintendents, Ken Klassen, who introduced this acronym as a short form for "well-being and well-becoming" during our time of collaboration.
4 See also the discussions of the WB2-Framework in chapters 5, 13, and 14 (this volume).

REFERENCES

Allport, G.W. (1964). The fruits of eclecticism – Bitter or sweet? *Acta Psychologica*, 23, 27–44. https://doi.org/10.1016/0001-6918(64)90073-3

Auhagen, A. (2000). On the psychology of meaning of life. *Swiss Journal of Psychology*, 59(1), 34–48. https://doi.org/10.1024//1421-0185.59.1.34

Baumeister, R.F. (1991). *Meanings of life*. Guilford Press.

Baumeister, R.F., & Newman, L.S. (1994). How stories make sense of personal experiences: Motives that shape autobiographical narrative. *Personality and Social Psychology Bulletin*, 20(6), 676–90. https://doi.org/10.1177/0146167294206006

Baumeister, R.F., & Vohs, K.D. (2002). The pursuit of meaningfulness in life. In C.R. Snyder & S.J. Lopez (Eds.), *Handbook of positive psychology* (pp. 608–18). Oxford University Press.

Bruner, J. (1990). *Acts of meaning*. Harvard University Press.

Christopher, J.C. (1999). Situating psychological well-being: Exploring the cultural roots of its theory and research. *Journal of Counseling & Development*, 77(2), 141–52. https://doi.org/10.1002/j.1556-6676.1999.tb02434.x

Cohen, D., & Kitayama, S. (Eds.). (2019). *Handbook of cultural psychology* (2nd ed.). Guilford Press.

Debats, D.L. (1996). Meaning in life: Clinical relevance and predictive power. *Journal of Clinical Psychology, 35*(4), 503–16. https://doi.org/10.1111/j.2044-8260.1996.tb01207.x

Emmons, R.A. (1999). *The psychology of ultimate concerns: Motivation and spirituality in personality.* Guildford Press.

Falkenberg, T. (2019). *Framing human well-being and well-becoming: An integrated systems approach.* http://wellbeinginschools.ca/paper-series/

Festinger, L. (1957). *A theory of cognitive dissonance.* Row, Peterson.

Frankl, V.E. (2006). *Man's search for meaning* (I. Lasch, Trans.). Beacon Press. (Original published 1946).

Harmon-Jones, E. (Ed.). (2019). *Cognitive dissonance: Reexamining a pivotal theory in psychology* (2nd ed.). American Psychological Association.

Hiley, D.R., Bohman, J., & Shusterman, R. (Eds.). (1991). *The interpretive turn: Philosophy, science, culture.* Cornell University Press.

Park, C. (2010). Making sense of the meaning literature: An integrative review of meaning making and its effects on adjustment to stressful life events. *Psychological Bulletin, 136*(2), 257–301. https://doi.org/10.1037/a0018301

Park, C.L., & Folkman, S. (1997). Meaning in the context of stress and coping. *Review of General Psychology, 1*(2), 115–44. https://doi-org.uml.idm.oclc.org/10.1037/1089-2680.1.2.115

Searle, J.R. (1983). *Intentionality: An essay in the philosophy of mind.* Cambridge University Press.

Seligman, M.E.P. (2011). *Flourishing: A visionary new understanding of happiness and well-being.* Free Press.

Steger, M.F. (2009). Meaning in life. In S.J. Lopez & C.R. Snyder (Eds.), *The Oxford handbook of positive psychology* (2nd ed.; pp. 679–87). Oxford University Press.

Steger, M. (2012). Making meaning in life. *Psychological Inquiry, 23*(4), 381–5. https://doi.org/10.1080/1047840X.2012.720832

Taylor, C. (1985). *Human agency and language: Philosophical papers 1.* Cambridge University Press.

Wong, P.T.P. (1998). Implicit theories of meaningful life and the development of the Personal Meaning Profile (PMP). In P.T.P. Wong & P.S. Fry (Eds.), *The human quest for meaning: A handbook of psychological research and clinical applications* (pp. 111–40). Erlbaum.

Wong, P.T. (2012). Introduction: A roadmap for meaning research and applications. In P.T. Wong (Ed.), *The human quest for meaning: Theories, research, and applications* (2nd ed.) (pp. xxvii–xliv). Routledge.

Yalom, I.D. (1980). *Existential psychotherapy.* Basic Books.

Zika, S., & Chamberlain, K. (1992). On the relation between meaning in life and psychological well-being. *British Journal of Psychology, 83*(1), 135–45. https://doi.org/10.1111/j.2044-8295.1992.tb02429.x

7 Well-Being of School Counsellors and School Psychologists

VIRGINIA M.C. TZE AND STEPHANIE BREKELMANS

Increasing attention is being paid to schools as sites for promoting well-being in children and adolescents. With this growing emphasis on developing and maintaining students' well-being, there is also a growing need to support the well-being of the school-based professionals who serve these student populations. According to the *American Psychological Association Dictionary of Psychology* (n.d.), well-being is defined as "a state of happiness and contentment, with low levels of distress, overall good physical and mental health and outlook, or good quality of life." According to self-determination theory (SDT; Ryan, 1995; Ryan & Deci, 2011), three basic psychological needs (i.e., autonomy, relatedness, and competency) are associated with well-being, with autonomy being a key ingredient in promoting well-being (Ryan & Deci, 2011). All three basic psychological needs impact school-based professionals' well-being, with autonomy being a particular area of concern. In this chapter, we focus on two kinds of school-based mental health professionals – school counsellors and school psychologists – who are often involved in supporting students' well-being.

When mental health and well-being are discussed in the context of schools, it is often in reference to the mental health and well-being of students (Lever, Mathis, & Mayworm, 2017). There is no doubt that attention should be paid to enhancing students' well-being. However, it is equally important to focus on the well-being of school-based professionals. In schools, teachers and principals are the core school staff members. Teachers, in particular, are the frontline professionals interacting with students on a regular basis. In a survey conducted by Harding et al. (2019) the authors found a positive association between teachers' and students' well-being whereby better teacher well-being relates to better student well-being while deficits in teacher well-being were associated with psychological distress in students. Additionally, lower depressive symptoms in teachers were found to be related to increased well-being of students. Findings from Harding et al. (2019) thus provide empirical support regarding the importance of promoting the well-being of school staff (e.g., Lever et al., 2017).

As was discussed by Lever et al. (2017), the well-being of these school-based professionals has an impact not only on the professionals themselves but also the student population that they serve. For instance, Laurie and Larson (2020) explained that teachers' well-being, in terms of stress and burnout, can affect their own physical fitness and job satisfaction as well as their students' achievement. In the school setting, school counsellors and school psychologists are often involved in supporting the well-being of students, and they are arguably at a higher risk of experiencing compassion fatigue (e.g., Lever et al., 2017) and role strain (e.g., Bardhoshi, Schweinle, & Duncan, 2014), which may affect their own well-being. School counsellors and school psychologists are often involved in helping students to manage strong negative emotions (e.g., anger and frustration) and challenging behaviours, which may contribute to their higher risk of burnout (Fradera, 2018; King, Subotic-Kerry, & O'Dea, 2018) and subsequently affect their well-being and professional work. Previous literature on the struggles with well-being that school counsellors and psychologists experience has focused largely on lack of support or resources in relation to burnout (e.g., Huebner, 1992; Lambie, 2007). For instance, in Simionato and Simpson's (2017) systematic review, the authors found that more than half of the psychotherapists (including counsellors and psychologists) they interviewed reported moderate to high levels of burnout, suggesting the importance to monitor these school-based mental health professionals' well-being. In the following section, we first provide a brief overview of the role of these professionals; we then discuss their emotional journey in their supportive role and explore ways to support their well-being.

Well-Being of School Counsellors

School counsellors play an integral role in fostering the well-being of the students in a school. As school counsellors are present working with children in the school on a regular basis, they act as a constant for fostering positive mental health in the students. School counsellors help foster well-being in students in multiple ways, including crisis interventions, talk therapy, liaising with family and community resources, and supporting under-represented students in programs such as science, technology, engineering, and math (Byrne et al., 2020; Cabell et al., 2021; King et al., 2018). Although school counsellors work to improve the well-being of the student population, they face their own struggles with mental health. This section will begin by looking at the education requirements and roles of school counsellors; it will then examine the challenges they face, ways to support their well-being, and, finally, the implications of what has been discussed.

Education and Roles of School Counsellors

The education requirements and regulation of school counsellors in Canada and in the United States vary by province, state, or territory (CCPA, 2012; U.S. Bureau of Labor Statistics, 2021). In Canada, all provinces and territories, with the exception of Quebec, require school counsellors to have a teaching licence (CCPA, 2012). However, while Quebec does not require a teaching licence it requires school counsellors to have a master's degree (CCPA, 2012). Newfoundland and Labrador and Prince Edward Island also have a mandatory master's degree requirement for school counsellors. In New Brunswick this requirement varies (CCPA, 2012). British Columbia, Manitoba, New Brunswick, Nunavut, Ontario, Quebec, and Saskatchewan have school counsellor specialization or certification available for those aspiring to be school counsellors (CCPA, 2012). In the United States licensed school counsellors typically have a master's degree in school counselling and have complete a practicum and written test (U.S. Bureau of Labor Statistics, 2021).

Given the teaching licence requirements across most of Canada, school counsellors are well-positioned to promote student well-being in the school system because of their knowledge in the fields of both education and mental health (ASCA, 2003). It is not uncommon to come across a school counsellor who started out teaching and later became a school counsellor in a school at which they had originally been teaching. Having background in both education and counselling in the school system is useful as school counsellors often engage with other stakeholders, especially teachers, in order to meet the needs of students (ASCA, 2003; Clemens, Milsom, & Cashwell, 2009). The American School Counselor Association's (2003) framework for school counselling states that the school counsellor's role should be designing and implementing counselling programs within the school. While school counsellors are able to effectively work in their role when they do not take on non-counselling tasks (ASCA, 2003), principals as school administrators are involved in determining day-to-day tasks of a school counsellor who is part of the school team (Clemens et al., 2009; Ruiz, Peters, & Sawyer, 2018). This means that school counsellors likely take on different roles, depending on the needs of a school, such as quasi-administrators or members of the leadership team, which, in turn, may have an impact on how their time is spent and what programs they implement specific to school counselling (Clemens et al., 2009).

Challenges Faced by School Counsellors

Given the way a school counsellor's role is determined, the potential for negative impacts on their mental health is significant. In a study conducted by Ruiz et al. (2018), there was only a 52 per cent agreement between principals and school counsellors with regard to appropriate counsellor activities. For instance, principals and counsellors disagreed on whether counsellors should occasionally perform bus, hall, or cafeteria duty, with a larger proportion of principals indicating that counsellors should take on these activities (Ruiz et. al., 2018), suggesting discrepancies between principals' and counsellors' views of the counsellor's role (Clemens et al., 2009). When these discrepancies emerge, the counsellor can experience role confusion (Clemens et al., 2009). Role confusion can have a substantial impact on the school counsellor's job satisfaction (Clemens et al., 2009). In addition to divergent views held by principals and school counsellors, changing economic and political trends can also have an impact on role uncertainty and confusion (Perkins, Oescher, & Ballard, 2010).

Role ambiguity has also been found to be associated with increased rates of burnout (King et al., 2018; Wilkerson & Bellini, 2006). For instance, taking on non-counselling duties, such as scheduling students for classes or substitute teaching, has been found to be associated with burnout in school counsellors (Bardhoshi et al., 2014; Moyer, 2011). School counsellors are exposed to high levels of stress on the job, making them vulnerable to experiencing burnout, but this is not exclusively related to role confusion (Butler & Constantine, 2005; Earle, 2017; Wilkerson & Bellini, 2006). Other factors that are found to be related to increased burnout in school counsellors include lack of supervision (Moyer, 2011), limited support in the school setting (Lambie, 2007), and heavy caseloads (Bardhoshi et al., 2014). The ratio of school counsellors to students frequently exceeds recommendations put forward by the Australian Psychological Association; these heavy caseloads not only put strain on counsellors but also reduce the accessibility of services for students (APS, 2016; King et al., 2018). A study conducted by King et al. (2018) explored factors that were associated with burnout in school counsellors working in secondary schools in Australia. Results of the study revealed that burnout was associated with increased workload, including appointments with students outside of regular school hours, dissatisfaction with mental health care provided by the school, and other work-related stresses (King et al., 2018).

Ways to Support School Counsellors' Well-Being

While school counsellors' work is supposed to foster good mental health in students, they, as mental health professionals, experience their own issues with well-being and are thus in need of support. There is often stigma around receiving help for mental health, perhaps even more so when one is considered to be a mental health professional(Evans & Payne, 2008). Seeking outside help may induce feelings of failure or incompetence. Therefore, reducing stigma surrounding receiving help for their mental health can help foster well-being in school counsellors (Evans & Payne, 2008).

Supporting school counsellors' well-being can be accomplished in multiple ways beyond encouraging counsellors to seek support and help. Given the importance of autonomy based on SDT (Ryan & Deci, 2011), it is clear that when school counsellors receive autonomy support in workplace settings that value their professional role, they will likely feel more connected within the school and that their counselling skills are put to good use in supporting the students who need to see them. For example, addressing school counsellors' role confusion requires a reduction in the discrepancy between the principal's and counsellor's view of the school counsellor's role (Clemens et al., 2009; Ruiz et al., 2018). Fostering a collaborative relationship between principals and school counsellors has been shown to reduce the discrepancy and therefore role confusion (Clemens et al., 2009; Ruiz et al., 2018). Clemens et al. (2009) looked at different approaches to fostering the relationship between principals and school counsellors. At the school level, principals and school counsellors can work on creating a collaborative relationship (Clemens et al., 2009). On a fundamental level, collaborative relationships between principals and school counsellors can be taught in education programs; as well, teaching school counsellors how to advocate for themselves supports their autonomy (Clemens et al., 2009).

In addition to reducing role confusion, reducing professional burnout is an important way to support school counsellors' well-being. King et al. (2018) put forwards a few ways to try to support school counsellors and reduce burnout. First, by measuring job overload, one can identify school counsellors who are at increased risk for burnout (King et al., 2018). When students require additional help outside of school hours, additional support should also be provided for the school counsellor to keep their workload at a manageable level (King et al., 2018). Second, school counsellors and other school members need to become more aware of burnout, and its associated risks and warning signs, as a preventive measure (King et al., 2018). Third, improving the allocation of resources in the school, such as improving the ratio of school counsellors to students, can help reduce the strain on school counsellors while also improving the mental health supports available to students (King et al., 2018).

Addressing role confusion and burnout in school counsellors is one way to support their well-being; encouraging self-care is another important strategy to consider. Guler and Ceyhan (2020) examined the implementation of an elective self-care course for undergraduate counselling and guidance students at a university in Turkey. Results showed that the self-care course helped increase these future counsellors' awareness of self-care while also helping them gain knowledge and skills related to self-care (Guler & Ceyhan, 2020). The course also facilitated practical application of the students' knowledge and skills (Guler & Ceyhan, 2020). As a result of taking the course, there was an increase in the counsellors' wellness (Guler & Ceyhan, 2020). These findings show that formal education/coursework in self-care can be beneficial in increasing the well-being of school counsellors. While an implementation of self-care courses for both future counsellors and practising school counsellors may be helpful in improving their mental health, much still remains to be done in this area (Government of Manitoba, 2019). For example, there is currently no mandatory or elective self-care course requirement to become a certified school counsellor in the province of Manitoba (Government of Manitoba, 2019).

Implications

School counsellors play an integral role in fostering the well-being of students, but the stresses of their job can take an emotional toll. While literature that looks at well-being and school counsellors largely focuses on school counsellors helping increase students' well-being, school counsellors' own mental health should not go unaddressed. While multiple factors affect a school counsellor's well-being, it becomes clear that the fostering of a collaborative relationship between principals and school counsellors and the provision of support and resources can help reduce role confusion and burnout, which in turn promotes the well-being of school counsellors. Additionally, formalized coursework in self-care can help increase school counsellors' knowledge of self-care as well as help them translate that knowledge into practical application. In addition to supporting school counsellors on a smaller scale, systemic changes, involving all levels of government, are required. Specifically, the provincial ministry of education can look at increasing funding to help schools improve the ratio of school counsellors to students so caseloads can be reduced. Improved funding can also help to reduce the amount of time that counsellors must devote to non-counselling activities. Individuals within the community can advocate for school counsellors by reaching out to their local provincial government representative. Finally, collaboration with local nongovernmental agencies can be utilized to provide continuity of care for students outside of school hours.

Well-Being of School Psychologists

School counsellors are typically present in the school buildings on a regular basis to support the learning and social-emotional development of students. There are a variety of other school-based professionals who are also essential in supporting the well-being environment in school settings. More specifically, these are clinical staff, such as school psychologists, school social workers, speech-language pathologists, occupational therapists, and physiotherapists. In this section, we discuss the importance of the well-being of school psychologists, who have a distinct role in supporting mental health concerns and implementing well-being programs in schools for students. First, we provide an overview of school psychologists' education and roles in school contexts. Second, we explain the emotional toll on school psychologists. Third, we explore several directions for promoting the well-being of school psychologists.

Education and Roles of School Psychologists

Like teachers, school psychologists undergo rigorous education. In the United States and Canada, school psychologists are required to hold a graduate degree, either a master's degree or a doctorate. According to the National Association of School Psychologists (2020) and the Canadian Psychological Association (CPA, n.d.), school psychologists receive specialized graduate preparation in psychology and education. Given their knowledge in child and adolescent development psychology, school-based intervention, and psychopathology, school psychologists provide school-based clinical services to the student population and assist teachers and families in supporting students. Not only do school psychologists provide diagnostic assessment services, they are also involved in case consultation, teacher consultation, in-service workshops, and tiered intervention based on the intensity of needs, supervision, and research (CPA, n.d.).

School psychologists are thus well-positioned in the school system to provide mental health and well-being support. As Eklund et al. (2017) has pointed out, because of the high number of young people presenting with mental health and behavioural concerns, school-based mental health support is a much-needed service. School psychologists hence find themselves in this vast mental health and well-being support arena. Even though school psychologists have expertise in the mental health domain, they typically do not provide just mental health and well-being support. School psychologists also provide an array of psychological services. While school psychologists are prepared to provide different psychological services, this also means that they have to meet multiple demands, possibly within a short period of time. For example, some students who exhibit mild-to-moderate mental health concerns may benefit from the support of school psychologists, but due to limited resources, these students may have to wait a long period of time before receiving the services they need.

Emotional Toll on School Psychologists

School psychology is a rewarding but demanding profession. School psychologists contribute knowledge and skills in developmental psychology, diagnosis and intervention, and mental health and well-being to support and work with students, parents, and teachers (e.g., Alahari, 2017). However, because of limited budgets and resources, typically one school psychologist serves multiple schools. Also, in their work, psychologists encounter many ethical dilemmas requiring difficult decisions, such as determining which students' needs are greater and should be regarded as priorities for psychological services (e.g., Huhtala, Kinnunen, & Feldt 2017). Huhtala et al. (2017) reported on a survey they had undertaken of 133 Finnish school psychologists regarding their experience of ethical dilemmas, the associated stress and frequency of ethical rumination, and their well-being (measured by vigour, exhaustion, and sleeping problems). The authors found that school psychologists can be categorized into one of three groups, namely, high, intermediate, and low ruminators. As suggested by the labels, these three groups of school psychologists differed mainly in their ethical rumination, which was measured by their response to a question about whether ethical dilemmas at work were kept affecting them during after-work hours. The high ruminators encountered ethical dilemmas more frequently and indicated that those ethical dilemmas were more likely to bother them after work hours (Huhtala et al., 2017). The intermediate group differed from the low ruminators on the intensity of stress and frequency of ethical rumination (Huhtala et al., 2017). Not surprising, the well-being of high ruminators suffered. In particular, these high-ruminating school psychologists felt more exhausted compared to their low-ruminating colleagues, and they also reported lower levels of vigour and poorer sleeping quality than the other two groups (Huhtala et al., 2017).

Like their educational counterparts – teachers and administrators – school psychologists are susceptible to stress and burnout. Stress and burnout among school psychologists are not new concerns. In 1988, Burden examined stress among school psychologists in three different countries – Australia, England, and the United States. It was found that the overall stress levels were similar among school psychologists in these different countries, while there were some slight variations regarding the intensity of stressors. However, moderate stress was reported in various situations, such as suicidal crisis, interpersonal relationship strain with principals and administrators, and dilemmas for meeting children's needs (Burden, 1988). Because Burden's work was descriptive in nature, how these various stressors affected school psychologists' well-being was not addressed. Huebner (1992) surveyed American school psychologists to examine what stressful events could predict burnout. Huebner (1992) found that lack of resources, time management, high risk to self and others, and interpersonal conflicts significantly predicted emotional exhaustion, whereas only lack of resources predicted depersonalization.

Supporting School Psychologists' Well-Being

Although school psychologists are experts in mental health and well-being, their work can take a huge emotional toll. Not only are school psychologists expected to conduct psycho-educational assessments requested by families and teachers, they are also involved in an array of different tasks (e.g., consultation on students' emotional and behavioural challenges, conducting individual or group therapy sessions to help students manage mental health issues, and crisis management). Facing multiple demands, school psychologists' abilities and skills to maintain their own well-being is crucial in order for them to support teachers, students, and families. Based on SDT (Ryan & Deci, 2011), it is reasonable to assume that when school psychologists work in autonomy-supportive schools, they are likely communicating their challenges to their teaching and clinical colleagues and getting much-needed support, which may result in more effective services for students.

One way to further support school psychologists' well-being is through mindfulness training and practice (Alahari, 2017). The rationale is that being mindful and in the moment expands school psychologists social-emotional skills, allowing them to be cognitively flexible and empathic when working with educators and parents (Alahari, 2017). It is particular true when school psychologists are being pulled by different demands and requests, such as which students should be assessed, given the limited resources and different priorities of teachers and administrators. As Alahari (2017) elaborated, through mindfulness practice, school psychologists' relationship with various stakeholders can be more proactive, especially when working relationships become strained due to different perspectives and priorities. In addition, being present and mindful also has a benefit to school psychologists' relationships to themselves, in gaining insights and awareness into their own thought processes and behavioural responses to various circumstances (Alahari, 2017).

George-Levi et al. (2020) recruited a group of school psychologists in Israel and examined their levels of burnout, loneliness, and sense of coherence. George-Levi et al. (2020) define a sense of coherence as the intrapersonal resources of seeing one's immediate yet challenging environment as "comprehensive, manageable and meaningful" (p. 3). A sense of coherence was found to buffer school psychologists' burnout only when their levels of loneliness are manageable. The benefit of embracing a high sense of coherence was not found when school psychologists felt lonely. This highlights the importance of enhancing school psychologists' social connectedness and their sense of coherence as a way to promote their well-being and combat burnout. While George-Levi et al. (2020) measured loneliness in general, the findings also coincide with the findings in Huhtala et al. (2017). While school psychologists can benefit by detaching themselves from their ethical dilemmas after work to attain better well-being, this is easier said than done. Hence, it would be important to explore avenues by which school psychologists can connect with their professional colleagues and discuss the various dilemmas they encounter (Huhtala et al., 2017), so that they too can benefit from collegial support and a sense of professional community.

In addition to mindfulness training and building a sense of community, self-care has been identified as an important element for school psychologists (e.g., Mann, Zaheer, & Kelly-Vance, 2019). As indicated by the American Psychological Association (APA, 2008), maintaining professional well-being is of utmost importance for school psychologists. Professional well-being helps school psychologists to be more vigilant about potential ethical issues in practice and more sensitive to students' needs, which is foundational to the profession as a whole. As the APA (2009) elaborated, self-care allows psychologists to maintain their well-being. While their suggestions associated with avoiding isolation and maintaining professional connection are similar to those of George-Levi et al. (2020), the APA Practice Organization (2009) and the APA (2009) include more self-care strategies. These self-care strategies include developing realistic work goals, attaining work-life balance, and being familiar with the occupational hazards of the profession (APA Practice Organization 2009; APA 2009). While the guideline applies to all psychologists, school psychologists may benefit from applying these strategies into their field, such as letting the school team know the response time frames for usual psychological requests, versus those requiring crisis intervention. As Schilling and Randolph (2020) found, practising school psychologists indicated the need for self-care to be taught, even in graduate programs, to prevent burnout within the profession.

Implications

While school psychologists are relied upon by school personnel to provide mental health care, the job that they do can exact a heavy emotional toll. For school psychologists to effectively and efficiently perform their tasks and contribute their expertise to serve the student population, their own well-being should not be neglected. While the literature on school psychologists' well-being is still in its infancy, there is emerging evidence that having access to various means of support helps to counter feelings of isolation and to strengthen their sense of professional connection. School psychologists are faced with multiple demands and stress can easily build up. Practising mindfulness may help these professionals to refocus on the present (by way of their thoughts and bodily reactions), thereby enhancing their capabilities to deal with complex and challenging situations. Noticing early warning signs of burnout and practising self-care may also be strategies for maintaining healthy well-being. In addition, at the school division level, superintendents should consider putting in place measures (e.g., regular protected time for a team of school psychologists to consult on issues which they encounter in the delivery of services) to foster school psychologists' professional connectedness. In many cases, more government funding would be needed to support and implement these goals.

Conclusion

The well-being of students in school has received increased attention in recent years; hence it is crucially important to address the well-being of the professionals who provide mental health intervention in school settings. In this chapter, we discussed the well-being of school counsellors and school psychologists; in particular we looked at conditions that may hinder their individual well-being and also at specific ways to support the growth and maintenance of their well-being. Building on Ryan and Deci's (2011) discussion, we have shown that when school counsellors and school psychologists are motivated and valued, they have more energy and positive experiences, leading to a greater feeling of competence. When administrators and decision-makers can provide autonomy support in the workplace, they are also more likely to support the other two basic psychological needs (Ryan & Deci, 2011). Thus school leaders can play a key role to play in supporting the well-being of these school-based professionals by creating and ensuring an autonomous-supportive work environment. School leaders such as principals and superintendents need to work with school-based professionals to ensure a collaborative work environment. Additionally, governing bodies need to look toward funding initiatives to help both school leaders and school-based professionals realize these positive changes. Likewise, members of the community can also play an important role in advocating for the well-being of these workers.

REFERENCES

Alahari, U. (2017). Supporting social-emotional competence and psychological well-being of school psychologists through mindfulness practice. *Contemporary School Psychology*, 21, 369–79. https://doi.org/10.1007/s40688-017-0154-x

American Psychological Association. (2008). Professional health and well-being for psychologists. https://www.apaservices.org/practice/ce/self-care/well-being?_ga=2.146464945.484772821.1602445118-70789940.1602445118

– (2009). *Self-care resources*. https://www.apaservices.org/practice/ce/self-care

– (n.d.). APA dictionary of psychology. Retrieved from 4 May 2021, from https://dictionary.apa.org/well-being

American School Counselor Association. (2003). The ASCA national model: A framework for school counseling programs. *Professional School Counseling*, 6(3), 165–8. www.jstor.org/stable/42732424

APA Practice Organization. (2009). *An action plan for self-care*. American Psychological Association. https://www.apaservices.org/practice/good-practice/Spring09-SelfCare.pdf

Australian Psychological Society. (2016). *Framework for the effective delivery of school psychological services*. https://www.psychology.org.au/getmedia/249a7a14-c43e-4add-aa6b-decfea6e810d/Framework-schools-psychologists-leaders.pdf

Bardhoshi, G., Schweinle, A., & Duncan, K. (2014). Understanding the impact of school factors on school counselor burnout: A mixed-methods study. *Professional Counselor*, 4(5), 426–43. https://doi.org/10.15241/gb.4.5.426

Burden, R.L. (1988). Stress and the school psychologist: A comparison of potential stressors in the professional lives of school psychologists in three continents. *School Psychology International*, 9, 55–9. https://doi.org/10.1177/0143034388091009

Butler, S.K., & Constantine, M.G. (2005). Collective self-esteem and burnout in professional school counselors. *Professional School Counseling*, 9(1), https://doi.org/10.1177/2156759X0500900107

Byrne, D., Carthy, A., & McGilloway, S. (2020). A review of the role of school-related factors in the promotion of student social and emotional wellbeing at post-primary level. *Irish Educational Studies*, 39(4), 439–55. https://doi.org/10.1080/03323315.2019.1697949

Cabell, A.L., Brookover, D., Livingston, A., & Cartwright, I. (2021). "It's never too late": High school counselors' support of underrepresented students' interest in STEM. *The Professional Counselor (Greensboro, N.C.)*, 11(2), 143–60. https://doi.org/10.15241/alc.11.2.143

Canadian Counselling and Psychotherapy Association. (2012). *Regulation for school counsellors by province*. https://www.ccpa-accp.ca/wp-content/uploads/2014/10/RegulationSchoolCounsellors_en.pdf

Canadian Psychological Association. (n.d.). *School psychology in Canada – roles, training and prospects*. https://cpa.ca/docs/File/Sections/EDsection/School%20Psychology%20in%20Canada%20-%20Roles,%20Training,%20and%20Prospects.pdf

Clemens, E.V., Milsom, A., & Cashwell, C.S. (2009). Using leader-member exchange theory to examine principal–school counselor relationships, school counselors' roles, job satisfaction, and turnover intentions. *Professional School Counseling*, 13(2), 75–85. https://doi.org/10.1177/2156759X0901300203

Cowan, K.C., & Rossen, E. (2013). Responding to the unthinkable: School crisis response and recovery. *Phi Delta Kappan*, 95(4), 8–12. https://doi.org/10.1177/003172171309500403

Earle, K.-M. (2017). Burnout in NSW school counsellors: Relationships between mindfulness, career-sustaining practices and work setting. *Journal *of Student Engagement: Education Matters, 7*, 71–96. https://paperity.org/p/82244270/burnout-in-nsw-school-counsellors-relationships-between-mindfulness-career-sustaining

Eklund, K., Meyer, L., Way, S., & McLean, D. (2017). School psychologists as mental health providers: The impact of staffing ratios and Medicaid on service provisions. *Psychology in the Schools, 54*, 279–93. https://doi.org/10.1002/pits.21996

Evans, Y.A., & Payne, M.A. (2008). Support and self-care: Professional reflections of six New Zealand high school counsellors. *British Journal of Guidance & Counselling, 36*(3), 317–30. https://doi.org/10.1080/03069880701729466

Fradera, A. (22 June 2018). *Burnout is common among psychotherapists – Now a review has identified the personal characteristics that increase the risk further.* https://digest.bps.org.uk/2018/06/22/burnout-is-common-among-psychotherapists-now-a-review-has-identified-the-personal-characteristics-that-increase-the-risk-further/

George-Levi, S., Schmidt-Barad, T., Natan, I., & Margalit, M. (2020). Sense of coherence and burnout among school psychologists: The moderating role of loneliness. *Current Psychology*. Advanced online publication. https://doi.org/10.1007/s12144-020-00766-5

Government of Manitoba. (2019). *School counsellor certification guidelines.* https://www.edu.gov.mb.ca/k12/profcert/pdf_docs/counsellor.pdf

Guler, D., & Ceyhan, E. (2021). Development of self-care behaviours in counsellors-in-training through an experiential self-care course: An action research. *British Journal of Guidance & Counselling, 49*(3), 414–34. https://doi.org/10.1080/03069885.2020.1740915

Harding, S., Morris, R., Gunnell, D., Ford, T., Hollingworth, W., Tilling, W. ... ... Kidger, J. (2019). Is teachers' mental health and wellbeing associated with students' mental health and wellbeing? *Journal of Affective Disorders, 242*, 180–7. https://doi.org/10.1016/j.jad.2018.08.080

Huebner, E.S. (1992). Burnout among school psychologists: An exploratory investigation into its nature, extent, and correlates. *School Psychology Quarterly, 7*(2), 129–36. https://doi.org/10.1037/h0088251

Huhtala, M., Kinnunen, U., & Feldt, T. (2017). School psychologists' ethical strain and rumination: Individual profiles and their associations with weekly well-being. *Psychology in the Schools, 54*(2), 127–41. https://doi.org/10.1002/pits.21992

King, C., Subotic-Kerry, M., & O'Dea, B. (2018). An exploration of the factors associated with burnout among NSW secondary school counsellors. *Journal of Psychologists and Counsellors in Schools, 28*(2), 131–42. https://doi.org/10.1017/jgc.2018.5

Lambie, G.W. (2007). The contribution of ego development level to burnout in school counselors: Implications for professional school counseling. *Journal of Counseling & Development, 85*(1), 82–8. https://doi.org/10.1002/j.1556-6678.2007.tb00447.x

Laurie, R., & Larson, E. (2020, May 12). *How does teacher stress and burnout impact student achievement?* EdCan Network. https://www.edcan.ca/articles/teacher-stress-and-student-achievement/#:~:text=Reduced%20motivation%20and%20achievement%3A%20Teacher,to%20succeed%2C%20lower%20grades

Lever, N., Mathis, E., & Mayworm, A. (2017). School mental health is not just for students: Why teacher and school staff wellness matters. *Report on Emotional and Behavioral Disorders in Youth, 17*(1), 6–12. https://www.civicresearchinstitute.com/online/article_abstract.php?pid=5&iid=1234&aid=8080

Mann, A., Zaheer, I., & Kelly-Vance, L. (2019). Self-care for school psychologists advancing social justice for youth. *Communique, 48*(4), 21–3. https://www.nasponline.org/publications/periodicals/communique/issues/volume-48-issue-4

Moyer, M. (2011). Effects of non-guidance activities, supervision, and student-to-counselor ratios on school counselor burnout. *Journal of School Counseling, 9*(5). http://www.jsc.montana.edu/articles/v9n5.pdf

National Association of School Psychologists. (2020). *Who are school psychologists?* https://www.nasponline.org/about-school-psychology/who-are-school-psychologists

Perkins, G., Oescher, J., & Ballard, M.B. (2010). The evolving identity of school counselors as defined by the stakeholders. *Journal of School Counseling, 8*(31). http://www.jsc.montana.edu/articles/v8n31.pdf

Ruiz, M., Peters, M.L., & Sawyer, C. (2018). Principals' and counselors' lens of the school counselor's role. *Journal of Professional Counseling: Practice, Theory & Research, 45*(1), 1–16. https://doi.org/10.1080/15566382.2019.1569321

Ryan, R.M. (1995). Psychological needs and the facilitation of integrative processes. *Journal of Personality, 63*(3), 397–427. https://doi.org/10.1111/j.1467-6494.1995.tb00501.x

Ryan, R.M. & Deci, E.L. (2011). A self-determination theory perspective on social, institutional, cultural and economic supports for autonomy and their importance for well-being. In V.I. Chirkov, R.M. Ryan, & K.M. Sheldon (Eds.). *Human autonomy in cross-cultural context: Perspectives on the psychology of agency, freedom, and well-being* (pp. 45–64). Springer.

Schilling, E.J., & Randolph, M. (2020). Voices from the field: Addressing job burnout in school psychology training program. *Contemporary School Psychology*. Advanced online publication. https://doi.org/10.1007/s40688-020-00283-z

Simionato, G.K., & Simpson, S. (2017). Personal risk factors associated with burnout among psychotherapists: A systematic review of the literature. *Journal of Clinical Psychology, 74*(9), 1431–56. https://doi.org/10.1002/jclp.22615

U.S. Bureau of Labor Statistics. (2021). *School and Career Counselors: Occupational Outlook Handbook: U.S. Bureau of Labor Statistics*. https://www.bls.gov/ooh/community-and-social-service/school-and-career-counselors.htm#tab-4

Wilkerson, K., & Bellini, J. (2006). Intrapersonal and organizational factors associated with burnout among school counselors. *Journal of Counseling & Development, 84*(4), 440–50. https://doi.org/10.1002/j.1556-6678.2006.tb00428.x

PART THREE

Contextualizing Well-Being and Well-Becoming in Schools

PART THREE

Contextualizing Well-Being and Well-Becoming in Schools

8 Well-Being in the Context of School Organizations

LESLEY EBLIE TRUDEL

Student well-being has become a major concern in today's schools and, according to the literature, deservedly so. This chapter takes an organizational perspective in order to contribute to the important dialogue on student well-being. Beginning with the notion that well-being is a global competency and fundamental human right around which education legislation and policies are to be developed, this chapter provides selected examples which illuminate the concept of well-being, not only as a foundational principle, but as a philosophical underpinning of school environments. Various Canadian provincial statutes and organizational frameworks pertaining to well-being in schools are examined through the relevant lenses of instruction, learning, safety, and accessibility. While there is no universally accepted definition for well-being, in this chapter, the term is defined with consideration of systemic contexts, initiatives, and activities that are undertaken to achieve healthy and vibrant communities. Additionally, the promotion of well-being is explored within the context of new frontiers in educational measurement and accountability. The chapter closes with a discussion of the tenets of educational leadership required to create, implement, and sustain conditions for well-being in schools. While perspectives and practices from different Canadian provinces are presented where helpful, examples are primarily drawn from school districts in Manitoba, Canada. Nonetheless, the perspectives and practices are addressed in a manner that can be applied beyond specific provincial jurisdictions.

Well-Being as a Foundational Perspective

Over the past decade, questions and concerns focused on student well-being have moved steadily to the centre of educational dialogue in Canada and around the world (Kempf, 2018). Given the rising levels and ubiquity of mental health challenges among youth (Mental Health Commission of Canada, 2016), the notion of well-being has gained momentum in school organizations as a means for enhancing student agency to meet the threshold at which learning can effectively occur (Ontario Ministry of Education, 2013; Wei & Kutcher 2014). In the School Effectiveness Framework (2013), the Ontario Ministry of Education indicates that well-being not only stands on its own as a powerful and essential condition for life, but also impacts student learning and school improvement. With Canada as a global leader in educational reform, boards of education and provincial ministries across the country have taken a lead in prioritizing student achievement and dispositions for positive well-being in an effort to promote learning that leads to success (Hargreaves et al., 2018). Further, according to the McConnell Foundation (2020) an emphasis on social-emotional well-being in the school setting can lead to an 11 percentage-point enhancement in academic achievement. The sole focus of systemic efforts toward student well-being cannot, however, remain solely on the promotion of human productivity.

Well-being underpins all aspects of the school environment (Ottawa-Carleton District School Board, 2015). Evidently, children and youth who are positively engaged in schools achieve greater resilience, have reduced likelihood of risk-taking behaviour, make more appropriate choices to support their learning, and acquire an increased capacity to meet challenges confronting them in society (Aldridge & McChesney, 2018; Boak et al., 2016; Marraccini & Brier, 2017; Rasberry et al., 2017). The World Health Organization (2020) describes well-being as "the state in which an individual realizes their own abilities, can cope with normal stresses of life, can work productively and is able to make a contribution to their own community." Accordingly, the McConnell Foundation (2020) believes it makes good sense to support school organizations in understanding the essential tenets of well-being. After all, the education system provides routine opportunities to address the concept of student well-being and offers the ideal environment in which to learn about strategies that support its instruction most effectively (Ontario Ministry of Education, 2016a).

Despite the national and international conversations about student well-being, educators have typically been untrained and inexperienced in the daily delivery and promotion of well-being in the classroom (Marko, 2015; Rodger et al., 2014). When teachers are unable to promote well-being as part of the instructional process, they become less effective, feel stressed, and experience compassion fatigue and burnout (Arens & Morin, 2016; Koenig et al., 2017). Santoro (2011) emphasized that teachers may also become demoralized if they are consistently unable to meet the challenges of their day-to-day work. Kempf (2018) advocated that teachers are best able to support students when they first acquire the capacity, support, and resources that are required to promote well-being in schools. Katz (2018), for example, has developed an enduring pedagogical framework, following universal design for learning guidelines, which assists teachers in responding to the social and emotional needs of students. In the "Three Block Model," Katz addresses capacity-building through suggested lesson plans, methods, and activities for skill development. Programming such as this is essential when bridging theory to practice and providing the necessary scaffolds for teachers to support well-being in classrooms. In addressing the challenges of service delivery in school organizations, this chapter explores the complex nature of well-being, from the perspectives of global competencies, human rights, legislation, policies, approaches, priorities, leadership practices, and programming. In so doing, contextual knowledge is enhanced to better prepare educators to become active participants and contribute to the dialogue on the instruction of well-being.

Well-Being as a Competency and Human Right

Student well-being is articulated in various global competency frameworks which outline key skills and dispositions for twenty-first century learning. Despite the fact that these frameworks have been part of the education landscape for over two decades, there remains deep interest in resiliency, creativity, inquisitiveness, and interpersonal proficiency (Griffin et al., 2012; Marzano & Heflebower, 2012; National Research Council, 2012; Tough, 2012). Global competencies are comprehensive sets of knowledge, attitudes, and skills that can be applied in a variety of scenarios, both locally and globally. The Canadian Council for Ministers of Education (CMEC, 2017) developed a competency framework and placed the concept of well-being within the category of global citizenship and sustainability. According to CMEC, well-being involves reflecting on diverse worldviews, as well as comprehending and attending to economic, ecological, and social issues, with an appreciation for differences and diverse perspectives. Student descriptors in the framework includes phrases such as "taking action to support quality of life both now and in the future," "promoting equity, respecting human rights and democracy," and "participating in networks in safe and socially responsible ways." Ultimately, the idea of what students should know is not only connected to how they should know it, but also to how students should be and feel as they learn and grow.

Internationally, the United Nations Convention on the Rights of the Child (1989) proposed six dimensions to measure and define child well-being. This included material well-being, health and safety, educational well-being, positive relationships with families and peers, reduced risk-taking behaviours and violence, as well as improved personal health and school life (Lee, 2009). The Convention was the first binding international agreement; each of its 54 articles encompass various aspects related to the civil, political, economic, cultural, and social welfare of children. As a result, the rights and well-being of children and youth are no longer seen as simply a moral commitment but as a legal obligation. In Canada, human rights are legally enforceable under the Charter of Rights and Freedoms (1982). According to the Canadian Public Legal Education Association (2020), the Charter is a "powerful legal tool that protects those living in Canada from breaches of specific rights and freedoms by federal and provincial governments" (p. 1). In relation to addressing well-being, section 7 of the Charter sets out fundamental political and civil rights for all individuals while section 15 outlines rights to equality, equal protection, and benefit of the law. The Canadian Human Rights Act (1977) and human rights codes across Canada are relevant to government bodies as well, but extend to breaches that affect individuals, organizations, and businesses. The Canadian Human Rights Act applies only to individuals who work for or receive benefits from the federal government, including within the jurisdiction of First Nations education. Nonetheless, both federal and provincial human rights codes prohibit discrimination on specific grounds and support a society where all individuals can participate equally. Legislation, policy, and the practice of education ministries and school districts must align with the Charter and with principles of human rights. In so doing, a climate of respect and understanding is created and the physical and mental well-being of staff and students within education communities is maintained.

Well-Being as a Legislated Provision

In Canada, school authorities, parents/legal guardians, and students have responsibilities set out in education legislation to ensure welcoming, safe, caring, and respectful learning environments. In Manitoba, education legislation, in the form of the Public Schools Act (2020b), is based on a foundational philosophy of inclusion, which supports the right of youth to learn in environments which value both their strengths and their uniqueness. The Manitoba "Philosophy of Inclusion" (2001) describes the importance of community members feeling accepted, valued and safe; it recognizes meaningful involvement, belonging, and equal access (which goes beyond physical location), and embraces the well-being of all. Representing an administrative perspective, the Manitoba Association of School Superintendents (MASS) published two position statements that provided understandings and recommendations pertaining to well-being in provincial schools (MASS 2012; 2019). Initially MASS focused on the needs of students who required intensive (tier 3) interventions for mental health concerns and called for government and social agencies to take action. Recently, however, MASS extended that focus to include all students, operationalizing the holistic concepts of well-being and well-becoming (Falkenberg & Ukasoanya, 2019).The latter position continued to include the needs of students with mental health concerns, but also outlined the importance of students' experiences when living their lives and developing capabilities for life now (well-being) and in the future (well-becoming). That said, MASS emphasized that the responsibility for this endeavour should be shared between educators, parents and legal guardians, as well as the community at large.

For many years, key themes of well-being, including those addressing human rights, health, poverty, environmental protection, and climate change, have been incorporated into Manitoba's education system through Education for Sustainable Development (2020a). ESD is an initiative linked to the United Nations Educational, Scientific and Cultural Organization (UNESCO). Every school in Manitoba has been encouraged to enlist ESD goals as part of their school planning process. In this regard, schools can prescribe the manner in which students will become responsible citizens, contributing to social, economic, environmental, and equitable quality of life in their communities. In 2013, amendments to the Public Schools Act required Manitoba School Boards to revise policy and practice in order to meet additional thresholds for safe and inclusive learning environments. New policies were required to ensure respect for human diversity, while existing codes of conduct were strengthened to include violence and bullying prevention strategies and responses. Further legislation impacting the well-being of Manitoba children and youth also became law in 2013. The Accessibility for Manitobans Act (2013) was devised to guide organizations in preventing and removing barriers in the workplace and in key areas of daily living. Furthermore, all school boards in Manitoba were required to have accessibility plans in place by November 2017. Aligning with the Charter of Rights and Freedoms and the Canadian Human Rights Act, The Government of Canada, along with the provinces of British Columbia, Nova Scotia, Ontario, and Quebec, worked toward devising standards within existing accessibility legislation to ensure inclusive and barrier-free environments (Doyle, 2020). Accessibility legislation not only demonstrated support for personal well-being for all children and youth, but also aimed at creating opportunities for children and youth with varying abilities.

Well-Being as a Systems Initiative

Although well-being is supported through human rights and legislation, it has been challenging to define this important foundational concept. Kempf (2018) queried whether it was a matter that is taught, a method or way of being, or perhaps an outcome in the curriculum. Spratt (2016) portrayed well-being as a "conflation of different concepts under one umbrella term" (p. 3) and added that ambiguity with these concepts could lead to confusion in practice. Bassett-Gunter et al. (2015) reported that most school districts rely on the definition from the Pan-Canadian Joint Consortium for School Health (JCSH, 2020). According to the JCSH (2020) comprehensive school health (CSH) is an "internationally recognized approach to supporting improvements in students' educational outcomes while addressing school health in a planned, integrated and holistic way" (para. 1). Moreover, the Alberta Teachers Association (ATA, 2019) reported that some districts might subscribe to the UNESCO definition of well-being or to that provided by the WHO (2020), whereas others may simply follow indicators supplied by provincial ministries of education or to criteria stipulated by funders. Needless to say, school organizations often find themselves needing to be flexible and responsive, depending on the terminology and descriptors of well-being that are in use at the time.

The ATA (2019) further indicated that school well-being initiatives in Canada have focused on systems-level change through advocacy for policy development and sustainable funding. That said, when considering national organizations such as Active at School, the Canadian Teachers Federation, the Canadian School Boards Association, EdCan Network, the JCSH, Physical and Health Education Canada, Recess Project, and Well Ahead, it is important to note that each organization collaborates closely with education ministries across Canada to influence the context of school health and well-being. For example, the EdCan Network (2020) indicates that the organization prioritizes well-being by connecting Canadian educators and partner groups by leveraging research and showcasing policy and practice. Furthermore, as can be observed when closely examining work of this nature, provinces and territories have subsequently focused on select initiatives or partnered with specific organizations to provide programming and supports to districts in the area of educational health and well-being. The ATA (2019) found that, in general, provincial well-being initiatives and activities across Canada have come about in a variety of ways. Organizations such as Ophea (2020) and Ever Active Schools (2020) have assisted in developing curriculum, providing resources (lesson plans, guides, and videos), connecting school districts with contacts that work in the field of well-being, creating and overseeing grant opportunities, as well as offering direct programming and certification plans for schools. Educators, in turn, have spent time on ministry committees advocating for and developing policies for well-being, participating in professional learning opportunities (webinars, workshops, conferences, and targeted training) and conducting action research in a supportive capacity for larger initiatives.

In Manitoba, Healthy Together Now (2020d) is an example of a regional, community-led well-being initiative that is facilitated and supported by the provincial government. Projects within this initiative operate in health authority regions and target Manitobans (including children and youth in schools) with prevention-related programming. School teams collaborate with ministry and health authority staff to build on, blend, or develop programming that reflects the unique needs of communities. For example, the program mobilizes knowledge in the area of prevention for a variety of chronic diseases. Manitoba also supports the Healthy Schools initiative (2020c) to promote physical, social, and emotional health in schools. Teams from various boards of education develop plans to identify ways of creating healthier environments within district schools. Grant funding can be requested for school- or district-based projects under priority health topics such as physical activity, nutrition, mental health promotion, substance abuse and addictions, sexual and reproductive health, as well as safety and injury prevention. School administrators typically request lead teachers or point persons on staff to represent, support, and advocate for student well-being. One of the most widely recognized ways of promoting student well-being is adopting a whole-school approach.

Well-Being as a Community Approach

When planning for inclusive, safe, and caring schools, the WHO (2020) and the International Union of Health Promotion and Education (2020) recommend the use of a whole-school approach. This method is multidimensional in nature and is implemented in a coordinated manner through shared leadership and engaged communities (e.g., Manitoba,

2017). In Manitoba, several evidence-based frameworks are considered when coordinating and leading a whole school approach to well-being. By addressing concepts relating to well-being within a systemic perspective, school communities can strengthen their efforts toward youth development (Ragozzino & O'Brien, 2009).

The most common frameworks that are used at a school or divisional level to approach well-being are the CSH Model, the Three-Tiered Model, and the social-ecological framework model, each of which will be described in turn. First, using the CSH Model, Morrison and Peterson (2013) refer to the whole-school setting and address well-being through pillars of social and physical environments, teaching and learning, healthy school policies, as well as partnership and services. Rather than focusing solely on bullying prevention initiatives, the researchers set out to cast a wider net in consideration of well-being and emphasize healthy relationships, digital citizenship, neurodiversity, school-based mental health, as well as suicide prevention and intervention. It is important to note that the CSH is a model that is commonly in use in Canadian schools.

Second, the Three-Tiered Model (Healthy Child Manitoba, 2013; Manitoba, 2011) – a holistic model commonly used in both education and health care settings – is used to facilitate well-being by categorizing and prioritizing students' strengths and needs. For example, planning for the primary tier is based on strengths of the entire school population and emphasizes school-wide expectations for safety and respect as a foundation for learning. At the secondary tier, planning practices are more responsive, proactive, and short-term for children and youth identified as experiencing difficulties. For students who require specialized and individualized responses, intensive supports, identified at the tertiary tier, are designed to mitigate existing and severe safety issues, to strengthen networks, and prevent further crises. This framework, which is shaped like a pyramid, is often used in planning a continuum of proactive supports for social-emotional learning in school districts.

Finally, from a social-ecological systems perspective (Ashiabi & O'Neal, 2015; Bronfenbrenner, 1977; Eriksson et al., 2018) educators are reminded that a sense of community and belonging assists students in maintaining social-emotional and psychological well-being. When planning for school safety, this third framework acknowledges the systemic and interactive relationships between students and their communities, families, peers, schools, and classrooms. Through social-ecological perspectives, planning can be focused, roles and responsibilities identified, and strategies established to address risk factors. It is clear that systemic models positively impact both education and health outcomes in schools (Bassett-Gunter et al., 2015). By identifying critical elements within those structures and establishing outcomes with measurable, evidence-based indicators, school districts can more accurately assess whether strategies and initiatives are successful.

Well-Being as an Educational Priority

In spite of the abundance of perspectives and frameworks available for application in Canadian schools, Short (2017) indicated that most school systems are not currently organized to embed well-being within educational priorities. Short added that for education ministries across the country, the dilemma of promoting well-being has been met with the equally difficult task of determining how to measure it. Stiglitz et al. (2009) suggested that in our performance-oriented society, metrics do matter. In other words, what is measured is valued and what is measured typically impacts what is done. From this standpoint, it is critical to acknowledge, regrettably, that concepts are dismissed when they are considered difficult to measure, small-scale, non-replicable, anecdotal, or subject to a lack of evidence (Borg, 2010, CUREE, 2011; Enthoven & de Bruijn, 2010; Wilkins, 2012). Bryk et al. (2011) argue, however, that relevant knowledge acquired by educators should be applied within the discussion of student achievement. In this regard, they coined the term *practice-based evidence*, a deliberate inversion of the familiar term *evidence-based practice*. Nelson and Campbell (2017) further remind us of the importance of taking a broad view of classroom evidence, balancing both qualitative and quantitative perspectives when providing indicators of student achievement.

With a key challenge being the need to conceptualize the idea of student success beyond the idea of academic achievement alone (Kempf, 2018), educators in Manitoba, for instance, are attempting to identify data which will inform student achievement in a holistic manner (Eblie Trudel, 2017). While Manitoba has identified well-being as a priority area for K-12 education, the province has yet to formally commit to its measurement as an aspect of student assessment. Nonetheless, this action signals a shift in discourse, from one based on achievement alone to one that takes into account the many contextual factors surrounding student progress (Falkenberg, 2015). The Ontario Ministry of Education (2014) has committed to identifying these contextual factors and finding ways of assessing well-being. This is a significant departure from typical practice, in that achievement drivers related to measurability or standardization historically involved only academic outcomes. The debate about what comprises well-being, measured as part of student learning, has now flowed into the broad politics of student assessment. While current curricular standards tests in the province have been admittedly too narrow to communicate student progress relating to well-being, the answer to shifting the concept of student success beyond traditional indicators of student assessment is clearly not to increase the number or widen the range of tests. In fact, increased assessment of any specific element in education would not guarantee accountability for, or improvement in, student outcomes.

In Ontario, the impetus for measurement began with the premise that greater well-being would lead to improved academic achievement in addition to enhancement of the common good for children and youth (Ferguson & Power, 2014; Ontario Ministry of Education 2016b, 2013, 2012). As a result, the shift from a paradigm of wellness promotion to more formal measurement of outcomes required analyses of specific elements and domains in order to effectively provide an assessment of well-being (Kempf, 2018). Ferguson and Power (2014) reviewed the evolution of instruments employed to measure well-being. Initially, from a population-level approach, school districts accessed data on well-being from aggregate assessments such as the Early Development Instrument (Janus & Duku, 2007; Janus & Offord, 2007), the Middle Years Development Instrument (Schonert-Reichl et al., 2012), and the Tell Them From Me Survey (The Learning Bar, 2020). A fundamental challenge was later identified in terms of the work required to develop reliable instruments and approaches for the measurement of individual, rather than from group-level, well-being indicators. The Education Quality and Accountability Office (EQAO, 2017) committed to the development of unique tools to better reflect individual metrics. The Ontario Ministry of Education has indicated that substantive challenges remain in measuring the well-being of students and, in particular, in measuring the impact of various well-being initiatives on individuals or groups of students (Huppert, 2014, 2017; White et al., 2017). Likewise, Alberta Education initiated similar revisions of programming in their Framework for Kindergarten to Grade 12 Wellness Education (2020) to more accurately assess and reflect student data on well-being. The proposed framework, which was to include assessment of school programming and high school credits in health and physical education, identified dimensions of wellness across all curricula and outcomes in specific wellness-related courses. Curriculum development is, however, being reworked under the current government. With that in mind, Ott et al. (2017) recommended more comprehensive approaches across multiple ministries and provinces to enhance resource development, training, and support and to determine optimal directions. Additional research is suggested to assist in determining the future course of action relating to the assessment of well-being in Canadian school organizations.

Well-Being as a Leadership Concept

Teachers play a key role in school improvement efforts with a focus on increasing student learning and achievement (Hargreaves & Fullan, 2012; Hattie 2009; Mincu, 2015; Marzano, 2003). Moreover, teacher leaders, that is, decision-makers within formal and informal leadership structures, are central to this process, given their integral understanding of the complexities of classroom dynamics (Mangin & Stoelinga, 2008). With the recent addition of student well-being to the school improvement agenda, greater importance has been placed on the role of leadership to achieve teacher well-being (Cherkowski & Walker, 2016, 2018; Greenberg et al., 2016). Ott et al. (2017) cautioned that while it might be tempting to infer that the well-being of students should be prioritized over that of educators, their research indicated that well-being was in fact an interdependent concept. Cherkowski and Schnellert (2017) affirmed that positive teacher well-being fosters personal agency, facilitates professional growth, improves classroom practice, and ultimately contributes to student achievement and school improvement. Cherkowski and Walker (2018) linked the contributions of organizational studies and positive psychology to school improvement, placing well-being and a reimagining of classroom instruction at the forefront(Dweck, 2006; Gergen, 2015; McGonigal, 2015). Teacher leaders, in this regard, are tasked with creating supportive environments that allow ideas to be shared, feedback to be received, and challenges to be solved collaboratively. Teacher leaders also benefit from attention to their well-being, which in turn impacts school improvement outside of the classroom (Margolis, 2012; Wenner & Campbell, 2017). Cherkowski and Walker (2016) reflected that teacher leaders gain a sense of well-being when they see the results of their work impacting their schools and communities. Promoting social-emotional competencies not only benefits school leaders but positively impacts all partners (Greenberg et al., 2016).

While there is a growing body of evidence related to positive leadership for well-being in organizations in general, there has been minimal research on positive leadership in educational settings (Cameron, 2008; Dutton & Spreitzer, 2014; Quinn, 2015). In their discussion paper for the Canadian Association for School System Administrators (CASSA), Short et al. (2017) identified gaps in leadership and resource development for mental health and well-being, indicating that a concerted effort is required to support leadership for mental health in schools. They recommended that a challenge of this nature would require input from school system leaders in addition to the development of a plan to coordinate capacity-building. Additionally, Manion et al. (2013) found that a survey of educational organizations revealed specific elements that impeded programming for well-being in Canadian schools. Challenges ranged from insufficient funding, poor planning, and shortcomings in educator knowledge, to limitations related to program access. With the dynamics couched in the context of effective school mental health, Short et al., (2017) further identified supports necessary to provide the foundations for student well-being. They emphasized the importance of school board commitments that reflect a culture of change and growth, the formation of teacher leadership teams that communicate a clear vision for the future, the development of processes through targeted professional learning communities, and the creation of continuous improvement plans at the district level to facilitate well-being.

Introduced in 2016, Manitoba's Framework for Continuous Improvement required school districts to incorporate accountability into their planning practices to ensure high levels of academic achievement for students. Within this process, districts were encouraged to examine student achievement results from provincial standards assessments and aggregate report card data to ensure that appropriate supports were in place for all students. School districts were also required to ensure that students were prepared as global citizens and supported in terms of personal growth, positive sense of self, and well-being. As mentioned earlier in the chapter, Manitoba currently has no formal mechanisms in place to measure success in the priority areas of citizenship and well-being. The framework does, however, promote collaborative inquiry and reflection, as well as enhancement of instructional leadership capacity. In this regard, Manitoba has provided an emergent response to concerns raised by Short et al. (2017) in the form of continuous improvement planning for well-being in school districts. Ultimately, the responsibility for well-being in educational organizations rests with government ministries, school boards, and education leaders who endeavour to work collaboratively to create a context where all community members have the opportunity to flourish.

Final Reflections

This chapter revealed essential details regarding the instruction of well-being from an organizational (school district) perspective. The chapter began with the discussion of well-being as a critical focal point on the agenda of school organizations across the country. Global competencies and human rights frameworks have placed well-being at the forefront for consideration in legislation, policy, and practice. Although well-being has been identified as an essential underpinning for student achievement, it is also regarded as a key ingredient in the development of resilience to cope with the daily stresses of life.

In spite of the relevance and importance of well-being, it was acknowledged that school boards and district staff have at times felt unprepared to address this concept in schools. Educators who are untrained in the area of well-being can experience compassion fatigue and eventually burnout. In order to mitigate these effects, teachers require assistance in building capacity to promote well-being in their classrooms. Education ministries and school systems are collaborating with partner groups to develop curriculum resources, facilitate professional learning for staff, and deliver well-being initiatives to students. While there is no common definition of well-being, most stakeholders agree that it is a holistic concept that is best achieved through a comprehensive, whole-school approach to safe, inclusive, and healthy learning communities.

Likewise, the promotion of well-being has emerged as a ministerial priority in certain Canadian jurisdictions. Whereas most education ministries and school systems have yet to organize ways to embed the concept within assessment practices, there has been initial work done in one province on the measurement of student well-being, employing population-level approaches and individual assessments through curricular outcomes. Many studies advise proceeding with caution, however, in terms of ensuring both qualitative and quantitative perspectives in the provision of student achievement indicators.

The final portion of the chapter featured a discussion of teacher leadership and its essential role in bringing well-being to life in school organizations. Emphasis was placed on the key role that teachers play in school improvement through instructional practice in the classroom. It was noted that teachers' own experience of well-being positively impacts student achievement. Further, the observation was made that teacher leadership is integral to ensuring both teacher and student well-being. A continuous improvement planning process in one Canadian province was highlighted to demonstrate the function of priority setting, collaborative inquiry, capacity building, and reflection in school systems. The conclusion was drawn that organizational commitment and teacher leadership are essential to the successful creation, implementation, and sustainability of programming for well-being in Canadian schools.

REFERENCES

Alberta. (2020, August 30). *Framework for kindergarten to grade 12 wellness education*. http://education.alberta.ca/teachers/program/pe.aspx

Alberta Teachers' Association. (2019). *School wellness and well-being initiatives across Canada. Environmental scan and literature review*. https://www.teachers.ab.ca/SiteCollectionDocuments/ATA/Publications/Research/COOR-101-27%20School%20Wellness%20and%20Well-being%20Initatives%20across%20Canada.pdf

Aldridge, J., & McChesney, K. (2018). The relationships between school climate and adolescent mental health and wellbeing: A systematic literature review. *International Journal of Educational Research, 88*, 121–45. https://doi.org/10.1016/j.ijer.2018.01.012

Arens, A., & Morin A. (2016). Relations between teachers' emotional exhaustion and students' educational outcomes. *Journal of Educational Psychology, 108*(6), 800–13. https://doi.org/10.1037/edu0000105

Ashiabi, G., & O'Neal, K. (2015). Child social development in context: An examination of some propositions in Bronfenbrenner's bioecological theory. *SAGE Open, 5*(2). https://doi-org.uml.idm.oclc.org/10.1177/2158244015590840

Bassett-Gunter, R., Yessis, J., Manske S., & Gleddie, D. (2015). Healthy school communities in Canada. *Health Education Journal, 75*(2), 235–48. https://cassalberta.ca/wpcontent/uploads/2018/10/Bassett_Gunter_etal_2015.pdf

Boak, A., Hamilton, H., Adlaf, E., Henderson, J., Wolfe, D., & Mann, R. (2016). *The mental health and well-being of Ontario students, 1991–2015: Detailed OSDUHS findings*. Centre for Addiction and Mental Health. http://www.camh.ca/-/media/files/pdf-osduhs/the-mental-health-and-well-being-of-ontario-students-1991-2015-detailed-osduhs-findings.pdf?la=en&hash=59BFD5B17408AAEE0E837E01048088ED51E558B2

Borg, S. (2010). Language teacher research engagement. *Language Teaching, 43*(4), 391–429. https://doi.org/10.1017/S0261444810000170

Bronfenbrenner, U. (1977). Toward an experimental ecology of human development. *The American Psychologist, 32*(7), 513–31. https://doi.org/10.1037/0003-066X.32.7.513

Bryk, A.S., Gomez, L.M., & Grunow, A. (2011). Getting ideas into action: Building networked improvement communities in education. In M.T. Hallinan (Ed.), *Frontiers in sociology of education* (pp. 127–62). Springer.

Cameron, K.S. (2008). Paradox in positive organizational change. *Journal of Applied Behavioral Science, 44*(1), 7–24. https://doi.org/10.1177/0021886308314703

Canada. Department of Justice. (1982). *Canadian Charter of Rights and Freedoms*. https://laws-lois.justice.gc.ca/eng/const/page-15.html

Centre for the Use of Research and Evidence in Education. (2011). Report of Professional Practitioner Use of Research Review: Practitioner Engagement in and/or with Research Coventry: CUREE [online]. http://www.curee.co.uk/files/publication/[site-timestamp]/Practitioner%20Use%20of%20Research%20Review%20-%20FINAL%2011_02_11.pdf

Cherkowski, S., & Schnellert, L. (2017). Exploring teacher leadership in a rural, secondary school: Reciprocal learning teams as a catalyst for emergent leadership. *International Journal of Teacher Leadership, 8*(1), 6–25.

Cherkowski, S., & Walker, K. (2016). Purpose, passion and play: Exploring the construct of flourishing from the perspective of school principals. *Journal of Educational Administration, 54*(4), 378–92. https://doi.org/10.1108/JEA-10-2014-0124

– (2018). *Teacher wellbeing: Noticing, nurturing, and sustaining flourishing in schools*. Word and Deed Press.

Council of Ministers of Education of Canada . (2017). *A pan-Canadian view on global citizenship and sustainability*. http://uis.unesco.org/en/blog/pan-canadian-viewglobal-citizenship-and-sustainability

Doyle, J. (2020). *A complete overview of Canada's accessibility laws*. https://siteimprove.com/en-ca/blog/a-complete-overview-of-canada-s-accessibility-laws/

Dutton, J., & Spreitzer. G. (2014). (Eds.). *How to be a positive leader: Small actions, big impact*. Berrett-Koehler.

Dweck, C. (2006). *Mindset: The new psychology of success*. Random House.

Eblie Trudel, L. (2017). *Towards fully appropriate public education in Manitoba: A 75-year journey*. Manitoba Education Research Network.

EdCan Network. (2020, 30 August). *Amplifying what works in Canadian education*. https://www.edcan.ca/

Education Quality and Accountability Office. (2017). *Results at a glance: EQAO's provincial elementary school report, 2016–2017*. http://www.eqao.com/en/assessments/results/assessment-docs-elementary/provincial-report-elementary-results-glance2017.pdf

Enthoven, M., & de Bruijn E. (2010). Beyond locality: The creation of public practice-based knowledge through practitioner research in professional learning communities and communities of practice. A review of three books on practitioner research and professional communities. *Educational Action Research, 18*(2), 289–98. https://doi.org/10.1080/09650791003741822

Eriksson, M., Ghazinour, M., & Hammarström, A. (2018). Different uses of Bronfenbrenner's ecological theory in public mental health research: What is their value for guiding public mental health policy and practice? *Social Theory & Health, 16*(4), 414–33. https://doi.org/10.1057/s41285-018-0065-6

Ever Active Schools. (30 August 2020). *Supporting healthy communities*. https://everactive.org/

Falkenberg, T., (2015). *Opening address at the working conference: Understanding and assessing wellbeing and well-becoming in Manitoba schools.* Faculty of Education, University of Manitoba, 19 November 2015. http://thomasfalkenberg.ca/wp-content/uploads/2020/07/Essay4.pdf

Falkenberg, T., & Ukasoanya, G. (2019). *Student well-being and well-becoming: A Position Paper.* http://mass.mb.ca/wp-content/uploads/2019/11/Discussion-Paper-on-Student-Well-Being-and-Well-Becoming-May-2019.pdf

Ferguson, B., & Power, K. (2014). *Broader measures of success: Physical and mental health in schools.* People for Education. https://peopleforeducation.ca/wp-content/uploads/2017/06/MWM-health.pdf

Gergen, K. (2015). *An invitation to social construction* (3rd ed.). Sage.

Greenberg, M., Brown, J., & Abenavoli R. (2016) *Teacher stress and health.* http://www.rwjf.org/content/dam/farm/reports/issue_briefs/2016/rwjf430428

Griffin, P., McGaw, B., & Care, E. (Eds.), (2012). *Assessment and teaching of 21st century skills.* Springer.

Hargreaves, A., & Fullan, M. (2012). *Professional capital: Transforming teaching in every school.* Teachers College Press.

Hargreaves, A., Shirley, D., Wangia, S., Bacon, C., & D'Angelo, M. (2018). *Leading from the Middle: Spreading learning, well-being, and identity across Ontario.* Council of Ontario Directors of Education.

Hattie, J. (2009). *Visible learning: A synthesis of over 800 meta-analyses relating to achievement.* Routledge.

Huppert, F.A. (2014). The state of wellbeing science: Concepts, measures, interventions, and policies. In C.L. Cooper (Ed.), *Wellbeing: A complete reference guide.* Wiley.

– (2017). Challenges in defining and measuring wellbeing and their implications for policy. In M. White, G. Slemp, & A. Murray (Eds.), *Future directions in wellbeing* (pp. 163–7). Springer.

International Union of Health Promotion and Education – IUHPE. (2020, 30 August). https://www.iuhpe.org/index.php/en/

Janus, M., & Duku, E. (2007). The school entry gap: Socioeconomic, family, and health factors associated with children's school readiness to learn. *Early Education and Development, 18*(3), 375–403. https://doi.org/10.1080/10409280701610796a

Janus, M., & Offord, D. (2007). Psychometric properties of the early development instrument (EDI): A teacher-completed measure of children's readiness to learn at school entry. *Canadian Journal of Behavioural Science, 39*(1), 1–22. https://doi.org/10.1037/cjbs2007001

Katz, J. (2018). *Ensouling our schools: A universally designed framework for mental health, well-being, and reconciliation.* Portage & Main Press.

Kempf, A. (2018). *The challenges of measuring wellbeing in schools: A review prepared for the Ontario teachers' federation*. https://www.otffeo.on.ca/en/wp-content/uploads/sites/2/2018/02/The-challenges-of-measuring-wellbeing-in-schools-Winter-2017-web.pdf

Koenig, A., Rodger, S., Specht, J. (2017). Educator burnout and compassion fatigue: A pilot study. *Canadian Journal of School Psychology, 33*(4), 259–78. https://doi.org10.1177/0829573516685017.

The Learning Bar. (2020, 30 August). *Understanding all aspects of your students' well-being*. https://thelearningbar.com/ourschool-survey/?lang=aue

Lee, Y. (2009). Child rights, child well-being, and child poverty. In J.E. Doek, A. Shiva Kumar, D. Mugawe, & S. Tsegaye (Eds.), *Child poverty: African and international perspective* (pp. 17–26). Intersentia.

Mangin, M., & Stoelinga, S. (2008). Teacher leadership: What is it and why it matters. In M. Mangin & S. Stoelinga (Eds.), *Effective teacher leadership: Using research to inform and reform* (pp. 1–9). Teachers College Press.

Manion, I., Short, K., & Ferguson, B. (2013). A snapshot of school-based mental health and substance abuse in Canada: Where we are and where it leads us. *Canadian Journal of School Psychology, 28*(1), 119–35. https://doi.org/10.1177/0829573512468847

Manitoba. (2001). Philosophy of inclusion. Student Services. https://www.edu.gov.mb.ca/k12/specedu/aep/inclusion.html

– (2011). *Towards inclusion: Supporting positive behaviour in Manitoba classrooms*. https://www.edu.gov.mb.ca/k12/specedu/behaviour/behaviour_document.pdf

– (2013). *The Accessibility for Manitobans Act, CCSM c A1.7*. https://www.canlii.org/en/mb/laws/stat/ccsm-c-a1.7/latest/ccsm-c-a1.7.html

– (2017). *Safe and caring schools: A whole school approach to planning for safety and belonging*. https://www.edu.gov.mb.ca/k12/docs/support/whole_school/document.pdf

– (2020a, 30 August). *Education for sustainable development - ESD*. https://www.edu.gov.mb.ca/k12/esd/

– (2020b). *The Public Schools Act*. C.C.S.M. c. P250. https://web2.gov.mb.ca/laws/statutes/ccsm/p250e.php

– (2020c, 30 August). *Healthy schools*. https://www.gov.mb.ca/healthyschools/

– (2020d, 30 August). *Healthy together now*. https://healthytogethernow.net/

Manitoba Association of School Superintendents. (2019). *Student mental health and student well-being and well-becoming*. http://mass.mb.ca/wp-content/uploads/2019/10/Student-Mental-Health-and-Student-Well-Being-and-Well-Becoming-2019.pdf

Margolis, J. (2012). Hybrid teacher leaders and the new professional development ecology. *Professional Development in Education, 38*(2), 291–315. https://doi.org/10.1080/19415257.2012.657874

Marko, K. (2015). *Hearing the unheard voices: An in-depth look at teacher mental health and wellness* (Master's thesis, University of Western Ontario). http://ir.lib.uwo.ca/etd/2804

Marraccini, M., & Brier, Z. (2017). School connectedness and suicidal thoughts and behaviors: A systematic meta-analysis. *School Psychology Quarterly, 32*(1), 5–21. https://doi.org/10.1037/spq0000192

Marzano, R. (2003). *What works in schools: Translating research into action.* Association for Supervision and Curriculum Development.

Marzano, R., & Heflebower, T. (2012). *Teaching and assessing 21st century skills.* Marzano Research Laboratory

McConnell Foundation. (2020, 30 August). *Helping integrate social and emotional wellbeing into K-12 education.* https://www.wellahead.ca/

McGonigal, K. (2015). *The upside of stress: Why stress is good for you, and how to get good at it.* Penguin.

Mental Health Commission of Canada. (2016). *The mental health strategy for Canada: A youth perspective.* https://www.mentalhealthcommission.ca/sites/default/files/2016-07/Youth_Strategy_Eng_2016.pdf

Mincu, M. (2015). Teacher quality and school improvement: What is the role of research? *Oxford Review of Education 41*(2), 253–69. https://doi.org/10.1080/03054985.2015.1023013

Morrison, W., & Peterson, P. (2013). *Schools as a setting for positive mental health* (2nd ed.). Pan-Canadian Joint Consortium for School Health.

National Research Council. (2012). *Education for life and work: Developing transferable knowledge and skills in the 21st century.* National Academies Press. https://www.nap.edu/resource/13398/dbasse_070895.pdf

Nelson, J., & Campbell, C. (2017). Evidence-informed practice in education: Meanings and applications. *Educational Research, 59*(2), 127–35. https://doi.org/10.1080/00131881.2017.1314115

Ontario Ministry of Education. (2012). *Stepping stones: A resource for educators working with youth aged 12 to 25.* http://www.edu.gov.on.ca/eng/document/brochure/SteppingStonesPamphlet.pdf

– (2013). *Supporting minds: An educator's guide to promoting students' mental health and wellbeing (draft version).*

– (2014). *Achieving excellence: A renewed focus for education in Ontario.* https://www.oise.utoronto.ca/atkinson/UserFiles/File/Policy_Monitor/ON_01_04_14_-_renewedVision.pdf

– (2016a). *Ontario's wellbeing strategy for education: Discussion document.* http://www.edu.gov.on.ca/eng/about/wellbeingpdfs_nov2016e/wellbeing_engagement_e.pdf

– (2016b). *21st century competencies: Foundation document for discussion.* http://edugains.ca/resources21CL/About21stCentury/21CL_21stCenturyCompetencies.pdf

Ophea. (2020). *Healthy schools, healthy communities*. https://www.ophea.net/

Ott, M., Hibbert, K., Rodger, S., Leschied, A. (2017). A well place to be: The intersection of Canadian school-based mental health policy with student and teacher resiliency. *Canadian Journal of Education, 40*(2), 1–30.

Ottawa-Carleton District School Board. (2015). *Framework for mental well-being*.

Pan-Canadian Joint Consortium for School Health (2020, 30 August). *Making the grade: Comprehensive school health framework*. http://www.jcsh-cces.ca/

Quinn, R. (2015). *The positive organisation: Breaking free from conventional cultures, constraints, and beliefs*. Berrett-Koehler.

Ragozzino, K., & O'Brien, M.U. (2009). *Social and emotional learning and bullying prevention*. National Center for Mental Health Promotion and Youth Violence Prevention. https://casel.org/wp-content/uploads/2016/01/3_SEL_and_Bullying_Prevention_2009.pdf

Rasberry, C., Tiu, G., Kann, L., McManus, T., Michael, S., Merlo, C., & Ethier, K. (2017). Health-related behaviors and academic achievement among high school students – United States, 2015. *Morbidity and Mortality Weekly Report, 66*(35), 921–7. https://doi.org/10.15585/mmwr.mm6635a1

Rodger, S., Hibbert, K., Leschied, A., Pickel, L., Stepien, M., Atkins, M.-A., Koenig, A., Woods, J., & Vandermeer, M. (2014). *Mental health education in Canada: An analysis of teacher education and provincial/territorial curricula*. Physical and Health Education Canada.

Santoro, D. (2011). Good teaching in difficult times: Demoralization in the pursuit of good work. *American Journal of Education, 118*(1), 1–13. https://doi.org/10.1086/662010

Schonert-Reichl, K., Smith, V., Zaidman-Zai, A., & Hertzman, C. (2012). Promoting children's prosocial behaviours in school: Impact of the Roots of Empathy program on the social and emotional competence of school-aged children. *School Mental Health, 4*(1), 1–21. https://doi.org/10.1007/s12310-011-9064-7

Short, K., Finn, C. & Ferguson, B. (2017). *System leadership in school mental health in Canada*. https://www.cassa-acgcs.ca/cms/lib/ON01929128/Centricity/Domain/30/CASSA-Discussion-Paper-System-Ldrship-in-School-MH.pdf

Spratt, J. 2016. Childhood wellbeing: What role for education? *British Educational Research Journal, 42*(2), 223–39. https://doi.org/10.1002/berj.3211

Stiglitz, J., Sen, A., & Fitoussi, J. (2009). *Report by the commission on the measurement of economic performance and social progress*. https://ec.europa.eu/eurostat/documents/8131721/8131772/Stiglitz-Sen-Fitoussi-Commission-report.pdf

Tough, P. (2012). *How children succeed: Grit, curiosity, and the hidden power of character*. Houghton Mifflin Harcourt.

United Nations General Council. (1989). *Convention on the Rights of the Child*. https://www.ohchr.org/en/professionalinterest/pages/crc.aspx

Wei, Y., & Kutcher, S. (2014). Innovations in practice: "Go-to" educator training on the mental health competencies of educators in the secondary school setting: A program evaluation. *Child and Adolescent Mental Health, 19*(3), 219–22. https://doi.org/10.1111/camh.12056

Wenner, J., & Campbell, T. (2017). The theoretical and empirical basis of teacher leadership: *A review of the literature. Review of Educational Research*, 8, 134–71. https://doi.org/10.3102/0034654316653478

White, M.A., Slemp, G.R., & Murray, A.S. (Eds.). (2017). *Future directions in wellbeing: Education, organizations and policy*. Springer.

Wilkins, R. (2012). *Research engagement for school development*. Institute of Education, University of London.

World Health Organization, (2020, 30 August). *Promoting mental health: Concepts, emerging evidence, practice*. https://www.who.int/mental_health/evidence/en/promoting_mhh.pdf

9 Well-Being and Well-Becoming in Inner-City Schools: Supporting Students' Wholistic Flourishing in Inner-City Communities

JEANNIE KERR

Students' well-being and well-becoming should be fundamental priorities in all educational contexts concerned with educating students to participate within and contribute to inclusive, flourishing societies. However, there are many ways of thinking of and for well-being and flourishing, and consideration of the concepts involved are generatively engaged with attention to particular contexts, social conditions, and histories. In my own teaching experiences, I have observed that students living with social inequalities face events and issues on a daily basis that impact their flourishing. The intense media coverage of COVID-19 and racialized police violence over the last few years has highlighted long-standing social inequalities experienced by Indigenous and racialized communities. These ongoing lived realities as experienced in inner-city communities impede flourishing, thus framing conceptions of well-being in schools in this context in very complex ways. However, what has received less exposure in popular media, and also within educational systems, is the incredible strength and resurgence of diverse communities that create *home* within urban, low-income contexts. Therefore, the ways well-being and well-becoming might be understood and fostered in schools should be carefully considered in relation to place, community, and located histories, and with a greater appreciation of community partnership. My extensive background in inner-city public schools as a white teacher, and currently researcher and teacher educator focused on educational inequalities, deeply informs my perspective on how schools might respond and foster well-being and well-becoming in the complex context of inner-city schools. In this chapter, I will discuss how well-being and well-becoming, conceived as wholistic flourishing, might be understood and addressed in the particular context of schools in Winnipeg's inner-city communities, and will also consider the implications in the Canadian and North American context.

Words Matter ... as Well as Who Is Saying Those Words

There are some words in this chapter that have diverse meanings that are often inaccurately assumed to be universally agreed upon. I choose my words carefully so that others are clear about what I am contending. First, the term *inner-city* is used pervasively within research, data collection, and schooling contexts to denote a core spatial area of concentrated poverty within an urban geography. However, the term is also entangled in problematic deficit discourses that exceed this economic-geographic meaning. Khoo (2017) argues that inner-city is a term that has complex, shared socio-cultural meanings associated with conceptions of race. Some scholars have shifted to the terms *urban* and even *centre-city* to avoid this deficit framing, tendering a distinction which in my view merely functions in the same racializing way. I believe that changing the term inner-city to other geographic descriptors will not change the problematic deficit attitudes that have become unfairly associated with the culturally and linguistically enriched communities in inner-city locations, communities that defy economic and political marginalization. I therefore use the term inner-city to draw attention to the reproduction of racialized poverty in urban geographies. Second, I tend to avoid using the word racism, and instead use the words racialized or racialization. Racism implies that there is a biological *thing* called race and that non-white people experience negative and pervasive effects based on being that so-defined race. Instead, racialization refers to the systemic and personal practices of sorting and defining people who are not white into what are socially constructed categories of race. Race is a social construction and not a reality. However, the practice of racializing people and communities creates problematic realities that reinforce ongoing inequalities in Canada and beyond. The power to racialize *others* emerges from histories of white supremacy and dominance through colonial forms of governance that continue to structure society (Tuck & Habtom, 2019; Wynter, 2003).

Clearly identifying the social and geographic location of the person who is speaking within these discussions is exceedingly important. I wrote this piece from my former home in West Broadway, which is an inner-city community in Winnipeg, Manitoba, located on the traditional land of the Anishinaabeg, Nêhiyawak, Dakota, Oji-Cree, and Dene peoples, and on the homeland of the Métis Nation (Huck, 2003). I worked at the University of Winnipeg and lived in this community from 2016 until 2021. I recently have moved to Vancouver and now work at Simon Fraser University, but continue to specialize in social justice concerns in education, and focus my research on inner-city educational contexts. Prior to completing my PhD at the University of British Columbia, I worked in an elementary school for 12 years in the culturally and linguistically vibrant Downtown Eastside neighbourhood of Vancouver. This community is known as an inner-city community due to its geographic location in urban Vancouver, and its history of political and economic marginalization. I am a monolingual white woman, and thus very typical of inner-city teachers (Marom, 2019a). I have been decidedly privileged in society and in my role in inner-city schooling, a place where the structures and culture of white normativity still prevail (Janzen & Cranston, 2016; Marom, 2019b). My parents immigrated to Canada from Ireland and Scotland, and I was the first family member born in Canada. I identify as a settler in Canada, and work to understand my responsibilities on treatied and unceded lands in the places I live and work. I share this information to clarify the experiences from which I speak, and some of the ways I participate within power structures. I sincerely hope that I can contribute to moving educational conversations beyond acknowledging identity, and toward capturing the complex, disparate ways that people are – or are not – invited to participate and share opportunities within a society based on their identity, culture, ethnicity, racialization, and experiences.

A Wholistic Conception of Well-Being and Well-Becoming in Schools

This chapter explores the nature of student well-being and well-becoming within schools in inner-city communities. Yet we first need to acknowledge that well-being is not a singular thing that all people picture in the same way, or a static state of being with an arrival point. In this sense, well-being implies an engagement with a *well-becoming* that is always in-process and on-the-way. The differences within conceptions of well-being and well-becoming can be profound, and these differences have the propensity to perpetuate ongoing inequalities in inner-city contexts. Thus, I pay particular attention to those conceptions of well-being that can engage the complexities and needs in that context. In listening to educational leaders, policy-makers, and researchers discuss well-being, I often hear it referred to as being almost synonymous with a state of mental health, using terminology that draws on common mental health discourses. These mental health discourses reflect and naturalize a contemporary, Eurocentric framework that understands mental health within a medical model of illness and disease experienced by an individual, and disregards the overwhelming impact of social inequalities on an individual's wellness (Rountree & Smith, 2016). In my view, an illness model of well-being does not capture the wholistic sense of being well. While there are multiple conceptions of well-being that do not engage with an illness model, I am guided in wholistic priorities for well-being through Indigenous frameworks that emerge from a "relational worldview" (Rountree & Smith, 2016, pp. 207–8), as well as pre-modernist Western conceptions of well-being understood as flourishing in community (Aristotle, 1998). I see these frameworks as being fundamentally informed by ethics, relationships, and community, and thus highly generative to inner-city educational contexts, contexts that in North America are noted for enriched linguistic, cultural and social diversities, as well as pronounced social inequalities for Indigenous, Black, and people of colour.

A Relational Worldview – Indigenous Frameworks for Well-Being

With regard to Indigenous relational frameworks of well-being, I am particularly influenced by Dr. Jo-ann Archibald, Q'um Q'um Xiiem (Stó:lō and St'at'imc) and her related research that theorizes well-being as achieving balance in the concerns of the emotional, intellectual, spiritual, and physical realms of human development within the context of community and relations (Archibald, 2008; Pidgeon, Archibald & Hawkey, 2014). This wholistic sense of well-being acknowledges the interconnected dimensions of being human, as well as the conditions of a person's well-being as always being relational and connected to social contexts. Her collaborative work conceptualizes the well-being of an Indigenous individual in the Canadian context in terms of relationship to family, provincial/federal governance structures, and First Nations communities, but, importantly, she frames these layers of relations as needing to be informed by the ethics of respect, responsibility, relevance, and support to well-being (see visual in Pidgeon, Archibald & Hawkey, 2014, p. 7). I believe this vision of Indigenous well-being could be generative to understanding well-being for all people, with attention to the particular complexity of the communities in which we are immersed, and the epistemic disruption of an illness model. I also appreciate the opportunity as a settler to be guided by philosophical frameworks that emerge from the wisdom of Indigenous traditions on the land which I live, as well as the direct mentorship I have received from Dr. Archibald in helping me understand this wisdom in more nuanced ways.

A framework known as the Circle of Courage is prominent in the context of Manitoba education, and similarly captures this wholistic sense of well-being in relation. This framework also emerges from Indigenous cultural values and knowledges, and considers the fundamental role of connectedness, and the need for children to be immersed in social contexts and circles of relations that nurture their well-being (Brendtro et al., 2019). Drawing on Lakota and Dakota cultural knowledges, this model is based on the Medicine Wheel, where "the shape of a simple circle reflects the interrelationship of all creation" (Brendtro et al., 2019, p. 27), and balances the human needs for experiencing belonging, mastery, independence, and generosity in cultivating well-being. This social-ecological perspective rejects illness models that stress individualized approaches, and notes that children's behaviour problems are "usually a symptom of *dis-ease* in the ecology rather than *disease* in the child" (p. 33). Medicine Wheel teachings are layered and varied in relation to different Indigenous Nations, yet commonly symbolize balance and harmony (Archibald, 2008).

I choose to be guided by Indigenous frameworks not only because of the cultural wisdom that emerges from their philosophies and knowledge systems, but also because of the disruption they provide to Eurocentrism. The mainstream illness and disease model for well-being is part of a much larger Euro-Western cultural commitment to abstract rationality, a key part of the power structure of continued colonial domination (Quijano, 2007). Through individualizing and abstracting the contemporary and historical experience of social life and inequalities in our ways of understanding well-being, dominant paradigms of illness are positioned to uphold current inequalities (DeFehr, 2016). I believe that a conception of well-being that is positioned to challenge social inequalities requires an explicit connection to societal experiences. In my view, abstract notions of well-being and well-becoming leave gaps that serve to perpetuate societal inequalities, and thus are problematic in inner-city educational contexts.

Flourishing in Community – Aristotle's Conception of Well-Becoming

Considering well-being and well-becoming from Indigenous wholistic perspectives helps to shed light on the interconnected nature of being and thus our well-being, but also draws in the layers of relations and ethics of governance in which well-being becomes possible within our schools in societies. In my view, well-being is a felt sense of having an opportunity for flourishing in a wholistic way. To consider these priorities from a Western perspective that is not immersed in modern illness models, I draw on Aristotle's ethics, developed thousands of years ago, an ethics built around the meaning and pursuit of a good and worthwhile life. I have grown to appreciate that Aristotle's ethical philosophy is not based in abstract ideas for an isolated individual but is built within a framework community and friendship. I also have recognized the significance of drawing on ideas that predate the problematic modernist ways of thinking of life and society in individualized, codifiable (rubrics, checklists), and rationalistic terms, and instead prioritize notions of wisdom based in wholism (Kerr, 2018). I understand it might also seem odd that I draw on Aristotle's work, as his ethics were only addressed to a community of elite white males. That said, I approach Aristotle's work with a more inclusive and socially just sensibility, but appreciate how my own social location as a privileged white woman haunts any attempt to minimize elitism. I also appreciate that many scholars diverge in how they interpret Aristotle's work, and I will briefly share my interpretation in relation to flourishing in community – or *eudaimonia*.

In his ethics, Aristotle was not primarily concerned with establishing rules for correct behaviour, but with cultivating goodness that is directed to a flourishing life in community (Kerr, 2013). This sort of flourishing is a form of living with a concern and attention for embodying what is good: "For the way we learn the things we should do, knowing how to do them, is by doing them" (NE 1103a33–34). From Aristotle's perspective, the good is not something that is relative to human interest or desire, but is a way of being and doing that is good because it "embodies or actualizes what *merits* being valued because it is good" (Vokey, 2001, p. 258). While a conception of goodness that ultimately relies on embodied wholistic experience, rather than rational justifications, can seem too open to be defensible, Aristotle believed this is where the guidance of the wise Elder – the *phronimos* – is key to ethical social structures. Aristotle states regarding practical forms of wisdom based in the good, "We shall get at the truth by considering who are the persons we credit with it" (NE 1140a24). Aristotle believed children can naturally be disposed to the good, but that they should be raised with embodied experiences of what is *kalon* (noble and fine) to cultivate their natural senses toward the good (NE Book II). The good is connected to being and doing well in community and exceeds individualized ways of considering social life. Aristotle's development of *eudaimonia* recognizes the human soul as an intellectual and emotional force in a physical body (NE Book VI).

I feel that Aristotle's ethics and account of *eudaimonia* capture the complexity of flourishing in community through a wholistic conception of well-being that draws together the mind, body, emotions, and spirit (Kerr, 2013). Aristotle's philosophy resonates with the wholistic conceptions of well-being from Indigenous informed philosophies that I mentioned earlier, including that of wisdom embodied by the Elder as knowledge holder (Archibald, 2008). I draw on both Indigenous and ancient Western conceptions of well-being and well-becoming in my attempt to bring together different knowledge systems, ones that reflect human complexity, value ethics as fundamental, and position well-being as contextual to the possibility of ethically informed governance in a community context. In inner-city contexts, this ethical governance is compromised by settler-colonialism. Inner-city schools committed to fostering well-being need to acknowledge the history and politics that have compromised ethical governance and that continue to negatively impact the well-being of their students.

Well-Being in Communities Experiencing Injustices and Inequalities: Theorizing Winnipeg's Inequalities

Since 2016, I have spent considerable time trying to understand the context and everyday realities in the inner-city of Winnipeg and within the schools. There is extensive research that frames Winnipeg as a *divided prairie city*. Lorch (2015) notes the spatial polarization of people in Winnipeg according to income level, where most low-income people in Winnipeg live to the north and west of the downtown core. Studying this spatial polarization over time, he notes the long-term and continuing pattern of spatial segregation. The main terminal of the CN Railway also physically divides the city between north and south with train tracks that are traversed by a limited number bridges. Kaufman (2015) considers how these spatialized income inequalities intersect with ethnicity and racialization. He concludes that within the city's neighbourhoods, the inner city, with its post-industrial high-rise buildings, is populated by low-income residents and has high representations of Indigenous people and recent immigrants. In contrast, the affluent neighbourhoods of Winnipeg are segregated to the south and the outskirts, and are mostly composed of white, Euro-descendant peoples. Kaufman concludes that Winnipeg is an economically and racially segregated city.

Heather Dorries (2019) draws attention to the settler-colonial framing of Winnipeg's urban space and how it is grounded in an ideology of white supremacy. Dorries highlights the ways that the damage-centred narratives of Indigenous peoples and the North End communities deflect attention from the systemic nature of these inequalities. These racialized geographic-spatial inequalities in Winnipeg can be framed through the lens of coloniality/modernity and settler-colonial scholarship. Decolonial scholarship theorizes that fifteenth-century European colonial expansion created a Euro-centred world power structure that remains with us today (Mignolo, 2007; Quijano, 2007). This power structure works to hide and/or justify its colonial violence through establishing a vision of modern European forms of thinking and social life as the arrival point of human history and civilization. Grosfoguel (2008) argues that this colonial-modernity structure maintains the initial hierarchies of the Euro-Western colonizing forces – white, male, able-bodied, Christian, and so on – and explains current racializing practices and knowledge hierarchies. The particular form of coloniality that manifests in Canada, and particularly the prairies, is settler colonialism. Dorries (2019) argues that settler colonialism is a type of colonialism that is based on a logic of elimination. In this way, "the colonizing force does not leave but rather seeks to replace Indigenous society with settler colonial society" (Dorries, 2019, p. 27). She similarly notes the structural nature of this form of colonialism: operating as an organizing feature of social life, it is enabled by an institutionalized racial hierarchy based in white supremacy and violence.

Approaching Well-Being and Well-Becoming in Inner-City Winnipeg Schools

The enriched cultural and linguistic diversity in Winnipeg's inner-city communities, combined with negative social and educational impacts rooted in settler colonialism, provides a unique lens through which to regard well-being and well-becoming in inner-city schools. The experiences of children in schools reflects the inequalities of the society that is reproduced within the schools. Winnipeg School Division's (WSD) publicly reported disaggregated student demographic data, as well as academic outcome data, draws attention to the continued inequalities of educational outcomes for Indigenous and newcomer students (WSD, 2020). Engaging with decolonial and settler-colonial theories allows us to see that societal and educational disparities in the inner-city are the present-day manifestations of colonial inequalities. The WSD in its submission to Manitoba's Commission on K-12 Education (WSD, 2019c) notes that neighbourhood poverty in Winnipeg schools is correlated with lower educational attainment, and calls out the lack of funding and coordination of supports throughout the provincial systems for perpetuating the conditions of poverty. Decolonial and settler-colonial theories allow us to deepen our analysis of these economic-opportunity gaps. Settler colonialism theory explains the over-representation of Indigenous peoples living in poverty in Winnipeg, and decolonial theory explains the migration of newcomers and refugees being displaced due to war, climate effects, and nation-state violence within the modern-colonial system. Together these theories shed light on inner-city educational inequalities. The recognition of racialized poverty and inequitable educational experience allows us to consider more deeply what educational systems might be able to do in supporting the wholistic well-being of inner-city students. The following story, shared in Kerr and Ferguson (2021), provides a metaphor for dominant educational approaches to student well-being in inner-city education.

Up the River, Down the River

A man is walking down the river and sees a child that seems to be in peril splashing in the water. Without hesitation, the man jumps in the river and saves the child, but then sees another child in similar circumstances. The man jumps back in the river and saves the next child, but then notices more and more children. The man is unwavering but exhausted; he implores passers-by to help him save the children in this down the river location. More people help, and the cycle continues – more children struggling in peril, more people saving them, more people exhausted. One woman walks away. Another woman who is pulling a child out from the water yells to the woman who is leaving: "Where are you going? We have to save these children!" The woman responds, "I'm going up the river to find out who is throwing these children in the river."

This story was shared with me in conversation with Dr. Vanessa Andreotti in our work together years ago, and a similar version which she also shared in one of her publications (Andreotti, 2012). This version is how I remember the story. I have been thinking deeply about it while working on a recent research project exploring mentorship of teacher candidates fulfilling practicum requirements in inner-city schools (Kerr & Ferguson, 2021). This particular story draws my attention to the nature and dynamics of teaching in inner-city schools. The people that work in this context engage with children that are often living without basic food and housing security; many of these children have at times been removed from their families/communities and are struggling with attendance and connection to the school. There are also very high levels of mobility where students move in and out of schools, and the teachers and students are part of a regularly shifting classroom community. The environment can at times be emotionally draining and chaotic. In my experience, the trope of *saving* children is a common one, and is often framed as saving them from their community and families. While the emotional experience of working with children without basic securities should never be discounted, this framing makes invisible the "up the river" sources of these challenges, as well as the strengths of the local communities. Absent from this framing is the racialized nature of the situation in which predominantly white teachers and administrators, who derive benefit from settler society, are working to *save* children that have suffered egregiously from the effects of settler colonialism. Ignoring the "up the river" causes serves to reinforce a damage-centred narrative of the local community and children, where the community is seen to be the source of the problems – while ignoring white supremacy and settler-colonial structural violence. The cultural and linguistic vibrancy of inner-city communities are also ignored within damage-centred narratives of community experience, and within Eurocentric, monolingual Euro-Western school structures.

Engaging again with the earlier conception of wholistic flourishing, schools should be guided by a relational ontology that recognizes a wholistic view of the student in community. In this conception, student well-being first requires students be recognized as whole individuals with needs for developing intellectual, emotional, spiritual, and physical wellness in a balanced way and through their own ways of seeing the world. Eurocentric approaches and illness/disease models continue to recreate the structural inequalities that form the context. This approach also recognizes that students are already embedded in relationships and structures that give their lives meaning and continuity. Their well-being is connected to their membership in community, and their flourishing requires that they be nurtured through the relations that structure their lives. Given the many ways in which settler colonialism has manifested in schools, it is incumbent on educators especially to respond to ethical obligations for respect, responsibility, and relevance in supporting students as members of communities. As schools are institutions that are deeply entangled in societal structures, well-being in schools should be approached in a way that engages students wholistically as unique human-beings immersed and entangled in communities, society, history, and politics. Due to the complexity and diversity of experience among communities, students, schools, and sets of relations, there can be no checkbox list that addresses this level of multiplicity. What I offer here are some perspectives and approaches. Some of these would be applicable to any context but are especially important in educational contexts with racialized and societal inequalities.

Collaborative Connections to Local Communities and Parents

Deficit perspectives – widely held in various sectors of society, especially among those in positions of power – inappropriately frame inner-city parents and communities as ultimately being a source of problems for children, rather than being deeply invested in the well-being of children. Such deficit discourses frame inner-city communities as inherently dangerous and rely on narratives of cultural deficit and hopelessness (Hugill & Toews, 2014; Dorries, 2019). This kind of framing positions inner-city communities and people as being in need of saving and avoids an analysis of the systemic forces that are the source of the problems. These ways of thinking are deeply entrenched and disregard the "up the river" causes that impede well-being and becoming in inner-city communities and schools. To support the well-being of students it is necessary to challenge these deficit perspectives and to build partnerships with parents and communities as they work to negotiate and challenge the societal inequalities that impact their lives. Perez (2019) draws attention to the idea that *home* is not just a physical shelter, but is also "the social world, familiar landscape, and spiritual, emotional-existential space" where lives are filled with meaning (p. 141). Looking at inner-city communities as an emotional-existential home challenges the notions of deficit that only see an impoverished community with endless obstacles and limited capacities. Families and community members that make the inner-city *home* operate from strength and resilience to systemic racialized inequalities rooted in settler colonialism and can meaningfully inform educational efforts that support well-being and well-becoming in schools from a place of knowledge and meaning. Learning from and collaborating with parents and local community organizations, in ways that honour their time and knowledge, is of the utmost importance to effecting positive change.

Curriculum in Inner-City Schools

While there is mandated curriculum in the Manitoba context, school districts, schools, and teachers have a great deal of latitude in choosing classroom resources and curricular materials. It is important to determine what the school is actually teaching through the in/formal curriculum in terms of who community members are and the nature of their experiences. What is the story being told regarding Indigenous peoples in North America, and world events that result in migration? Are notions of poverty, classism, and racializati curriculum? The curriculum needs to be careft perspectives and meritocracy narratives, as wel that setter colonialism is made invisible throu ers," normalizing settler-colonial systems, and claims and histories. To support students' flourishing, the significant issues that frame students' lives need to be part of the curriculum. Students are better positioned to understand and challenge inequalities when they are engaged in a curriculum that helps them understand the sources of the inequalities that impact their lives, families, and communities.

To address this ongoing racialized educational disparity, schools need to engage and develop curriculum that supports meaning-making that moves beyond the limitations of Eurocentric frames of knowledge and that is relevant to the students and community. The Eurocentric nature of the curriculum is commonly portrayed as "neutral" and "culture-free" (Battiste, 2005; Kerr, 2014; Marker, 2006), rather than as culturally specific to Euro-descendant sensibilities and as a form of cognitive imperialism (Battiste, 2013). The curriculum in Manitoba schools follows dominant patterns across North America; that is, it is centred on a Euro-Western approach to knowledge that relies on rationality and abstraction. Knowledge systems that recognize embodied knowledge, and where the idea of the *good* is located within Elders and knowledge holders as sourced from the land, are often dismissed or presented as supplementary or for private consumption (Kerr 2014; Marker, 2006).

There is a robust body of research literature on the benefits of culturally responsive curriculum and pedagogy in addressing disparities of academic achievement in inner-city schools (Gay, 2014). This literature suggests that curriculum in inner-city schools should reflect the students' cultural backgrounds. I would argue that everyone requires culturally responsive curriculum, but the curriculum in North American systems of schooling is dominated by Euro-Western cultural knowledges, values, and perspectives. Making the claim that Indigenous and students of diverse ethnicities need culturally responsive curriculum suggests that Euro-descendant students are not already being culturally accommodated. Curriculum needs to also be interrogated for a more balanced representation of cultural views, perspectives, and peoples, and the knowledges that inform them. A wholistic approach that honours the intellectual, emotional, spiritual, and physical aspects of being human requires experiential learning that has students immersed in experience and place, and that is not abstracted. When looking at the curriculum of the school we can ask several questions: Who are positioned as the knowledge holders in the school's curriculum? Does this balance reflect the local, and also global, diversities of knowledges? What forms of knowledge are being put forward through the authorship of both curriculum documents as well as learning resources? In what ways are supposed culture-free knowledges circulated in the school? How are students being invited to experience their learning?

There is a long-standing curricular debate concerning the use of skill-based curriculum, and this debate takes on more complexity in the context of schools in low-income neighbourhoods. Martusewicz et al. (2015) assert that instructional methods connect to societal hierarchies. They note a dominant pattern in which children in higher social class neighbourhoods learn more exploratory-enriched ideas in schools that require critical and creative thinking, and those in lower social class neighbourhoods are more likely to be subjected to didactic methods and rote learning, with a focus on developing skills and following directions. These methods are a key part of the ways schools engage in systemic reproduction of class-based inequalities. Based on my experiences, I would argue that there needs to be a careful *balance* within an enriched curriculum, with a focus on the skills necessary to access that curriculum. Engaging a curriculum that ultimately does not give students the skills to access materials which will help them understand and address the inequalities that affect their lives, or the mathematical skills to access desired careers, will ultimately serve to reproduce the current marginalization of inner-city students. A realistic and engaged conversation with students, and with parents in the school community about their own desires for access and opportunity to post-secondary systems for their children, should inform the collective way forward. Conversely, a curriculum that is dominated by skill-based approaches and lacks meaning for students will result in disengagement. A curriculum that is led from the perspective of creating meaningful and rich learning opportunities, yet supported by the development of skills to engage multiple forms of knowledge with student and parent priorities in mind, is more likely to support wholistic well-being of students in inner-city schools. Again, a wholistic conception of students requires a balancing of their needs.

Pedagogy in Inner-City Schools

Curriculum and pedagogy are fundamentally entwined. Drawing on Young's forms of oppression, Kelly (2012) elaborates how K-12 teachers can understand and practically counter cultural imperialism, marginalization, systemic violence, exploitation, and powerlessness in the Canadian settler-colonial context through both curriculum and pedagogy. I would highlight that a curriculum engaged beyond Euro-Western commitments requires pedagogies that are responsive to the cultural knowledges informing that curriculum. In my experience in British Columbia, the emphasis on the First Peoples' Principles of Learning, as developed by BC First Nations Elders and knowledge holders, effectively engaged Indigenous resources in curriculum (Chrona, 2014). In the Winnipeg context, the Circle of Courage (as mentioned earlier) and the Seven Sacred Teachings (see, e.g., MFNERC, n.d.) are widely shared and reflect Indigenous pedagogical priorities. Curriculum scholar Dwayne Donald (2011) cautions that such teachings and pedagogies can become reified when cut-off from the wisdom and teachings that inform them. Therefore, careful attention should be made to keeping close connections between the teachings and the philosophies. The inner city is typically a highly multilingual context, yet teachers in inner-city schools are often monolingual English speakers. Stewart and Martin (2018) advocate for curriculum and pedagogy that is responsive to the social and linguistic experiences of newcomers and refugees, maintaining that students are more than the trauma they have experienced. Within dominant educational systems, speaking a language other than English is usually considered to be a deficit in need of fixing, rather than an asset to be cultivated in a globalizing world (Lam, 2019). Children coming to school with one or more languages should not have to replace their language(s) with English, but to include English in their linguistic repertoire. Language and culture are deeply tied. Colonialism not only disrupts and imposes upon non-Euro-Western knowledge systems, it also imposes English and displaces other languages (Zavala, 2016). Attention to reclaiming Indigenous languages, as well as enriching multilingual linguistic experience, is important in supporting the well-being of children and communities. Multimodal and trans-language curricular and pedagogical approaches that support the learning of language *and* content, while also encouraging the ongoing development of the child's home language(s), are crucial in supporting the wholistic well-being of students (Early & Marshall, 2008; Lam, 2019; Orellana & Garcia, 2014), and have proved to be successful in inner-city educational contexts (Early & Kendrick, 2017). Supporting home languages in schools also supports and deepens connections to parents and communities, and creates an avenue to expand culturally responsive curriculum that is locally relevant and that engages students wholistically.

Conclusion

Efforts to support well-being and well-becoming in schools need to be carefully considered in relation to place, community, and located histories, and with a greater appreciation of community partnership. The wholistic conception of well-being as flourishing in community that is advanced in this chapter for inner-city schools is meant to capture the complexity of inner-city students as complex individuals who require meaningful education that addresses and recognizes them as immersed community members with unique access to different knowledge systems. This relational framing of well-being also helps educators to recognize the ethically impoverished context that is created through settler colonialism and Eurocentricity in schools, and to recognize the ethical imperative to address the school context in aid of student flourishing. Schools not only support individual students but serve as key institutions that can contribute to societal well-being through their role in the wholistic flourishing of students. Educators from outside the local community need to realize that they are coming into a vibrant *home*, one where they can learn from an enriched, dynamic, and diverse inner-city community. I have suggested that any efforts toward promoting well-being and well-becoming in inner-city schools need to recognize the enriched context of the community, but must also understand that the inequalities that are experienced by children and community members are the result of systemic problems emerging from the structures of coloniality and settler colonialism. In particular, the deficit perspectives that are entrenched in society need to be dismantled. I offered ideas for ways that educators might connect with parents and community, and to support reforms in curriculum and pedagogy. Most of these recommendations would be valuable for any school – not only inner-city schools. However, I must emphasize that educators who do not work in inner-city schools should also be attentive to what is being argued in this chapter. A primary source of inequalities for inner-city communities emerges from the ways that economically privileged people have been taught to see and participate in society, and how they have been taught to normalize societal inequalities and dominance. I live in a settler-colonial society that is seldom recognized as such within systems of schooling. While there is no magic bullet to end social inequality, we can consider the ways in which we are perpetuating current inequitable structures. Thus, I would conclude that to support inner-city students' well-being and well-becoming is to disrupt the dominant narratives that students in other parts of the same city are exposed to, and that they be supported in learning to recognize that their privileges are indeed connected to inequalities experienced by others. In this time in history, marked by COVID, climate change, and political turmoil, it has never been clearer to me that we will all do well when we take care of each other and are focused more on the collective well-being than on clinging to what we have. As educators, we can all work toward addressing well-being and well-becoming with a broader view of how we are all connected.

REFERENCES

Andreotti, V. (2012). Education, knowledge and the righting of wrongs: Other Education. *Journal of Educational Alternatives, 1*(1), 19–31. https://doi.org/10.1007/978-94-6300-729-0_8

Archibald, J. (2008). *Indigenous storywork: Educating the heart, mind, body and spirit*. UBC Press.

Aristotle. (1998). *The Nicomachean ethics* (trans. D. Ross, Rev. J.L. Ackrill, & J.O. Urmson). Oxford University Press.

Battiste, M. (2005). You can't be the global doctor if you're the colonial disease. In P. Tripp & L. Muzzins (Eds.) *Teaching as activism: Equity meets environmentalism* (pp. 121–33). McGill-Queen's University Press.

– (2013). *Decolonizing education: Nourishing the learning spirit*. Purich Publishing Limited.

Brendtro, L., Brokenleg, M., & Van Bockern, S. (2019). *Reclaiming youth at risk: Future of promises* (3rd ed.). Solution Tree Press.

Chrona, J. (2014). *Background of First Peoples Principles of Learning and current contexts*. (Web log content). https://firstpeoplesprinciplesoflearning.wordpress.com/background-and-current-context/

DeFehr, J. (2016). Investing mental health first aid: The problem of psychocentrism. *Studies in Social Justice, 10*(1), 18–35. https://doi.org/10.26522/ssj.v10i1.1326

Donald, D. (2011). *On making love to death: Plains Cree and Blackfoot wisdom*. https://www.ideas-idees.ca/blog/making-love-death-plains-cree-and-blackfoot-wisdom

Dorries, H. (2019). "Welcome to Winnipeg": Making settler colonial urban space in"'Canada's most racist city." In H. Dorries, R. Henry, D. Hugill, T. McCreary, & J. Tomiak (Eds.) *Settler city limits: Indigenous resurgence and colonial violence in the urban prairie West* (pp. 25–43). University of Manitoba Press.

Early, M., & Kendrick, M. (2017). Multiliteracies reconsidered: A "pedagogy of multiliteracies" in the context of inquiry-based approaches. In R. Zaidi & J. Rowsell (Eds.) *Literacy lives in transcultural times* (pp. 43–57). Routledge.

Early, M., & Marshall, S. (2008). Adolescent ESL students' interpretation and appreciation of literary texts: A case study of multimodality. *Canadian Modern Language Review, 64*(3), 377–97. https://doi.org/10.3138/cmlr.64.3.377

Gay, G. (2014). *Culturally responsive teaching: Principles, practices and effects*. In H.R. Milner & K. Lamotey (Eds.) *Handbook of urban education* (pp. 353–72). Routledge.

Grosfoguel, R. (2007). The epistemic decolonial turn. *Cultural Studies, 21*(2-3), 211–23. https://doi.org/10.1080/09502380601162514

— (2008). Decolonizing political economy and post-colonial studies: Transmodernity, border thinking, and global community. *Eurozine*. http://www.eurozine.com/articles/2008-07-04-grosfoguel-en.pdf

Huck, B. (2003). *Crossroads of the continent: The forks of the Red and Assiniboine Rivers*. Heartland Associates.

Hugill, T., & Toews, O. (2014). Born again urbanism: New missionary incursions, Aboriginal resistance and barriers to rebuilding relationships in Winnipeg's North End. *Human Geography, 7*(1), 69–84. https://doi.org/10.1177/194277861400700112

Kaufman, A. (2015). Who lives where in 2011: Demographics of a divided city. In J. Distasio & A. Kaufman (Eds.) *The divided prairie city: Income inequality among Winnipeg's Neighbourhoods, 1970–2010* (pp. 26–36). Institute of Urban Studies, University of Winnipeg. http://winnspace.uwinnipeg.ca/handle/10680/822

Kelly, D. (2012). Teaching for social justice: Translating an anti-oppressive approach into practice. *Our Schools, Our Selves, 21*(2), 135–54.

Kerr, J. (2013). Pedagogical thoughts on knowing bodies: The teacher educator encounters the Elder and the Phronimos. (Doctoral dissertation, University of British Columbia). https://open.library.ubc.ca/cIRcle/collections/ubctheses/24/items/1.0165675

— (2014). Western epistemic dominance and colonial structures: Considerations for thought and practice in programs of teacher education. *Decolonization: Indigeneity, Education & Society, 3*(2), 83–104.

— (2018). Challenging technocratic logics in teacher education: Seeking guidance from Indigenous and Aristotelian traditions. *Research in Education, 100*(1), 83–96. https://doi.org/10.1177/0034523718762169

Kerr, J. & Ferguson, K.A. (2021). Engaging ethical relationality and Indigenous storywork principles in research methodology: Addressing settler-colonial divides in inner-city educational research. *Qualitative Inquiry, 27*(6), 706–15. https://doi.org/10.1177/1077800420971864

Khoo, J. (2017). Code words in political discourse. *Philosophical Topics, 45*(2), 33–64.

Lam, M. (2019). Effects of Canada's increasing linguistic and cultural diversity on educational policy. *Journal of Contemporary Issues in Education, 14*(2), 16–32. https://doi.org/10.20355/jcie29370

Lorch, B. (2015). Spatial polarization of income in a slow-growth city. In J. Distasio & A. Kaufman (Eds.) *The divided prairie city: Income inequality among Winnipeg's neighbourhoods, 1970–2010* (pp. 14–25). Institute of Urban Studies, University of Winnipeg. http://winnspace.uwinnipeg.ca/handle/10680/822

Manitoba First Nations Education Resource Centre. (n.d.). *Middle years health*. https://mfnerc.org/middle-years-health/

Marker, M. (2006). After the Makah whale hunt: Indigenous knowledge and limits to multicultural discourse. *Urban Education, 41*(5), 482–505. https://doi.org/10.1177/0042085906291923

Marom, L. (2019a). Under the cloak of professionalism: Covert racism in teacher education. *Race Ethnicity and Education, 22*(3), 319–37. https://doi.org/10.1080/13613324.2018.1468748

– (2019b). Whiteness and teacher education. In M.A. Peters (Ed.), *Encyclopedia of teacher education*. Springer. https://doi.org/10.1007/978-981-13-1179-6_199-1

Martusewicz, R., Edmundson, J., & Lupinacci, J. (2015). *Ecojustice education: Toward diverse democratic, and sustainable communities* (2nd ed.). Routledge.

Mignolo, W. (2007). Coloniality of power and decolonial thinking. *Cultural Studies, 21*(2–3), 155–67. https://doi.org/10.1080/09502380601162498

Noguera, P.A. (2017). Introduction to "Racial inequality and education: Patterns and prospects for the future." *Educational Forum, 81*(2), 129–35. https://doi.org/10.1080/00131725.2017.1280753

Orellana, M.F., & García, O. (2014). Language brokering and translanguaging in school. *Language Arts, 91*(5), 386–92.

Perez, L.E. (2019). Where the heart is and where it hurts: Conceptions of home for people fleeing conflict. *Refugee Survey Quarterly, 38*, 139–58. https://doi.org/10.1093/rsq/hdz001

Pidgeon, M., Archibald, J., & Hawkey, C. (2014). Relationships matter: Supporting Aboriginal graduate students in British Columbia, Canada. *Canadian Journal of Higher Education, 44*(1), 1–21. https://doi.org/10.47678/cjhe.v44i1.2311

Quijano, A. (2007). Coloniality and modernity/rationality. *Cultural Studies, 21*(2–3), 168–78. https://doi.org/10.1080/09502380601164353

Rountree, J., & Smith, A. (2016). Strength-based well-being indicators for Indigenous children and families: A literature review of Indigenous communities' identified well-being indicators. *American Indian and Alaska Native Mental Health Research, 23*(3), 206–20. https://doi.org/10.5820/aian.2303.2016.206

Starblanket, T. (2018). *Treaties: Negotiations and rights*. http://ourlegacy.library.usask.ca/sites/ourlegacy.library.usask.ca/files/Starblanket_updated2018.pdf

Stewart, J., & Martin, L. (2018). *Bridging two worlds: Supporting newcomer and refugee youth*. CERIC Foundation House.

Tuck, E., & Habtom, S. (2019). Unforgetting place in urban education through creative participatory visual methods. *Educational Theory, 69*(2), 241–56. https://doi.org/10.1111/edth.12366

Vokey, D. (2001). *Moral discourse in a pluralistic world*. University of Notre Dame Press.

Winnipeg School Division. (2019a). *School demographics report 2018/2019*. https://www.winnipegsd.ca/About%20WSD/deptservices/research

-planning-technology-services/researchevaluation/SiteAssets/Pages
/Demographic-Reports/Student%20Demog%20Rpt%2018_19.pdf
– (2019b). *Continuous improvement report 2018/2019 and plan 2019–2020*.
https://www.winnipegsd.ca/About%20WSD/K-12%20Framework
%20for%20Continuous%20Improvement/Documents/WSD
%20Continuous%20Improvement%20Report%202018-2019%20and%20Plan
%202019-2020.pdf
– (2019c). *Submission to Manitoba's Commission on Kindergarten to Grade 12 Education*. https://www.winnipegsd.ca/About%20WSD/WSD
%20Submission%20to%20Manitobas%20Commission%20on%20Kindergarten
%20to%20Grade%2012%20Education/Pages/Default.aspx
– (2021). *Continuous improvement report 2020/2021*. https://sbwsdstor.blob.core
.windows.net/media/Default/medialib/wsd-framework-for-continuous
-improvement-report-2021-2022.55b81625830.pdf
Wynter, S. (2003). Unsettling the coloniality of being/power/truth/freedom: Towards the human, after man, its overrepresentation – an argument. *New Centennial Review*, 3(3), 257–337. https://doi.org/10.1353/ncr.2004.0015
Zavala, M. (2016). Decolonial methodologies in education. In M. Peters (Ed.) *Encyclopedia of educational philosophy and theory* (pp. 361–6). Springer.

10 Developmental Evaluation as a Tool for Promoting Well-Being in Schools: A Case Study

CAMERON HAUSEMAN, THOMAS FALKENBERG,
JENNIFER WATT, AND HEATHER KREPSKI

In recent years school divisions and ministries of education across Canada have been investing more time and resources into initiatives aimed at improving the well-being of staff and students (e.g., Alberta Teachers' Association [ATA], 2019; Bassett-Gunter et al., 2015). These efforts are informed by the compelling links between student well-being and positive academic and non-academic outcomes (Putwain et al., 2015, 2020), as well as the high rates of stress, burnout, and emotional exhaustion that teachers and administrators are reporting (Berkovich & Eyal, 2015, Hauseman, 2021; Kokkinos, 2007; Ryan & Tuters, 2015). For example, researchers have cited well-being as a key characteristic associated with positive levels of student engagement (Herbert, 2017; Nelson et al., 2020), as well as a prerequisite for maximizing students' academic and non-academic outcomes (Gray et al., 2017; Miller et al., 2013).

In this chapter, we use data collected from a partnership project between our university research team and a Manitoba school division's student success team to illustrate why developmental evaluation can be an effective approach for refining and upscaling programs that are intended to promote well-being in schools. This research is unique as it focused solely on the perceptions of evaluation users about the evaluation process, rather than on those of the evaluators. The findings of this study both reinforce prior observations about the utility of developmental evaluation and offer new insights about the benefits and challenges of using the approach to upscale and refine programs in K-12 education contexts. Prior to the genesis of the partnership project, the school division had engaged in a number of unconnected individual well-being initiatives that, although effective in individual schools, failed to gain traction across the division. Further, the impact of the individual well-being initiatives at the successful schools diminished over time due to personnel changes at the school level as administrators, teachers, and other staff members moved to different schools over time.

Our university-based team, composed of the four authors, began working with the school division partner in November of 2018 to support the division's intention of upscaling its well-being initiatives throughout the whole division. Over the 2018–19 academic year, the school division asked teachers to provide information about the specific strategies they were using to promote and support student well-being in each of their classes. Partnering with our university team seemed like a practical way for the school division to move forward, as the division lacked the means to analyse the amount of qualitative data generated from these efforts.

Using data generated from interviews with school division–level staff, this chapter describes participants' experiences with the developmental evaluation process engaged in at the school division by answering the following overarching research question: What are the benefits and challenges associated with the developmental evaluation supports provided in an effort to assist the school district's leadership team with expansion work?

Well-Being

While student well-being has become a more prominent focus in Canadian school education, few school organizations actually use a definition of well-being to both guide their activities and/or evaluate the effectiveness of these activities (Alberta Teachers' Association [ATA], 2019). At the same time, definitions of well-being vary widely (see, for instance, Falkenberg, 2014). The contested nature of well-being can present challenges for evaluating programs and initiatives aimed at promoting well-being in schools and other settings. Navigating competing definitions of any construct can put content validity at risk by making it difficult for researchers and evaluators to develop holistic and comprehensive measures. Attempts to evaluate well-being initiatives may lack content validity if the definitions that evaluators are working from are too narrow to represent the range of meanings implied in some conceptions of well-being. Further, when researchers are engaged in traditional evaluation approaches, it is vital that the program model is stable and its various concepts and assumptions are well-defined and presumably measurable or observable, or else the evaluation will fail (Patton, 1994, 1999, 2010, 2016). Without a stable model and clear definitions of the social problems that a program is attempting to improve, summative evaluation cannot accurately determine the overall value of a program, and formative evaluation will fail to lead to strategies that can improve programming (Patton, 1994, 1999, 2010, 2016). Since these traditional approaches to evaluation are not well-suited to evaluate innovative programs that respond to social programs in complex and ambiguous environments, developmental evaluation has emerged as an approach that has specifically been designed for an environment that is characterized by uncertainty and ambiguity. The flexible nature of developmental evaluation makes it ideal for evaluating programs aimed at improving well-being and other social conditions that are subjective and difficult to define. The next section elaborates on this approach to program evaluation.

Developmental Evaluation

Over the past two decades, developmental evaluation has emerged as a strategy for supporting innovative programs in achieving positive outcomes by adapting and responding to changing conditions in the complex environments or systems in which they operate. Schools, school systems, and school districts stand to benefit from developmental evaluation as they are subject to societal shifts and operate within complex policy and micropolitical systems (Anderson et al., 2016; Peurach et al., 2016; Poth et al., 2012). For example, widespread awareness of the importance of well-being has altered the purposes and goals of public schooling in many jurisdictions (e.g., Ontario Ministry of Education, 2014). Further, school systems have long been recognized as complex systems influenced by many factors, ranging from federal and provincial laws and policies to individual goals and desires (Cooke & Rousseau, 1981; Mital et al., 2014).

Before moving forward, it is important to mention that developmental evaluation is complementary to, and is not intended to replace, summative or formative and other approaches to evaluating social programs and policy. Summative evaluations are designed to determine overall value, and formative evaluations are aimed at honing, fine-tuning, and stabilizing a program model. Development evaluation, on the other hand, "supports innovation development to guide adaptation to emergent and dynamic realities in complex environments" (Patton, 2010, p. 1). These complex environments (Patton 2010, 2016) are characterized by high levels of conflict and uncertainty about how to solve key social problems. Complex issues that unfold in turbulent environments can make it difficult for innovative program developers and other primary intended users to illustrate the relationships between inputs, outputs, and short-, medium-, and long-term outcomes. The "turbulence" surrounding complex issues renders logic models and several other traditional program evaluation tools inadequate for use in evaluating innovative programs. Uncertainty and complexity can also lead to difficulty determining attribution and suggest a need for program developers to be innovative, adaptive, and responsive to societal shifts as well as changes in the political and policy climates (Gamble, 2008; McDonald, 2016; Patton, 1994, 1999, 2010, 2016). In addition to being responsive to programmatic contexts and championing innovative solutions, a key practice associated with developmental evaluation is generating data in real time to facilitate rapid feedback and a focus on program development (Fagen et al., 2011; Lawrence et al., 2018; McDonald, 2016; Patton, 1994, 1999, 2010, 2016). Patton (2010) began his seminal text, *Developmental Evaluation*, by highlighting how developmental evaluations have a distinct purpose, similar to how formative and summative evaluations are conducted with certain goals and information needs in mind. Patton (2010) proposes the following five purposes as appropriate for developmental evaluation:

1. Supporting ongoing program development through adaptation or innovation by being responsive to changing conditions in the complex environment in which the program operates.
2. Adapting effective principles to a local context.
3. Responding rapidly to a sudden change or crisis by implementing meaningful solutions to help those most in need.
4. Upscaling innovative programming or innovations.
5. Obtaining feedback about the effectiveness of major systems change initiatives and how innovations can be adapted to broaden impact. (Patton, 2010, pp. 21–2)

Given that the purposes and uses of developmental evaluation differ from more traditional evaluation approaches, evaluators are required to engage in different practices than when they conduct summative and formative evaluations. For example, Patton (1994, 1999, 2010, 2016) noted that the role of the evaluator in developmental evaluation is to spur dialogue and discussion and facilitate data-informed decision-making. Similarly, other scholars have noted that developmental evaluations compel evaluators to become integrated into the program development team by stimulating discussion, promoting evidence-informed approaches, and bringing their expertise in interpreting data to the table (Lam & Shulha, 2015; Peurach et al., 2016; Poth et al., 2012).

Although developmental evaluation fills a specific niche for innovative program developers, scholars and practitioners have noted several challenges to this approach. Time management and the subsequent blurring of boundaries surrounding the evaluators' role are key challenges highlighted in the literature (Gamble, 2008; Lawrence et al., 2018; Poth et al., 2012). In this case, a heavy time investment from the evaluators can prove very beneficial to program development, but the collaborative nature of developmental evaluation can allow users to become over-reliant on the evaluators and their expertise (Poth et al., 2012). Another challenge involves evaluation users' familiarity with more traditional approaches to evaluation: high levels of familiarity can lead users to question the impartiality of the evaluators and the rigour associated with developmental evaluation activities (Gamble, 2008; Patton, 2010; Poth et al., 2012). Developmental evaluation has also been criticized for focusing too much on program development and building evaluative capacity within organizations at the expense of collecting meaningful data about results and effectiveness (Gamble, 2008).

Context

This research was conducted in Winnipeg, Manitoba, Canada. Our partnership with the school district began in November 2018 and is still ongoing. As set out in the Canadian Constitution, public education in Canada is a provincial responsibility, though the federal government has an obligation to fund and maintain schools on federal First Nations reserves and military bases (Council of Ministers of Education, Canada, 2019; Pollock & Hauseman, 2015). This means that there is no national-level education strategy, and the provinces are responsible for developing the goals and purposes of public schooling in their jurisdictions. In Manitoba, well-being has been identified as a priority area of focus for public schooling (Manitoba Education, 2020). The provincial government's decision to make well-being for staff, students, and other stakeholders a goal of schooling seems to be informed by the recent pan-Canadian and international awareness around well-being and its importance to school success (Bryson et al., 2019; Gray et al., 2017; Miller et al., 2013). For example, other provinces have also made promoting well-being a goal of their publicly funded school systems (Ontario Ministry of Education, 2014).

The strong connections between well-being, student achievement, and other desirable outcomes (Bryson et al., 2019; Gray et al., 2017; Miller et al., 2013), combined with localized concerns about increased rates of student anxiety and mental health concerns, provided educational leaders with the impetus to focus on well-being within their respective school divisions. For example, the school divisional partner that participated in this project began to use data gathered from student surveys, such as the "OurSCHOOL" survey, to develop an understanding of the school-based factors that influence student well-being. Also, in the school division several unconnected initiatives to promote the well-being of staff, students, and other stakeholders were implemented but failed to gain a foothold in all of the schools in the division. When we entered the partnership, the division settled on a three-tiered approach to promoting student well-being. The first tier involved (a) using the curriculum as an opportunity to discuss strategies students can use to promote their own well-being, (b) designing student-friendly physical spaces at the school, (c) creating extracurricular activities and clubs, and (d) developing relationships within the school community to promote well-being for all students. The second tier involved divisional student services and learning support personnel providing classroom teachers with strategies to support their students' well-being when requested by the teacher. Finally, the third tier involved providing intensive and individualized interventions for students with particular well-being needs. These third-tier supports were individualized to meet the specific needs of each student and often involved intensive collaboration between students, parents, teachers, clinicians, school administrators, and community supports. We initially worked to assist division leaders to analyse data gathered around the different types of approaches, supports, and interventions provided across the three tiers in all classrooms throughout the division.

Methods

Several developmental evaluation activities took place since the partnership began in November 2018. Developmental evaluation activities included an analysis of qualitative well-being data the district collected at the school and classroom levels during the previous academic year and conducting focus groups with school leaders involved in previous well-being initiatives. We also guided district staff through a descriptive inquiry process that allowed them to clarify the goals of the expansion project and its intended outcomes, as well as outline challenges and supports that could influence well-being throughout the district.

Before moving forward, it is important to mention that our data collection and analysis methods were constrained by research ethical concerns. These concerns relate to the delineation between the research methods used to gather data to inform the developmental evaluation supports provided, and the actual developmental evaluation activities that we engaged in throughout this expansion process. This means that we have to rely solely on the interviews with division staff to describe the developmental evaluation activities, rather than on our own recollections. This, however, had the advantage of helping us provide an accurate reflection of participants' experiences of using developmental evaluation to develop and refine school-based well-being initiatives.

The Interviews

We conducted a total of four interviews with four school district staff who were members of the partnership. The interviews focused on three key areas related to each participant's work with the partnership as well as their experiences with upscaling the well-being initiatives within their school division. For the first focus area, participants were asked to describe the educational context in both their school division and the province of Manitoba more broadly. For the second focus area, participants were asked to share their experiences with the development evaluation support provided throughout the upscaling partnership work. Finally, for the third focus area, participants were asked about their roles and responsibilities in the upscaling process and the school division more generally. For the purpose of this chapter, we report on findings based on participants' responses in the second focus area.

Each staff member who participated in the interviews indicated that they were involved in the development and/or implementation of the well-being initiatives that the developmental evaluation sought to refine and upscale throughout the rest of the division. There was some variation in the roles and responsibilities of the interview participants, as well as their demographic characteristics. For example, one of the interview participants occupied a leadership role within the district and the three remaining interviewees reported directly to that individual. Further, the individual who occupied a leadership role identifies as male, while the three staff that report to him identify as female.

Data Analysis

We conducted qualitative analysis in two distinct yet complementary stages. The first stage involved reading the interview transcripts and engaging in a process called *open coding*. Developing a familiarity with the dataset and crafting initial categories are key aspects of the open coding process (Robson & McCartan, 2016). The second stage of data analysis involved taking these initial categories and interpreting the data in an effort to draw conclusions about the developmental evaluation process – often referred to as *analytical coding* (Robson & McCartan, 2016). Engaging in the analytical coding process was important, as it provided us with a framework for formulating overarching themes and subthemes from the initial categories developed during the earlier open coding process.

Findings

When asked to comment on their involvement with the developmental evaluation processes, activities, and supports, all participants indicated that their experience had generally been positive and resulted in a meaningful contribution to program development. Participants in this study identified several benefits and some challenges associated with collaborating with our university evaluation team and the use of developmental evaluation to support the upscaling of well-being initiatives in their school division. The benefits and challenges that participants associated with engaging in developmental evaluation are described below.

Benefits

Participants described several ways in which they saw the support process working. These benefits involved the use and analysis of data to identify gaps in service delivery and program implementation, and a recognition of the importance of developing and refining programs to maximize impact and outcomes rather than moving on to something new. An additional benefit discussed in the interviews was that the evaluation team brought an impartial and external perspective to the developmental evaluation work and guided the process. Each of these benefits are discussed below.

DATA USE AND INTERPRETATION

All four participants discussed how the data collection and analysis features of the developmental evaluation process have been especially beneficial aspects of the partnership. For example, one of the staff members described the benefits associated with having members of the university team analyse and summarize programmatic data that had been collected throughout the school year:

> I've never been involved with it before but what I see in terms of the support you guys have provided is taking the data, whatever that is, so stuff that we've provided to you, what the school teams provided, the profiles.

> Taking that data and being able to summarize it in a really usable format that's clear and makes sense and I think that's been really valuable for our team.

Gaining assistance in the analysis and interpretation of programmatic data has allowed participants to better identify gaps in program implementation. Another interviewee described how the data analysis is used to guide discussions and support evidence-based decision-making about the upscaling process and facilitate further program development:

> I mean you've done tons. You've done some data analysis already. Thank you for the work you did there. In just crunching some data you've helped frame the consultations ... and you collate all the data. Well, the collating of data ... looking at some stuff, it's great. It's just great to have that support.

This participant shared that the support around interpreting and using data has been especially valuable.

STICKING WITH THE PROGRAM

It became clear during the interviews that several different initiatives aimed at promoting the well-being of staff and students within the school division had already taken place. Though well intentioned, some of those initiatives, and the various activities associated with them, failed to gain a foothold across the division. Changes in priorities led to new initiatives and areas of focus. Conversely, participants described how the entirety of the developmental evaluation process helped them recognize the importance of staying with the general focus of the divisional concern for well-being in schools. For example, one of the staff members explained that the developmental evaluation provided a means for keeping them on track:

> I have to say, [another team member] likes to go ... all of a sudden there's a new idea? You saw that with [them] wanting to do another school with well-becoming ... wait a minute, we haven't even gotten to where we needed to be with this one! We've just done it for a year and now we have a new admin and there's all these opportunities with that information that could still further inform what we're doing, or even whether it's around something concrete like how to implement zones or whether it's about doing research and implementing a project and walking through the steps; we're learning and we're not there yet. There's so much more to add to it and so I was going to dig my heels in really hard on that one.

According to this participant, a key benefit of engaging in the developmental evaluation process involved commitment to an ongoing effort to refine and develop programming, rather than simply moving on to different opportunities when they arise. Committing to this process also gave staff members a voice and the opportunity to advocate for staying the course. According to another staff member, the fact that they were engaging in the developmental evaluation process provided them with arguments that can be presented to division leadership:

> Sometimes the six of us have a somewhat different perspective than [leadership] has and that's good. Because [they] see things differently than we do, from a different level and that's [their] way of processing. But I think sometimes we will end up going in a different direction before we're ready to and, again, I think that's if we use the last meeting – sort of saying, "Well, we need to follow this through," just helped a little bit to stay on and let's see this whole cycle through a whole round instead of hopping to something new. And I think we do that too much in education.

In this case, a key benefit of developmental evaluation has been the team's ability to stick with the program and buffer the division from engaging in new initiatives related to well-being prior to seeing the end result of the current upscaling process. Avoiding the distractions that can come with shifting goals and competing priorities may not have been possible without the addition of impartial and external perspectives.

IMPARTIAL AND EXTERNAL PERSPECTIVE

Several participants cited collaborating with researchers who are external to the school division as another benefit. Division staff indicated that, because our university team was not immersed in the day-to-day operations of the school division, we could provide an impartial perspective on the upscaling process. For example, one staff member discussed how it can be difficult to make objective decisions about program refinement and development when a person has an emotional connection to a given initiative:

> Because when you're immersed in it, there's always an emotional connection. If you are part of an initiative, it will be always harder to let go of something or you may not necessarily see another perspective. And I think those schools that were present – knowing that the university helped guide that – I think that was also important for them, that they could answer those questions without feeling that it was the division collecting that and then interpreting it the way they want. There's an impartiality to having a partnership.

This participant appreciated that engaging in the developmental evaluation process exposed them to outside perspectives, which increased the credibility of the upscaling initiatives among school staff and others at the division. Another staff member echoed this idea, stating that "having a partnership with the university to come in, who is impartial, is always a good thing. I think that is a really important connection." Based on these findings, our university team was able to provide an outside eye throughout the upscaling of the school division's efforts to promote well-being.

GUIDING THE PROCESS

The partnership also allowed school division staff to take a step back and allow the university team to guide the developmental evaluation process. This was the first time several of the participants had engaged in developmental evaluation activities and processes. Participants appreciated having "critical friends" embark on this journey with them. One of the staff members indicated that having our team guide the process was one of the most beneficial aspects of engaging in the process:

> For me, developmental evaluation, the power of that, is having experts in what they do journey alongside, forcing you to articulate things and then helping you to realize the things that you need to dig deeper in, or you can't explain, or can't answer the question. When you guys ask me a question, then all of a sudden everything is lighting up and you're going, "Yeah, that's a good question!" I'm going to think about that. Which is even doing this, even going through this process. So developmental evaluation to me strictly adds developmental. You're getting someone to help you develop your thinking on a project.

This participant felt that having our university team lead the developmental evaluation process helped spur program development in ways that would not have been possible if the division had embarked on these efforts alone. Similarly, another staff member described how the collaborative nature of the developmental evaluation process was especially beneficial:

> I think that there are lots of conversations back and forth – it's not just us talking and you guys listening and then pulling it and then saying, "Well, okay, so you told us this is what we're doing," but you bring that back and then we talk about, "Well, what does that mean and where are we going to go next?" And everyone around the table is comfortable talking about it.

This staff member found that having our team guide the developmental evaluation fostered a high level of collaboration, which increased their level of comfort in sharing insights as well as with the process more broadly. Participants also felt that having our university team guide the developmental evaluation process increased the credibility of the activities in which the school division staff engaged. For example, one of the participants mentioned that a key developmental evaluation activity involved having a large information-gathering session with principals and vice-principals who were involved in the school division's previous well-being initiatives. They indicated that senior leadership likely acquiesced and provided the principals and vice-principals with release time to participate in the developmental evaluation activities because the partnership with a university team added a sense of importance to the activity:

> Pulling people out of schools is a very delicate topic in the division right now. So, if [I] had just wanted to pull them out to do this work, it may have been more challenging than to say, "Oh, I'm engaged in research with the [university team]. We have agreed to this and [the superintendent] signed off on it and now it's going to occur because the CEO wants it to occur. And, so, you need to do this." Does that make sense?

According to this participant, having our university evaluation team involved added credibility and urgency to the request to have principals and vice-principals participate in the information-gathering session.

Challenges

Although all of the participants described feeling that the developmental evaluation process was a positive experience, during the interview they discussed three key challenges to the engagement with the developmental evaluation process. The first is that some team members had difficulty maintaining a focus on refining, developing, and upscaling the well-being initiatives and committing to these efforts, and would prefer to move on to new initiatives. The other challenges included a lack of time to engage in developmental evaluation activities during the school year and a sense of uncertainty regarding the next steps in the developmental evaluation process.

DIFFICULTY STAYING THE COURSE

Although participants indicated that the emphasis on sticking with the program was a key benefit, some felt it would be a challenge for their team to commit to staying the course. For example, one staff member discussed how the school division members of the partnership have a tendency to move on from projects and initiatives too quickly:

> I think [leadership] saw the opportunity for other schools to get involved without seeing the details of the project being seen to the finish. So, I think what you guys bring is helping us to stay the course – to see it through to the end of something. And I think that will be important to us. Because it will be easy just to quickly say, "Oh well, we've got what we need, we're fine. We'll go this direction."

This participant felt that it would be a challenge for their team to stay committed to developing and improving the well-being initiatives that were already underway, rather than moving to new opportunities.

LACK OF TIME

Participants also cited a lack of time to participate in meetings and other activities during the school year as another challenge they had to overcome during the developmental evaluation process. It appeared that participants were so busy balancing competing priorities and managing day-to-day concerns that they had little time left to think about making decisions about refining or changing aspects of programs. For example, one participant indicated that the pace of the school year offers little time for rumination, and that they have to "fight" for mental bandwidth and headspace:

> I'll probably come back in the fall with new thoughts. Because there's space for thinking over the summer. It will be an interesting thing because during a school year, there is little space for thinking. You fight for that space and in the summer, in the shower, there are a lot of spaces. Even on vacation the things that rumble around back there in your unconscious, so sure, when I come back in the fall, I'll already have some things that I think we need to do next. It goes quickly. It surprises me how quickly it goes.

This staff member highlighted that it can feel like the school year goes by quickly, leaving little time and space to ponder programmatic decisions. A lack of time to make decisions can also create uncertainty around the next steps for various programs.

UNCERTAINTY SURROUNDING NEXT STEPS

The final challenge the participants identified involved uncertainty surrounding the next steps – specifically, how the developmental evaluation activities and the data generated by those activities will be used to further inform project development. One participant stated:

> I think looking at the information and knowing what to do with it, how to categorize it [is a challenge]. I don't think we've come to the evaluation part yet very well. We're still doing some gathering phases, so evaluation is probably the next piece. But I would think that how we evaluate it would also be ... like what do we want to get out of it? And that will determine how we evaluate it, too – or where we want to go with it will determine how we evaluate it. Because you can gather data, but what you do with it is a bit of a challenge.

As developmental evaluation was a new approach for many in the school division, the ambiguity associated with the approach and the process was challenging for some participants.

Discussion

Including Patton's seminal books and articles (e.g., Patton, 1994, 1999, 2010, 2016), much of the literature surrounding developmental evaluation focuses on the experiences of the evaluators (e.g., Lam & Shulha, 2015; Peurach et al., 2016; Poth et al., 2012). By highlighting the perceptions and experiences of developmental evaluation users, this research is unique and helps fill a glaring gap in the literature on developmental evaluation as a program evaluation approach. Prioritizing the voices and perspectives of evaluation users provided us with an opportunity to highlight how the role of the evaluator (or evaluation team) influences the developmental evaluation process. For example, participants in this evaluation found the assistance we provided valuable, which is aligned with Patton's (2010) experience using developmental evaluation and is also supported by findings reported in other research studies (Lam & Shulha, 2015; Peurach et al., 2016; Poth et al., 2012). However, our participants' experience differed from the evaluation users working with Poth et al. (2012) and Patton (2010, 2016), who associated developmental evaluation with a decreased sense of rigour. Our four interviewees emphasized that the process was beneficial to program development and implementation, and that working with an external university team provided an impartial perspective and lent an air of prestige and legitimacy to their efforts. The differences in how evaluation users perceived the rigour associated with developmental evaluation may be a function of their experience engaging in different program evaluation approaches and methodologies. For example, the school division participants were well-versed in K-12 assessment and evaluation practices but had little experience with traditional approaches to program evaluation that call for evaluators to maintain an "arm's length" from the evaluation users. The fact that these school division staff lacked experience engaging in formative or summative forms of program evaluation could explain why their perceptions of rigour were so different from those found in the literature.

According to the interviewees, a key benefit to emerge from the developmental evaluation process they were involved in was sticking with the program and staying the course. By disregarding their inclination to move on to new initiatives, participants were able to lean in and further refine their existing well-being programs. As one participant mentioned, educators are prone or feel pressure to move on to new initiatives before the maximum benefits are realized. By throwing the proverbial baby out with the bathwater, they may be doing a disservice to students who are not able to benefit from the maximum impact of these programs. Further, school systems that continually demand teachers, principals, and other educators implement new programs can contribute to initiative overload (Pollock & Hauseman, 2015) as well as to the work intensification individuals in these roles currently experience (Hauseman et al., 2017).

Prior research has demonstrated that evaluators must invest a great deal of time and energy into developmental evaluation activities for their efforts to be successful. For example, Poth et al. (2012) discussed how evaluators can experience an increased time commitment when engaged in developmental evaluation efforts if evaluation users become over-reliant on the evaluators' input when making key programmatic decisions. Patton (1994, 1999, 2010, 2016) also noted that developmental evaluation requires a heavy time commitment. The findings of our study indicate that the time issue cuts both ways: Participants outlined several benefits associated with their experience, but it is important for evaluators to remember that they and those they are working with need to put in a great deal of work and energy to achieve those positive outcomes. If evaluators and evaluation users are not willing to invest in the developmental evaluation process and learn from it, then all parties would be better served by engaging in a process evaluation or in another approach to ongoing program development and refinement.

It is also important to note that the COVID-19 pandemic occurred during this developmental evaluation, introducing additional turbulence and complexity to its implementation (Gurr & Drysdale, 2020). The pandemic exacerbated the existing challenges related to well-being in schools, further intensified the work of teachers and other school staff (Hauseman et al., 2020), condensed the amount of time available to engage in developmental evaluation activities, and created additional uncertainty about next steps.

Conclusion

Well-being is increasingly becoming a core focus of schooling, but the reasons why individuals experience ill-being and fail to achieve a sense of well-being are complex and interrelated. In our partnership project we used developmental evaluation as a framework to guide a school division in Winnipeg throughout the process of analysing and upscaling their well-being initiatives prior to the COVID-19 pandemic. The positive experiences our participants have reported so far are encouraging and point to the potential of developmental evaluation to continue supporting the design, implementation, and evaluation of school-based initiatives aimed at promoting well-being. Our research also hints at the potential for developmental evaluation to address subsequent well-being initiatives as well as an array of complex issues in contemporary education systems that require innovative solutions.

The findings of this study indicate that generating real-time data that can be quickly analysed is one area where developmental evaluation thrives and K-12 education struggles. Some data sources in education, including large-scale assessment or standardized test results, have a muted influence on classroom instruction and program development, in part because it takes too long to get the data in the hands of classroom teachers and other staff members who work with students or schools more generally, or because the data are not classroom or student-specific. Inviting our development evaluation team to analyse this division's dataset allowed our participants to identify effective classroom- and school-level interventions that can be upscaled to other classrooms, individual schools, or an entire division. Developmental evaluation is also uniquely suited to assisting educators in responding and adapting to societal shifts, such as changing perceptions surrounding the importance of well-being. In these ways, developmental evaluation can assist school divisions in refining programs to maximize their impact and best meet the needs of staff and students.

ACKNOWLEDGMENTS

We would like to express our appreciation to those school divisional personnel who collaborated with us on the partnership project and to those, in particular, who gave so generously of their precious time to be interviewed by us for the study reported upon here. We would also like to acknowledge the financial support of the study through a grant from the UM/SSHRC Explore Grants Program.

REFERENCES

Alberta Teachers' Association [ATA]. (2019). *School wellness and well-being initiatives across Canada: Environmental scan and literature review.* https://www.teachers.ab.ca/SiteCollectionDocuments/ATA/Publications/Research/COOR-101-27%20School%20Wellness%20and%20Well-being%20Initatives%20across%20Canada.pdf.

Anderson, R.C., Guerreiro, M., & Smith, J. (2016). Are all biases bad? Collaborative grounded theory in developmental evaluation of education policy. *Journal of Multidisciplinary Evaluation*, 12(27), 44–57. https://doi.org/10.56645/jmde.v12i27.449

Bassett-Gunter, R., Yessis, J., Manske, S., & Gleddie, D. (2015). Healthy school communities in Canada. *Health Education Journal*, 75(2), 235–48. https://doi.org/10.1177/0017896915570397

Berkovich, I., & Eyal, O. (2015). Educational leaders and emotions: An international review of empirical evidence 1992–2012. *Review of Educational Research*, 85(1), 129–67. https://doi.org/10.3102/0034654314550046

Bryson, A., Stokes, L., & Wilkinson, D. (2019). Who is better off? Well-being and commitment among staff in schools and elsewhere. *Education Economics*, 27(5), 488–506. https://doi.org/10.1080/09645292.2019.1623178

Cooke, R.A., & Rousseau, D.M. (1981). Problems of complex systems: A model of system problem solving applied to schools. *Educational Administration Quarterly*, 17(3), 15–41. https://doi.org/10.1177/0013161X8101700304

Council of Ministers of Education, Canada. (2019). *Some facts about Canada's population.* https://www.cmec.ca/299/education-in-canada-an-overview/index.html

Fagen, M.C., Redman, S.D., Stacks, J., Barrett, V., Thullen, B., Altenor, S., & Neiger, B.L. (2011). Developmental evaluation: Building innovations in complex environments. *Health Promotion Practice*, 12(5), 645–50. https://doi.org/10.1177/1524839911412596

Falkenberg, T. (2014). Making sense of western approaches to well-being in an educational context. In F. Deer, T. Falkenberg, B. McMillan, & T. Sims (Eds.), *Sustainable well-being: Concepts, issues, and educational practices* (pp. 77–94). Education for Sustainable Well-Being Press. https://www.eswb-press.org/

Gamble, J.A.A. (2008). *A developmental evaluation primer.* The J.W. McConnell Family Foundation. https://mcconnellfoundation.ca/wp-content/uploads/2017/07/A-Developmental-Evaluation-Primer-EN.pdf

Gray, C., Wilcox, G., & Nordstokke, D. (2017). Teacher mental health, school climate, inclusive education and student learning: A review. *Canadian Psychology/psychologie canadienne, 58*(3), 203–10. https://doi.org/10.1037/cap0000117

Gurr, D., & Drysdale, L. (2020). Leadership for challenging times. *International Studies in Educational Administration, 48*(1), 24–30.

Hauseman, C. (2021). Strategies secondary school principals use to manage their emotions. *Leadership and Policy in Schools, 20*(4), 630–49. https://doi.org/10.1080/15700763.2020.173421

Hauseman, C., Darazsi, S., & Kent, S. (2020). Collaboration, communication and wellness: Response to the COVID-19 pandemic in Manitoba schools. *International Studies in Educational Administration, 48*(2), 70–7.

Hauseman, D.C., Pollock, K., & Wang, F. (2017). Inconvenient, but essential: Impact and influence of school–community involvement on principals' work and workload. *School Community Journal, 27*(1), 83–106.

Herbert, A. (2017). Closing the rhetoric reality gap: Effectively implementing engagement and well-being policies in Queensland state secondary schools. *International Journal of Innovation, Creativity and Change, 3*, 124–39.

Kokkinos, C.M. (2007). Job stressors, personality, and burnout in primary school teachers. *British Journal of Educational Psychology, 77*(1), 229–43. https://doi.org/10.1348/000709905X90344

Lam, C.Y., & Shulha, L.M. (2015). Insights on using developmental evaluation for innovating: A case study on the cocreation of an innovative program. *American Journal of Evaluation, 36*(3), 358–74. https://doi.org/10.1177/1098214014542100

Lawrence, R.B., Rallis, S.F., Davis, L.C., & Harrington, K. (2018). Developmental evaluation: Bridging the gaps between proposal, program, and practice. *Evaluation, 24*(1), 69–83. https://doi.org/10.1177/1356389017749276

Manitoba Education. (2020). *Mandate, mission, vision and priority areas.* https://www.edu.gov.mb.ca/edu/mandate.html

McDonald, H. (2016). Developmental evaluation: A tool to support innovation. *Evaluation Matters – He Take Tō Te Aromatawai, 2*, 79–97. https://doi.org/10.18296/em.0012

Miller, S., Connolly, P., & Maguire, L.K. (2013). Well-being, academic buoyancy and educational achievement in primary school students. *International Journal of Educational Research, 62*, 239–48. https://doi.org/10.1016/j.ijer.2013.05.004

Mital, P., Moore, R., & Llewellyn, D. (2014). Analyzing K-12 education as a complex system. *Procedia Computer Science, 28*, 370–9. https://doi.org/10/1016/j.procs.2014.03.046

Nelson, R.B., Hemmy Asamsama, O., Jimerson, S.R., & Lam, S.F. (2020). The association between student wellness and student engagement in school. *Journal of Educational Research and Innovation, 8*(1), 1–26.

Ontario Ministry of Education. (2014). *Achieving excellence: A renewed vision for education in Ontario*. https://www.oise.utoronto.ca/atkinson/UserFiles/File/Policy_Monitor/ON_01_04_14_-_renewedVision.pdf

Patton, M.Q. (1994). Developmental evaluation. *Evaluation Practice*, 15(3), 311–19. https://doi.org/10.1177/109821409401500312

– (1999). Organizational development and evaluation. *Canadian Journal of Program Evaluation*, 14(3), 93–114.

– (2010). *Developmental evaluation: Applying complexity concepts to enhance innovation and use*. Guilford Press.

– (2016). What is essential in developmental evaluation? On integrity, fidelity, adultery, abstinence, impotence, long-term commitment, integrity, and sensitivity in implementing evaluation models. *American Journal of Evaluation*, 37(2), 250–65. https://doi.org/10.1177/1098214015626295

Peurach, D.J., Glazer, J.L., & Winchell Lenhoff, S. (2016). The developmental evaluation of school improvement networks. *Educational Policy*, 30(4), 606–48. https://doi.org/10.1177/0895904814557592

Pollock, K., & Hauseman, D.C. (2015). Principal leadership in Canada. In H. Arlestig, C. Day, & O. Johansson (Eds.), *A decade of research on school principals: Cases from 24 countries* (pp. 211–44). Springer International Publishing. https://doi.org/10.1007/978-3-319-23027-6_11

Poth, C., Pinto, D., & Howery, K. (2012). Addressing the challenges encountered during a developmental evaluation: Implications for evaluation practice. *Canadian Journal of Program Evaluation*, 26(1), 39–48.

Putwain, D.W., Daly, A.L., Chamberlain, S., & Sadreddini, S. (2015). Academically buoyant students are less anxious about and perform better in high-stakes examinations. *British Journal of Educational Psychology*, 85(3), 247–63. https://doi.org/10.1111/bjep.12068

Putwain, D.W., Loderer, K., Gallard, D., & Beaumont, J. (2020). School-related subjective well-being promotes subsequent adaptability, achievement, and positive behavioural conduct. *British Journal of Educational Psychology*, 90(1), 92–108. https://doi.org/10.1111/bjep.12266

Robson, C., & McCartan, K. (2016). *Real world research*. John Wiley & Sons.

Ryan, J., & Tuters, S. (2015). Leadership and emotions: Promoting social justice. In S. Clarke & T. O'Donoghue (Eds.), *School leadership in diverse contexts* (pp. 173–90). Routledge.

11 A Complex Adaptive Systems Approach to Well-Becoming in Schools

THOMAS FALKENBERG, HEATHER KREPSKI, CAMERON HAUSEMAN, AND JENNIFER WATT

A school principal and three of her teachers attend a conference on well-becoming in schools. They get inspired and go back to their school division and share their learning and their ideas on the important role of student well-becoming with the rest of the school staff. More teachers get inspired. The principal provides release time to a group of teachers who want to develop further the notion of student well-becoming as a central focus of their teaching. As teachers develop their teaching ideas further, more teachers become interested in these ideas and want to join the initial group of teachers. The principal shares this development with other principals in the division.

The vignette illustrates two important points about change processes in school educational contexts (see, for instance, James, 2010; Redding et al., 2017). First, educators' ideas that motivate their work (e.g., student well-becoming as a central focus of teaching) and organizational decisions that create a social context within which any enacting of such ideas operates (e.g., provision of release time for teachers) are two core forces for change in schools and school divisions. Second, the actions that result from educators enacting the ideas that motivate their work *dynamically interact* with "organizational behaviour" that creates the social context for such actions (e.g., increased interest in the work of the initial teacher group and spreading the word about this work beyond the school). This dynamic interaction creates an important *context* for a school division's concern for well-becoming in schools. The present chapter focuses on this dynamic interaction as a context for the school division's concern for well-being in schools.

Contextualizing the concern for well-becoming in schools is not a theory-neutral undertaking. Such an undertaking is biased from the beginning by the "lens" that we use to understand the inquiry itself and then how we decide to undertake the inquiry. We suggest in this chapter that the lens should be a system-theoretical lens, because if we want to intentionally impact change at the school systems level, we need to account for the adaptive complex systems nature of school divisional dynamics (e.g., Fullan, 1993, 1999, 2003; see also Glouberman & Zimmerman, 2002, for the same argument brought to bear to the reform of the Canadian health care system).

This chapter develops the conceptual and theoretical framework for understanding well-becoming in schools as a developmental process of and within complex adaptive systems. We particularly focus on change processes within school divisions, which in Canada are charged with the implementation of the responsibilities of provincial governments for public education. To this end, we first outline a complex adaptive social system (CASS) philosophy, with particular focus on the conceptualization aspect for such a philosophy. Then, we draw on a study linked to a project in which the chapter authors collaborated with a particular school division that engaged in a change process of bringing a new focus on well-becoming into the school-based work of the school division. We draw on data from this study to illustrate the change dynamics within a school division understood as a CASS. Finally, we argue with reference to the first two sections of the chapter that using a CASS lens is a productive approach for inquiring into the change dynamics of school divisions as a crucial context for any concern for well-becoming in schools.

A Complex Adaptive Social Systems Philosophy

Complex adaptive social systems (CASS) are special cases of complex adaptive systems (CAS), which in turn are special cases of complex systems (CS). Examples of complex systems that are not adaptive are "a hurricane or a turbulent rushing river" (Mitchell, 2009, p. 13). An example of a CAS that is not a CASS is an ecosystem as understood by an ecologist (Westley et al., 2002). There are different definitions of CASs in circulation (see Wallis (2008) for a list of 20 different versions of CAS theory). The purpose of this section is to explicate the particular version of a CASS (as a special case of a CAS) that we make use of in the remainder of the chapter.

To begin, we draw on Mitchell (2009), who defines a CAS as "a system in which large networks of components with no central control and simple rules of operation give rise to complex collective behavior, sophisticated information processing, and adaptation via learning or evolution" (p. 13). Refining Mitchell's general definition of a CAS,

Gerrits (2012) identifies the following three "principal properties common to most definitions" (p. 56) for (human-based) CASSs:

> First, *systems emerge through interactions between heterogeneous actors, but not by superimposed control or deliberate design* [emphasis added]. This means that if actors engage in repeated interaction of any type, structures and processes will emerge and become (somewhat) persistent. Over time, a system will be established out of those interactions ...
>
> The second common aspect of complex adaptive system[s] is the *adaptive nature of actors in such systems* [emphasis added]. Structure, processes and norms are not cast in iron, but are the collective response of individual actors to the incentives presented from within and outside the system. ... If a system emerges out of interactions, it follows that it becomes *dynamic* and *adaptive* through the aggregated behaviour of its constituent actors ...
>
> The third aspect concerns the *non-linear relationship between what happens at the level of the individual actors and the behavior of the entire system* [emphasis added]. The adaptive moves of actors are mutually different as each actor has a (somewhat) different criterion for what constitutes a better individual fit. These adaptive moves shape the system's behavior but the two do not share a linear relationship. (Gerrits, 2012, pp. 56–7)

For human-based CASSs, these principal properties take the following form, which will be elaborated upon in the remainder of this section. The components of the system are humans, who are the social actors of the system. The networks of the system are the concrete communicative interactions between the social actors. Out of repeated human communicative interaction emerges a system structure that together with the network of interacting social actors makes up a social system. While the social structure puts constraints on and provides affordances for communicative actions of social actors of the system through its norms and rules, the actual communicative interactions between social actors are underdetermined by the social system because of the agency of social actors (Martin, Sugarman, & Thompson, 2003). For the social system to continue functioning despite this underdetermination, the social system needs to be adaptive: the system responds to system-internal (social agents) and system-external (systems environment) perturbations by adapting its structure in response to such perturbations as needed. However, how the system as a whole adapts to perturbations cannot be predicted from knowing what happens at the level of individual communicative interactions between social actors. Figure 11.1 shows the

Figure 11.1. The organization of a complex adaptive social system

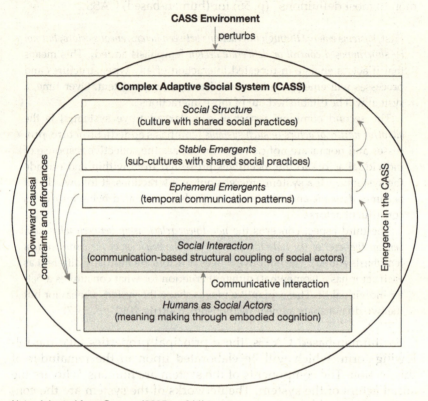

Note: Adapted from Sawyer (2005, p. 211).

organization of a CASS. In the following sections, the different components of the organization will be discussed in more detail.

Humans as Social Actors and Their Interaction

COMMUNICATION: STRUCTURALLY COUPLING SOCIAL ACTORS

Within a CASS, humans are considered in their functioning as social actors within the social system. As social actors of a CASS they interact with other social actors of the same CASS through communication: "For humans, interaction is essentially communicational and social systems can therefore be seen as networks of recurring conversations (series of interlocked communications)" (Mingers, 1999, p. 36). A communication is an event in time and space. Verbal and non-verbal forms of communication during face-to-face encounters are only one type of forms of communication. Other types that are especially relevant to organization-based CASSs are discussed by Gerrits (2012):

> From this perspective, the organization of government is essentially shaped through communicative connections between people. Bureaucratic communications are distinct from informal communications because much of the former is captured in protocols, standard operating procedures and organizational identities expressed in such protocols. However formalized, commands and acknowledgments, norms and accountability transferred through the bureaucratic system are still communicative acts that are subject to the same dynamics of other kinds of communication. (pp. 52–3)

What makes communicative acting *systemic* interaction are the downward-causal constraints and affordances (see figure 11.1; on the notion of *affordances* relevant here, see, e.g., Ramstead et al., 2016) that the social system puts on the *expectations* that a social actor involved in the communication can have for the quality of their experience. In other words, when one social actor communicates (interacts) with another social actor within a given social system, then each of them can have certain expectations about the quality of their interaction. These expectations arise from the constraints and affordances that the social structure provides to social actors within the social system. For instance, if in an encounter between two strangers in a Canadian city one of them says "Excuse me!" while pointing to a map in their hand and looking at the other person, the map holder can rightly have the expectation that the other person will stop walking with the intention of inquiring about the map holder's apparent need for help with directions. The appropriateness of these expectations derives from the affordances and constraints provided to the social actors through the verbal and gestural language system that is part of the social structure of the social system.

Following Maturana and Varela (1980, 1998), we say that two communicating people are "structurally coupled" or engaged in "coordinated actions," and it is the social structure of the social system which *structurally* couples the two human beings as social actors in the particular instance. This structural coupling of social actors within a social system is built upon a circular relationship between social actors, who generate/reaffirm the social system's structure, and the social structure of the social system, which constrains and provides affordances for the communication of social actors of that specific social system in specific situations (see also Mingers, 1999, pp. 6, 36).

THE AGENCY OF SOCIAL ACTORS

Humans as social actors are not like rocks on a beach. The latter are at the mercy of the waves and are predictably and passively moved around by the moving water, while the former engages *with agency* with the affordances and constraints of the respective social system. What does such agentic engagement look like and what is the basis for it? To answer this question, we draw on the work of Grawe (2004), who has developed an integrated and sophisticated theory of human mental functioning grounded in systems thinking. We see human agency arising from this very mental functioning and outline the systemic basis for such functioning and, thus, human agency. Following Falkenberg (2019), we will call this systemic base the "bio-psychic system."

Human mental functioning is materially grounded in the biological qualities of our neurological system, of which the brain is the centre. In other words, the human psychic system is what it is because we are living (biological) beings of a certain type. At the heart of our existence as living systems are experience and behaviour. Simplified, it is through experience that we know of a world (an outer and inner world) and it is through behaviour that we engage in that world. Both experience and behaviour are closely connected. We are linked to a world outside of us through the receptors of our sense organs only. But these neural signals give rise to neurological activation patterns from which different types of experiences at different systems levels emerge: experiencing sensations (e.g., coldness), experiencing configurations (e.g., a chair), experiencing change/movement (e.g., a car driving by), experiencing sequences (e.g., a melody), experiencing relationships (e.g., a causal relationship), experiencing actions (e.g., someone buying something), experiencing principles (e.g., a person as being nice), and experiencing systems (e.g., a voting system in a democracy).[1] These hierarchically organized levels of experience form a complex system. In line with the social system represented in figure 11.1, a level of experience "constrains" its lower levels of experiences. For instance, if I perceive someone buying something (action), then that constrains how I experience two movements of the two people involved in the action: one putting an object on the counter causes the other person to look for the price tag; that is, I perceive a causal relationship between the two movements.

Systemically, human behaviour is linked to these hierarchically organized levels of experience through feedback loops in the following sense: "Behavior, then, does not function to create certain objective conditions or end products, but instead is aimed towards achieving and maintaining subjective perceptions of very specific qualities" (Grawe, 2004, pp. 151–2). In other words, each human behaviour is what it is because it is an attempt to address an actual or expected incongruence between desired experience and actual experience – and that applies to each level of experience. For instance, I grab a glass of water because I want to experience the state of not feeling thirsty anymore. Our perceptions (experiences) are goal-oriented and our behaviours are perception (experience)-oriented, thus, "both behavior and perceptions are oriented towards attaining certain desired perceptions" (Grawe, 2004, p. 152). These desired experiences are determined by what Grawe (2004) calls motivational schemes: we desire to experience what we perceive, how we act, and how we feel emotionally to be in line with certain perceptual, action, and emotional tendencies that we have formed, and to be in line with goals that we have set for ourselves.

We use this sketch of the human bio-psychic system and its functioning to explicate in what sense humans as social actors have agency. Bio-psychic systems are linked to social systems in two ways. First, from birth on, humans are embedded into social systems, whose social practices and communication patterns (see figure 11.1) provide the experiential feedback loops through which motivational schemes (the perceptual, action, and emotional tendencies and goals) are formed. Second, through one's behaviour in social settings, one engages with these social practices and communication patterns by providing experiential input to other social actors. Human agency is grounded in the specifically human capability of self-understanding "that permits a deliberative, reflective activity in selecting and choosing, framing, and executing actions" (Martin et al., 2003, p. 114). In other words, humans "are capable of reflective, intentional thought and action directed outward and inward" (p. 114). This capability of self-understanding, together with other mental capabilities like imagination and memory, allows human beings to imagine different types of experiences for themselves, especially at the action, principle, and system levels. The potential and actual engagement of these capabilities manifest human agency, which, when enacted, contributes to the dynamic of social systems, for instance, through behaviour in social settings that violates experiential expectations that other social actors have of that individual's behaviour based on social practices and communication patterns assumed for that social system. More on the dynamic of social systems below.

Social Structures

A CASS has two major levels (see figure 11.1): one is "the biophysical level" (shaded) and the other is the "emergents level" (non-shaded). The two components of the organization of a CASS at the biophysical level are the social actors and a network of interactions (communications) between the social actors. Within the *structure* of a specific CASS, these components are concrete entities (social actors) and concrete events (interactions). They have a specific place in space and time.

The social interactions of the social actors give rise to emergent phenomena at the emergents level in the way described above. It is not the social actors' agency per se that gives rise to the emergents, but rather the interaction between the social actors. Following Sawyer (2005), we distinguish between ephemeral emergents, stable emergents, and the social structure per se as three different types of emergents. Ephemeral emergents are more momentary, relatively short-lived, while stable emergents are more enduring. The more stable emergents develop from the interaction of ephemeral emergents. Out of the interaction of the more stable emergents develops the social structure of the social system. We introduce the three types of emergents that relate hierarchically to each other (see figure 11.1), because "by introducing these intermediate levels and the corresponding notion of collaborative emergence, [we avoid] ... mak[ing] too large a jump from the individual to the structural level" (Sawyer, 2005, p. 211). Some examples of emergents at these intermediate levels are "families, clubs, organizations (and subcultures within them) and other informal but enduring networks" (Mingers, 1999, p. 35).

The *structure* of a CASS provides the social system with its constraining and affording properties for the interactions of the social actors of the CASS. As explicated above, these constraints and affordances manifest themselves in the form of expectations that the social actors have and can afford to have for their experiences as they engage in their social interactions. It is these expectations that social actors have in a concrete situation that make the interactions (communications) with a specific CASS "structural."

> Luhmann (1995, ch. 8) recognises that lying behind or underneath social systems is the idea of social *structure*. Both interaction and society are essentially *temporal* – they consist of *events* that occur and must then lead to further events. How can this process happen? And, in particular, what controls the potentially enormous range of possibilities that could potentially follow on [sic]? Clearly, there must be some constraints in operation and this is what Luhmann means by social structure – a complex of *expectations* that constrain the possibilities for particular events following others ... Going out for a meal involves the expectation of having to pay for it at the end. (Mingers, 1999, p. 38)

A CASS is *organizationally closed* in the sense defined by Maturana and Varela (1998): the communicative interactions of social actors lead to further communicative actions and communicative interactions are understood in such a way that they only generate other interactions that are part of the CASS. This feature is central to understanding the dynamics within CASSs, as we will see next.

The Dynamics of CASSs

The interactions between social actors with agency, together with the downward causal constraints and affordances and the emergence within a CASS, create the *inner dynamics* for the CASS. This inner system dynamic is characterized by two processes. One is a process of maintaining the system and its structure: "The mutually reinforcing nature of social networks means that they are inevitably conservative in the sense that they operate so as to maintain their present organizational relations" (Mingers, 1999, p. 36). Social actors of a social system interact (communicate) with each other in alignment with the downward causal constraints and affordances established by the social structure and its sub-emergents. As such, the interaction reinforces the system's structure of constraints and affordances. The second process is a structural change in response to perturbations of the interaction patterns by social actors who interact with other social actors in ways that run counter to the expectations that the social structure suggests to social actors. Because CASSs are operationally closed, *any* system change

> can only come about through a change in the behaviour of the participants – it cannot be imposed in some sense by the system ... An individual may enter a social network and not become structurally coupled to it, instead altering the behaviours of the other members by becoming structurally coupled to them in the course of co-ordinations of action that do not confirm the social system. Or, already existing members can reflect upon their experiences in other domains and choose to modify their own behaviours, thus realising an altered social network. (Mingers, 1999, p. 36)

The inner dynamics of a social system – as a communication network of social actors of the system – can only change through a change in the communication relationship between the system's social actors. Mingers's (1999) quotation above exemplifies two ways in which such change in the communication relationships within the system can happen. One is through non-system actors who communicatively interact with system members in a way that lead to changes to the bio-psychic system of the system member – and such change leads to changes in the communicative interactions with other system members by the exertions of agency by the system member. To account for the operational closure of CASSs, it has to be kept in mind that any perturbation of a CASS by its environment, as in this example, is mediated by the bio-psychic system of the humans that are social actors of the CASS. Not all environmental perturbations lead to system change, though. The second example is a system change that happens when a system member exerts their agency, like the social actor reflecting upon their experiences in other domains and then "perturbing" the system's structure in a way that leads to system change. We can say that this second form of system change happens through *system-internal perturbations*, while the first form of system change in Mingers's example happens through *system-external perturbations*.

In response to some of the (system-internal or external) perturbations, the social system *adapts*, for instance, when it is perturbed by the exertion of agency by social actors of the social system. On the other hand, it is a constitutive feature of a social system that its structure perturbs the bio-psychic systems of its social actors, and, in response, the social actors need to adapt. These reciprocal perturbations cannot be disentangled to arrive at a linear chain of causation; rather the two systems *co-evolve*. The concept of systems co-evolution is central to describing and understanding the dynamics of systems interactions (Gerrits, 2012; Norgaard, 1984, 1994).

Human beings are members of several different social systems. Each of these social systems co-evolves with a person's bio-psychic system as just described. It is this bio-psychic system that indirectly links the different social systems. It is through this indirect link that we can say that the different social systems that a person is a social actor of *indirectly perturb each other* and as such *indirectly co-evolve*.

School Divisions as Complex Adaptive Social Systems

Complex systems approaches have been utilized to understand schooling processes and schools as organizations (e.g., Abraham, 2003; Bakker & Montessori, 2016; Isaacson & Bamburg, 1992; Fidan & Balci, 2017; Keshavarz et al., 2010; Mennin, 2007; Osberg et al., 2008). Some of the more recent educational change literature has moved to a complex system perspective, arguing that educational change processes are best understood as an adaptive process of a complex system (e.g., Mason, 2008; Morrison, 2010; Nespor, 2002).

We build on this notion in this section, where we utilize the conceptual and theoretical framework that we described in the previous section to understand school divisions as CASSs. To this end, we draw on data from a study that the authors undertook and that is described in more detail in chapter 10 of this book. We use these data to illustrate the structural and dynamic features of school divisions when viewed through a CASS lens.

The Organization of a School Division as a Complex Adaptive Social System

There are three basic "components" in the organization of a school division as a CASS: the CASS-relative environment; the social actors and their social interactions; and the social emergents that "build up" the social structure of the CASS. We describe each and use data from the study to illustrate, in particular, the dynamic nature of school divisions as CASSs.

CASS ENVIRONMENT

The social systems environment of a school division is made up of anything that can perturb the social system. As the theoretical framework outlined above suggests, that can only happen through changes to the social actors, which can only happen through perturbations of their bio-psychic systems. In the study, the participants identified a number of perturbations of the school division, which we want to cluster into two types of perturbations. The first type is linked to the fact that each social actor within the school division is also a social actor in a number of other social systems than the school division, for instance professional organizations and province-wide committees. In alignment with the theoretical framework, we have characterized perturbations of a social system as perturbations of the bio-psychic systems of the humans that are the social actors. Changes in the bio-psychic system of a human being in response to certain experiences as social actor in one CASS, like a province-wide organization, potentially impact the way in which the human being behaves and acts as a social actor in another CASS, like a school division.

The second type of perturbation of a school division consists in individual acts of perturbations of the bio-psychic system of humans who are social actors in the school division. In the study, participants identified, among others, the following examples of perturbations of this second type: engaging with speakers invited to give presentations in the school division; attending a workshop or conference outside of the school division; being informed about governmental decisions, like budgetary decisions; reading media articles. Following is a quotation that illustrates the first in this list of examples:

> They had brought in sort of external experts who worked directly with teachers and in their classrooms and developing practices around good practice in developing writers, and in math and numeracy development. There were some really good practices and approaches that were used by those external experts who came in. So the first round with the instructional support team was carrying through with those projects and using those sort of support tools to continue to grow capacity in our teachers. (P2)

What both types of perturbations have in common is that they are mediated by perturbations of the bio-psychic system of humans who are social actors in the respective school-divisional CASS. What distinguishes the two types of perturbations is the social-systems status of this bio-psychic perturbation. In the first type, the bio-psychic perturbation arises as part of social couplings of a social actor in a different social system, like a principal's membership in a provincial organization, while in the second type, the bio-psychic perturbation arises through the social coupling of a social actor *within* the social system in focus, like a principal's engagement with reform work in their school division.

SOCIAL ACTORS, THEIR AGENCY, AND THEIR STRUCTURAL COUPLING

Through their social interaction, social actors of a CASS create, maintain, and transform the social emergents, including the social structure of the CASS. In a school division as a CASS, the social actors are typically the students, the teachers and administrators, other staff in schools and other divisional units, and the parents. As is the case for all social actors in social systems, their agency impacts how they engage in their function as social actors. In alignment with the systems-theoretical framework outlined above, motivational schemes and self-understanding are core elements of this agency. For social actors in school divisions, both are often characterized by a vision of educational goals and purposes to support students' learning and development, as is illustrated in the following example from the study:

> Yes, and I don't need the personal recognition. I'm not looking for the personal, I'm looking for the systemic shift recognition. That's what's exciting, that's what keeps me motivated. I'm getting it. The mental health promotion, that was huge to see everybody there and see them all using it, the calls I get, the information people are asking for and then I've been

going to some of those schools that were pilot schools and helping them do it over again or overview and that's great to see. It's really good to see something take off. That's very motivating. (P4)

As the system-theoretical framework suggests, what makes human beings social actors of a particular social system is their structural coupling with other social actors of that social system. Such structural coupling happens through concrete communicative interaction within the constraints and affordances of the social system in which they are social actors. We draw on study data to illustrate two aspects to be considered when understanding structural coupling in school divisions as CASSs.

First, parts of social structures are *power structures* that manifest themselves through particular types of expectations.[2] The following example from the study data illustrates two types of structural coupling that are grounded in power structures. The first suggests expectations from the perspective of the social actor who "officially sets the agenda" and the second suggests expectations from a social actor who does not officially set the agenda for a change process:

Because change is hard and if you don't create the appropriate readiness and dissonance, and resonance, and all those cycles of things I was talking about. When I was a principal it was easy. My building. I set the agenda. I wander around. That was a piece of cake. Being [in division-wide administrator position] is harder, because you pick your moments. You try and get on agendas, you try and do that, and everyone's got their own agendas. (P1)

A second aspect of social coupling that needs to be understood is *the quality and history of interaction of those that are structurally coupled.* For instance, in the study participants showed concern for the negative impact of staff turnover on the change process, suggesting that the quality and history of the social interaction between particular social actors are important for understanding structural coupling between social actors in a social system.

EPHEMERAL AND STABLE EMERGENTS

Following the systems-theoretical approach outlined above, the social emergents – of which the social structure is the most stable – arise from the communicative interaction patterns of the social actors of the social system. While we use the more common language and say that, for instance, meeting structures, families of schools, and divisional policies are social emergents, in accordance with the outlined CASS philosophy we would need to say more accurately that meeting structures, families of schools, and policies are social practices in the form of structures of behavioural expectations.

We draw on study data to provide examples of some ephemeral and some stable emergents in the context of school divisions as CASSs. The first kind of emergent is a shared understanding across the school division of how to view student behaviour:

> I think we've come a long way in understanding behaviour and so I'm talking from my experience in education over the last 30 years. I would say it's moved from more of a behavioural approach to an understanding of children's needs and that behaviour is not just what you see, it's what's behind the behaviour. Seeing it from a developmental perspective for children in the whole area of brain development, understanding that more. So lots of those pieces coming in over time. (P4)

What has emerged "over the last 30 years" is a new view of how to understand student behaviour, namely one that sees student behaviour as an expression of underlying needs (e.g., Rosenberg, 2000), and thus requires educators to inquire into the underlying motivation of the behaviour rather than judging and responding to the behaviour on its own. At least in the eyes of the study participant, this view of student behaviour in the school division is a fairly stable emergent.

Another study participant points to a recent extensive process of developing division-wide strategic goals:

> First it was again a broad community consultation through thought exchange and then emerging themes came from that and then all the leadership team got together and we used the circle of courage format to take these priorities and ideas and flush them out into strategic goals into different quadrants of the circle of courage and then we took that to the board. (P1)

These division-wide goals, despite the broad consultative process, would initially be best understood as *ephemeral* emergents until they have been adopted widely across the school division. At that time, these strategic goals become *stable* emergents or even part of the social structure of the school division.

Similarly, the development and communication of division-wide policies – mentioned by study participants – should initially be understood as ephemeral emergents until the expectations linked to these policies become stable through the adopting of the expectations that make up the policies across a broader group of social agents. Within the outlined CASS philosophy, a school-divisional policy is not adopted when the school board passes the policy or the superintendent's office releases a policy, but rather when social actors across the social system align their expectations for their own and other social actors' behaviour with those expressed in the respective policy.

The Dynamics of School Divisions as CASSs

In alignment with the theoretical framework outlined above, school divisions as CASSs are operationally closed, while being interactionally open to system-external perturbations. These system-external perturbations are mediated by the bio-psychic systems of human beings that are social actors in the CASS that is the school division. In other words, the agency of the social actors in a school division is a school division's potential for its development.

Two types of "agency dynamics" in the changing of a school division's social structure can be distinguished and found in the study data: top-down agency and ground-up agency. The former is illustrated in the study when participants point to changes initiated by the school division's leadership, while the latter is illustrated when participants talk about their own contributions to systemic changes.

As part of the study, participants were also asked to consider challenges to systems change. Participants provided two examples: challenges that come through personnel changes and challenges that arose through a lack of shared understanding. The latter challenge is exemplified through this quotation from one study participant, who points to perceived different understandings arising from different professional practices and backgrounds:

> I do still think that there is not always a real detailed understanding of how clinicians work and so that's my other point, is sometimes there's that us versus them dynamic. Like teachers and clinical staff. Often it works very well, but there still can sometimes be that you're a clinician, you have not taught in a classroom or that kind of thing. And I think sometimes when you are the leader and it comes back to you. (P2)

Finally, the study data also provide illustrative examples for the co-evolution of systems:

> So that is the work of the senior leadership team with the leaders of schools. So that's where we engage in all kinds of learning and

conversation and collaboration with the leaders of our schools. And then of course they as leaders also work in families of schools, so they get a chance to work collaboratively with the high school and their surrounding community schools that connect to that high school, they get time together to talk about issues in their broader community and around transition and things. (P1)

This quotation illustrates how subsystems of the school system that is a CASS co-evolve because the same humans are social actors in both subsystems.

A CASS Approach to Well-Becoming in Schools

The first section of this chapter provided an outline of a complex adaptive social systems philosophy, with a particular focus on the development of a conceptual framework. The second section drew on our study focused on systems understanding of a particular school division in order to exemplify and conceptualize school divisions as CASSs. This third and final section argues why understanding school divisions as CASSs is a productive approach to inquiring into the dynamics of school divisions.

To argue why understanding school divisions as CASSs is a productive way of inquiring into the dynamics of school divisions, we want to apply a central argument for using a systems lens for social organizations more generally. The argument is as follows: If we are dealing with a complex adaptive social system, then any intervention needs to give consideration to the complexity of the system's dynamics. If not, an intervention may not work as intended and for the identified purpose: "The tendency is to make single-variable interventions or to create inventions without regard for their impact on other parts of the systems, to ignore internal mechanisms that facilitate adjustments, or to fail to balance objectives" (Westley et al., 2002, p. 117). In other words, it is productive to understand school divisions as CASSs, because when we want to intentionally and systemically intervene in the dynamics of school divisions, we have a better chance of giving consideration to the complex nature of that dynamics.

Understanding school divisions as CASSs allows us:

- to recognize social structure(s) of school divisions that create constraints and affordances for its social actors (students, teachers, administrators, parents, etc.) to act (engage with each other in communicative interaction);

- to recognize that different social (sub)structures in school divisions emerge from the interaction of the actors in the school division and that those emergents are stable to different degrees;
- to recognize continuous change dynamics for the social (sub)structure(s) and the social actors' bio-psychic systems that are the foundations for their acting based on systems-internal interactions between actors in the school division and external perturbations of the social system;
- to recognize a co-evolution of social (sub)structure(s) and the bio-psychic systems that give rise to the acting of the social actors within the constraints and affordances of the social (sub-)structure(s).

We now provide some examples of insights about the change dynamics in school divisions that come directly from understanding school divisions as CASSs, some of which are illustrated in the previous section through reference to study data.

The CASS phenomenon of co-evolution provides two such insights. First, because of co-evolution, we cannot simply expect that there are "change programs that work" out there, that is, programs which when simply applied lead to a desired change outcome at a school divisional level. The emergence of new social structures in CASSs – which is what change at the school divisional level is about – is in principle unpredictable because they result from co-evolution. For this reason, developmental evaluation is a powerful systems change tool – a case that we make in chapter 10 of this book. Second, staff turnover in a school or school division is a huge challenge to the pursuit of system goals, because with new staff the co-evolution of the social system (school or school division) and the bio-psychic systems (social agents) is interrupted: one component of this co-evolution, namely the bio-psychic systems, is replaced with the consequence of newly created systems-internal perturbations through the introduction of new social agents that bring different bio-psychic systems to the social interactions.

Third, progress and success for systems change efforts need to be defined relative to the systems status at given times and in relation to its preceding system states. Structural changes in CASSs only happen relative to an immediately preceding systems state, which itself only happens relative to an immediately preceding system state, and so on. This is the systems-theoretical justification for the insight that we might overlook success if we define it absolutely, that is, in a context-independent way. What it means to be successful in achieving a goal depends on how we define success: for instance, as improvement relative to the current system state or as an endpoint of certain measurable attributes. In terms of a school system, a reappraisal of a systems change goal "midstream" may need to happen because the particular systems development made the original change goal questionable.

Fourth, from a systems-theoretical perspective, all perturbations that provide for externally initiated systems changes should be understood as mediated through individual social actors. This means that any change to a CASS through system-external perturbation requires that a social actor of that system create that perturbation.

In this section, we have argued that understanding school divisions as CASSs is a productive way of inquiring into the dynamics of school divisions, because it allows us to recognize the complex phenomena at work in complex systems, which in turn will allow us to be responsive to these phenomena when trying to influence the directions of school divisional change. From a systems-theoretical perspective, such intentional influencing is an ongoing process, because a social system (for instance, a school division) never stands still. It is constantly perturbed and adapts to such perturbations as appropriate.

This understanding of school divisions as constantly perturbed social systems is particularly important for school divisional change efforts that are concerned with well-becoming in schools, because the idea of well-becoming in schools as a focus of school educational reform is a much more vague, and thus controversial, endeavour than focusing educational reform on raising test scores or on raising graduation rates. As such, reform efforts linked to well-becoming in schools are much more challenged by the complexity of the dynamics of school divisions, and any such reform efforts will benefit from a CASS-perspective on school divisions as described in this chapter.

ACKNOWLEDGMENTS

We would like to express our appreciation to those school divisional personnel who collaborated with us on the partnership project and to those, in particular, who gave so generously of their precious time to be interviewed by us for the study reported upon here. We would also like to acknowledge the financial support of the study through a grant from the UM/SSHRC Explore Grants Program.

NOTES

1 Here, Grawe (2004) draws on Powers's control theory (Powers, 1973).
2 We acknowledge the centrality of power structures to the dynamics of CASSs. Exploring those dynamics in more detail, however, goes beyond the scope of this chapter.

REFERENCES

Abraham, J.L. (2003). Dynamic systems theory: Application to pedagogy. In W. Tschacher & J.-P. Dauwalder (Eds.), *The dynamical systems approach to cognition: Concepts and empirical paradigms based on self-organization, embodiment, and coordination dynamics*. World Scientific Publishing. https://doi.org/10.1142/5395

Archer, M.S. (1995). *Realist social theory: The morphogenetic approach*. Cambridge University Press. https://doi.org/10.1017/cbo9780511557675

Bakker, C., & Montessori, N.M. (Eds.). (2016). *Complexity in education*. Sense Publishers.

Falkenberg, T. (2019). *Framing human well-being and well-becoming: An integrated systems approach*. www.wellbeinginschools.ca/paper-series

Fidan, T., & Balci, A. (2017). Managing schools as complex adaptive systems: A strategic perspective. *International Electronic Journal of Elementary Education*, 10(1), 11–26. https://doi.org/10.26822/iejee.2017131883

Fullan, M. (1993). *Change forces: Probing the depths of educational reform*. Routeldge Falmer.

– (1999). *Change forces: The sequel*. Falmer Press.

– (2003). *Change forces with a vengeance*. RoutledgeFalmer.

Gerrits, L. (2012). *Punching clouds: An introduction to the complexity of public decision-making*. Emergent Publications.

Glouberman, S., & Zimmerman, B. (2002). *Complicated and complex systems: What would successful reform of Medicare look like?* Commission on the Future of Health Care in Canada. https://doi.org/10.3138/9781442672833-004

Grawe, K. (2004). *Psychological therapy*. Hogrefe & Huber.

Isaacson, N., & Bamburg, J. (1992, November). Can schools become learning organizations? *Educational Leadership*, 50(3), 42–4.

James, C. (2010). The psychodynamics of educational change. In A. Hargreaves, A. Lieberman, M. Fullan, & D. Hopkins (Eds.), *Second international handbook of educational change: Part 1* (pp. 47–64). Springer.

Keshavarz, N., Nutbeam, D., Rowling, L., & Khavarpour, F. (2010). Schools as social complex adaptive systems: A new way to understand the challenges of introducing the health promoting schools concept. *Social Science & Medicine*, 70, 1467–74. https://doi.org/10.1016/j.socscimed.2010.01.034

Martin, J., Sugarman, J., & Thompson, J. (2003). *Psychology and the question of agency*. State University of New York Press.

Mason, M. (2008). What is complexity theory and what are its implications for educational change? *Educational Philosophy and Theory*, 40(1), 35–49. https://doi.org/10.1002/9781444307351.ch3

Maturana, H.R., & Verela, F.J. (1980). *Autopoiesis and cognition: The realization of the living*. D. Reidel Publishing Company. https://doi.org/10.1007/978-94-009-8947-4

– (1998). *The tree of knowledge: The biological roots of human understanding* (2nd ed.). Shambhala.

Mennin, S. (2007). Small-group problem-based learning as a complex adaptive system. *Teaching and Teacher Education, 23*, 303–13. https://doi.org/10.1016/j.tate.2006.12.016

Mingers, J. (1999). Information, meaning, and communication: An autopoietic approach to linking the social and the individual. *Cybernetics & Human Knowing, 6*(4), 25–41.

Mitchell, M. (2009). *Complexity: A guided tour*. Oxford University Press.

Morrison, K. (2010). Complexity theory, school leadership and management: Questions for theory and practice. *Educational Management Administration & Leadership, 38*(3), 374–93. https://doi.org/10.1177/1741143209359711

Nespor, J. (2002). Networks and contexts of reform. *Journal of Educational Change, 3*, 365–82. https://doi-org.uml.idm.oclc.org/10.1023/A:1021281913741

Norgaard, R.B. (1984). Coevolutionary development potential. *Land Economics, 60*(2), 160–73. https://doi.org/10.2307/3145970

– (1994). *Development betrayed: The end of progress and a coevolutionary revisioning of the future*. Routledge.

Osberg, D., Biesta, G., & Cilliers, P. (2008). From representation to emergence: Complexity's challenge to the epistemology of schooling. *Educational Philosophy and Theory, 40*(1), 213–27. https://doi.org/10.1002/9781444307351.ch14

Powers, W.T. (1973). *Behavior: The control of perception*. Aldine.

Ramstead, M.J.D., Veissière, S.P.L., & Kirmayer, L.J. (2016). Cultural affordances: Scaffolding local worlds through shared intentionality and regimes of attention. *Frontiers in Psychology, 7*, article 1099. https://doi.org/10.3389/fpsyg.2016.01090

Redding, C., Cannata, M., & Haynes, K.T. (2017). With scale in mind: A continuous improvement model for implementation. *Peabody Journal of Education, 92*(5), 589–608. https://doi.org/10.1080/0161956X.2017.1368635

Rosenberg, M.B. (2000). *Nonviolent communication: A language of compassion*. PuddleDancer Press.

Sawyer, R.K. (2005). *Social emergence: Societies as complex systems*. Cambridge University Press.

Wallis, S.E. (2008). Emerging order in CAS theory: Mapping some perspectives. *Kybernetes, 37*(7), 1016–29. https://doi.org/10.1108/03684920810884388

Westley, F., Carpenter, S.R., Brock, W.A. Holling, C.S., & Gunderson, L.H. (2002). Why systems of people and nature are not just social and ecological systems. In L.H. Gunderson & C.S. Holling (Eds.), *Panarchy: Understanding transformations in human and natural systems* (pp. 103–19). Island Press.

PART FOUR

Curricularizing Well-Being and Well-Becoming in Schools

12 Finding Meaning in Life through School Mathematics

THOMAS FALKENBERG

Searching for and experiencing meaning in life is an ongoing existential undertaking for human beings (e.g., Frankl, 1946/2006; Yalom, 1980; Wong, 2012). In many conceptions of human flourishing, meaning in life is a fundamental consideration (e.g., Ryff, 1989; Seligman, 2011). If "the concept of well-being is to capture what humans aim for when they exert their agency to live their lives one way rather than another" (Falkenberg, 2014, p, 78), then we are existentially concerned about developing and experiencing meaning in life, because meaning in life is a core component of what it means to live a flourishing life.

Some conceptualizations of human flourishing (e.g., Nussbaum, 2011; Sen 2009) are explicit about the importance of developing capabilities and having opportunities to engage these capabilities in order to be able to live a flourishing life. I subscribe to this notion (see Falkenberg, 2019) and thus to the idea that we need to *learn* to live a flourishing life. If we, as I do, consider the developing and experiencing of meaning in life a core component of what it means to live a flourishing life, then we also need to *learn* to develop and experience meaning in life. With schooling being society's main organizational structure to guide children to learn what society values, it stands to reason that schools should provide opportunities to children to develop the capabilities linked to being able to live a flourishing life. With the understanding that finding meaning in life is a component of what it means to live a flourishing life, this mandate of school education includes also the concern for students to find and experience meaning in life, as students and future adults.

In countries of the Global North, teaching and learning is primarily structured around the teaching and learning of traditional subject matters, like mathematics, natural sciences, English language arts, and social studies. That means that unless this curricular focus changes, helping students with their seeking, developing, and experiencing meaning in life will have to be undertaken primarily *as part of* the teaching and learning of traditional subject matters. This chapter contributes to an inquiry into what this could look like by inquiring into ways in which the teaching and learning of mathematics might be able to contribute to students finding meaning in life.

For this inquiry, I proceed as follows. First, I outline some general conceptual assumptions about meaning in life that frame the inquiry. Second, I identify different types of meanings that are central to the teaching and learning of mathematics in school. Third, I select one such type of meaning and illustrate how it can provide opportunities in the teaching and learning of mathematics for students to develop and experience meaning in life.

Some Conceptual Assumptions about Meaning in Life

In this section, I outline a few conceptual assumptions about meaning in life, as relevant to the purpose of this chapter. For this, I draw on chapter 6 (this volume), where I develop the conception of meaning in life within a particular framework of understanding human well-being, which I call the Well-Being and Well-Becoming Framework, WB2 Framework for short (Falkenberg, 2019). In this framework, living a meaningful life is a core component of human well-being, and accordingly, I have labelled the conception of meaning in life (MIL) in chapter 6 (this volume) with "MIL_{WB2}."

For the purpose of this chapter, it suffices to explicate two core conceptual ideas for understanding meaning in life as developed in chapter 6. The first core idea is taken from Baumeister (1991), who suggests that the human need for meaning in life can be analysed as four separate needs, namely the need for purpose, the need for values, the need for efficacy, and the need for self-worth. He suggests that we can derive meaning in life from each.

The second core conceptual idea, which is in one form or another found in the literature on meaning in life, is that meaning in life involves two distinct aspects of human functioning: understanding and being motivated. Finding meaning in life means that we understand or comprehend our life, for instance, we understand what our life options are and how to efficaciously pursue some of these options. However, finding meaning in life means not just that we understand but also that we are motivated to pursue those options to efficaciously engage our abilities in our pursuits. As illustrated in this example, the distinction between an understanding and a motivational aspect of meaning in life applies to each of the four needs of purpose, values, efficacy, and

Table 12.1.

	MIL_{WB2} as understanding	MIL_{WB2} as motivational
purpose	... I understand how my present life experiences are linked to my past life experiences and how they provide me with specific options of living my life in the immediate and long-term future.	... I am motivated to live my life along specific immediate, mid- and long-term future life options available to me.
values	... I understand what values I subscribe to and how they guide and justify how I live my life in pursuit of my life's purpose.	... I am motivated to live my life in accordance with the values I subscribe to in pursuit of my life's purpose.
efficacy	... I understand what capabilities are required to live my life toward its purpose in accordance with the value system I subscribe to.	... I am motivated to develop, engage, and get better with capabilities required to live my life toward its purpose in accordance with the value system I subscribe to.
self-worth	... I understand that and how my finding meaning through purpose, justified by a value system I subscribe to and made possible for me to actually pursue by my efficacy, provides me with a sense of self-worth.	... I am motivated through a sense of self-worth to live my life toward its purpose in accordance with the value system I subscribe to.

Note: Table 12.1 is taken from chapter 6 (this volume).

self-worth, creating the eight conceptual components of what it means to have meaning in life (within the WB2-Framework), that is, MIL_{WB2}, as presented in table 12.1.

Humans are meaning-making beings (see chapter 6, this volume). When a mathematics teacher speaks of polyhedrons or has students engage in particular activities to develop mathematical competencies, the students need to make sense (grasp the meaning) of mathematical objects and processes, like polyhedrons and multiplication of decimal numbers, as well as the meaning of activities they are asked to engage in in the learning of mathematics, like the representation of number relationships in a bar graph. I suggest that it is this range of meanings, relevant in the teaching and learning of mathematics, that can serve as the means through which mathematics learners can be provided with opportunities to develop and experience MIL_{WB2} (table 12.1). The next section presents in a systematic structure such a range of meanings.

Meanings in the Teaching and Learning of School Mathematics

Howson (2005) identifies a number of meanings that are relevant in the teaching and learning of school mathematics. Expanding on his conceptual distinctions, I want to suggest a range of meanings that are relevant in the teaching and learning of mathematics in schools (see table 12.2).

Table 12.2 shows how these meanings can be structured. Generally, the meanings fall into two groups: those that focus on what makes up the subject matter, that is, mathematics, and those that focus on aspects of what it means to study mathematics. In table 12.2, these groups of meanings are labelled *subject-focused meanings* and *meanings focused on studying mathematics*, respectively.

The four subject-focused meanings (M1a, b, c, d; see table 12.2) relate to each other as follows. It is through mathematical activities that people engage with the mathematical objects, concepts, and processes; at the same time, mathematical objects, concepts, and processes are defined through the way they allow for certain ways of engagement. Competencies required for competent engagement in mathematical activities that engage mathematical objects, concepts, and processes define what it means to be mathematically literate. The structure created through the two preceding relationships defines the structure of the discipline of mathematics.

The four meanings focused on studying mathematics (M2a, b, and M3a, b) fall into two subcategories, which are a reflection of the ambiguity of *meaning* in the English language. If something has meaning for a person, then this could refer to the person *understanding* that something or it could refer to the something having *relevance* to the person; for instance, it might have relevance to the person's life as a teacher. Studying mathematics is a type of human activity and as such, both types of meaning are relevant: meanings referencing cognitive aspects of making sense of that activity (M2a, b) and meanings referencing the motivational (relevance) aspect of engaging in that activity (M3a, b). Both types of meaning complement each other: understanding makes relevance possible and relevance motivates understanding. My understanding of what it means to study mathematics (M2a) makes studying mathematics (intrinsically) relevant to me (M3a), and the relevance of studying mathematics to me motivates me to (further) understand what it means to study mathematics. Understanding mathematics learning activities as I study mathematics (M2b) makes the mathematical object, concepts, and processes involved in the learning activities relevant to me (M3b).

Table 12.2. The different meanings of *meaning* for a student learning mathematics in school

Meaning refers to...		
subject-focused meanings		M1a: ... the meanings of mathematics as a discipline
		M1b: ... the meanings of mathematical objects, concepts, and processes
		M1c: ... the meanings of mathematical activities
		M1d: ... what it means to be mathematically literate
meanings focused on studying mathematics	understanding	M2a: ... what it means to study mathematics
		M2b: ... the meanings of mathematics learning activities
	relevance/ significance	M3a: ... the relevance of studying mathematics
		M3b: ... the relevance of mathematical objects/ concepts

Even though all eight meanings listed in table 12.2 play a role in students' engagement with school mathematics, students might not have explicit knowledge of what that meaning is. Nevertheless, these meanings are not just always present in students' engagement with school mathematics, they also provide constraints and affordances (in a systems-theoretical sense; see chapter 11, this volume) for how students engage in the learning of mathematics. The following draws on two meanings (M1a and M2a) to provide illustrative examples for such constraints and affordances.

If the discipline of mathematics means to a student a set of facts about abstract entities that are established by professional mathematicians, then learning mathematics means for the student to understand *their* meaning of the objects and *their* way of engaging with these objects, and there is only one right way, namely *their* way. The student's engagement with mathematics is constrained by those meanings and those ways of engagement. On the other hand, if the discipline of mathematics means for a student a human endeavour that has historically led to quite different and incompatible ways of understanding of what mathematics is and how best to engage with it, then learning mathematics means for the student that there is not just one way of understanding mathematics or doing mathematics, and that there is a chance that the student comes up with ways of solving mathematical problems and engaging with mathematical ideas in novel ways that deviate from the ways presented in the textbook and known to the teacher.

Let's assume that learning mathematics means for me the following: to study examples of a particular type of mathematical problem together with a particular way of solving it, and then to apply this process to a problem of the same type in order to get the already established answer to the problem. Based on this meaning of what it means for me to study mathematics, I expect in my learning of mathematics to see good enough examples that I can easily abstract a rule from, and I expect that the new problems I am facing are similar enough that I have a reasonable chance of getting the already established answer to the problem. That means that it can frustrate my learning of mathematics if I face a non-routine mathematical problem, that is, a problem for which no routine way of solving it is available to me. On the other hand, if studying mathematics means for me solving non-routine problems, the solution for which has meaning to my life at some level, then I expect that I might have to productively struggle as I tackle the problem – an experience that is real all too often when we engage with mathematical problems in our life outside of school.

What understanding students develop for each of the eight meanings relevant in the teaching and learning of mathematics in school (Table 12.2) does matter greatly to students' lives (and thus they need to matter to teachers of mathematics), because of the way in which these meanings can and do impact how the teaching and learning of mathematics can contribute to the development and experience of meaning in life, that is, to what matters to students in their lives, as students and later as adults. The rest of this chapter develops this argument further.

On the Meaning of Mathematics as a Discipline

In 1941, the American mathematicians Richard Courant and Herbert Robbins published their influential book *What Is Mathematics?*, which is still in print more than 80 years later (Courant & Robbins, 1996). The chapters of the book are dedicated to different fields of the mathematical sciences, like the number system and topology, with the mathematics content that one would typically find in a university-level textbook.

In answer to the question of *What is mathematics?* mathematician and philosopher of mathematics Reuben Hersh offers what he has called the Platonic view of mathematics:

> That standard version [of the Platonic view of mathematics] says mathematical entities exist outside space and time, outside thought and matter, in an abstract realm independent of any consciousness, individual or social. Today's mathematical Platonism descends in a clear line from the doctrine of Ideas in Plato. (Hersh, 1997, p. 9)

Hersh (1997) suggests that "Platonism ... is the most pervasive philosophy of mathematics" (p. 9). It is, however, not the only philosophy of mathematics and, thus, not the only way in which one can respond to the question of what mathematics is. An alternative that Hersh (1997) introduces and discusses is the humanistic philosophy of mathematics, which builds on "the idea of mathematics as a human creation" (p. 182).[1] The humanistic paradigm of understanding mathematics as a discipline sees mathematics as something that is done by humans, as a human endeavour.

The irony is that even Platonists like Courant and Robbins will acknowledge mathematics as a human endeavour but then not link that relationship to mathematics as a discipline. At the beginning of their book, they write:

> Mathematics as an expression of the human mind reflects the active will, the contemplative reason, and the desire for aesthetic perfection. Its basic elements are logic and intuition, analysis and construction, generality and individuality. Though different traditions may emphasize different aspects, it is only the interplay of these antithetic forces and the struggle for their synthesis that constitute the life, usefulness, and supreme value of mathematical science. (Courant & Robbins, 1996, p. xxi)

In the first few pages of their book, Courant and Robbins (1996) make the case that the history of mathematics shows that "creative minds forget dogmatic philosophical beliefs [about the nature of the mathematical objects that mathematicians are studying] whenever adherence to them would impede constructive achievement" (p. xxv). However, they then spend the rest of the over 500 pages of their book describing only what mathematicians have to say about these mathematical objects, leaving aside any connection to the constructive and sometimes controversial and divisive process itself.

The opposite can be found in *Proofs and Refutations* by the Hungarian philosopher of mathematics and science Imre Lakatos (1976), who argued, in the words of Hersh (1997), that

> mathematics, like natural science, is fallible. It too grows by criticism and correction of theories, which may always be subject to ambiguity, error, or oversight. Starting from a problem or a conjecture, there's a search for *both* proof and counter-examples. Proof explains counter-examples, counter examples [sic] undermine proof. Proof isn't a mechanical procedure that carries an unbreakable chain of truth from assumptions to conclusion. It's explanation, justification, and elaboration, which make a conjecture convincing,

while the counter-examples make it detailed and accurate. Each step of the proof is subject to criticism, which may be mere skepticism or may be a counter-example of a particular argument. (Hersh, 1997, pp. 211–12)

Mathematics from this humanistic view is a disciplined way of asking questions about particular state of affairs that we are interested in, that we acknowledge as "real," and where *the process* in which we engage in to answer these questions is as much a part of the discipline as the responses to the questions.

Why should the distinction, for instance, between a formalistic (Platonic) and a humanistic philosophy of mathematics matter to school mathematics? It should matter, because "the philosophy of mathematics held by the teacher can't help but affect her teaching" (Hersh, 1997, p. 238), a dynamic which is empirically supported through a number of studies, although the relationship between teachers' types of beliefs about mathematics as a discipline is not linearly linked to teachers' ways of teaching mathematics (see, for instance, Hoz & Weizman, 2008; Thompson, 1984). I will call a comprehensive set of assumptions about the teaching and learning of mathematics a *philosophy of mathematics education* (Ernest, 1991; Hersh, 1997). This can then be expressed as follows: How one understands mathematics as a discipline impacts one's philosophy of mathematics education, which in turn impacts how one teaches mathematics. But the impact works also the other way around: When we teach mathematics in a particular way, we teach mathematics as a particular discipline, that is, with a particular philosophy of mathematics, whether we are aware of it or not.

How a teacher teaches mathematics impacts the experiences that students have in learning mathematics, which in turn impacts the way these experiences provide an opportunity for students to develop and experience meaning in life. This means that what mathematics as a discipline means to the teacher *and* to the student impacts how the teaching and learning of mathematics can contribute to students finding meaning in life through the learning of mathematics. When we teach mathematics, we do so using particular pedagogical approaches. The task of this chapter can be reformulated as follows: How might the meaning that we give to mathematics as a discipline in our teaching of mathematics help students develop meaning in life (MIL_{WB2}, to be more precise), and what kind of pedagogical approach might we adopt?

In the next section, I respond to this question by illustrating how a humanistic approach to the teaching of mathematics – suggesting a humanistic philosophy of mathematics – can provide a foundation for helping students develop and experience meaning in life.

Teaching and Learning Mathematics for MIL$_{WB2}$: Focusing on Mathematics as a Discipline

In the introduction to this chapter, I suggested that meaning in life is not something like a treasure that we unearth, but is rather something that we develop as we interact with the world around us, and that there is an aspect of *learning* involved, as in any such interaction. I suggested that if schools want to contribute to students developing meaning in life, MIL$_{WB2}$ to be more precise, they would need to do so through their teaching of core subject areas, like mathematics. For mathematics education to contribute to students developing and experiencing meaning in life, I suggested, teachers of mathematics can draw on the meanings that are already linked to the teaching and learning of mathematics (see table 12.2). In this section, I present how that might be done, focusing on the meaning of mathematics as a discipline.

Before I do so, however, I need to clarify the following. Developing meaning in life seems to be quite different from learning a subject matter. The latter involves processes that are much more predictable in their outcomes than the former and thus are much easier to plan. For instance, if we engage students long enough in meaningful activities that involve the solving of particular mathematical problems, they will generally develop the capability of solving these types of problems. However, in whatever meaningful activities we engage students in around helping them develop meaning in life, there might be nothing that they get out of such engagement for their meaning in life. On the other hand, a one-time conversation with a classmate about that classmate's interest in playing chess might spark a student's interest in learning chess, leading to a lifelong love of playing chess, and giving the student purpose, value, efficacy, and self-worth in their life, that is, meaning in their life. This means that we have to understand that the way in which the teaching and learning of a subject, like mathematics, can contribute to helping students develop meaning in life is more about facilitating exposure to and awareness of opportunities for developing purpose, value, efficacy, and self-worth in their life in the learning of the subject than it is about developing learning outcomes, designing learning activities, and assessing the achievement of learning outcomes. While there are clearly many examples of students who have developed meaning in life through their experiences with mathematics education – those working as mathematicians or doing research in mathematical physics might be examples – there are many more who do the opposite, namely developing no or negligible understanding of the meanings listed in Table 12.2, finding no or negligible relevance in the activities in the mathematics classroom, turning their back on mathematical thinking when the option is available, and developing their own meaning in life in anything but mathematical thinking.

In light of this understanding, what follows considers approaches to teaching mathematics that are linked to particular ways of understanding the discipline that *make it more likely* that more students – beyond those already so inclined – would develop meaning in life through learning mathematics. Whether what I suggest here is indeed achieving the intended increase in likelihood is an empirical question that requires empirical investigations; therefore I will have to provide plausibility arguments in this chapter.

The next subsection articulates the specific task in light of the MIL_{WB2} framework used. Then I provide a concrete example of humanizing mathematics education that exemplifies a humanistic philosophy of mathematics as well as a pedagogy that reflects a humanistic understanding of the discipline of mathematics. Using this example, I then provide a plausibility argument for how such humanizing mathematics education indeed can contribute to students developing and experiencing MIL_{WB2}.

Linking Meaning of Mathematics as a Discipline to the Four MIL_{WB2} Needs

As outlined above, the four MIL_{WB2} needs are the needs for purpose, values, efficacy, and self-worth. For the meaning that mathematics as a discipline has for a student to contribute to developing and experiencing MIL_{WB2} for the student, that meaning has to

- provide purpose to the student's life; and/or
- contribute to a value system that allows the student to justify actions and make decisions they take in living their lives toward that purpose; and/or
- contribute to defining capabilities that they need to engage in these justified actions and to make these decisions; and/or
- provide a basis for their sense of self-worth.

That means that the question of the disciplinary status of mathematics has to be moved from the meta-mathematical level, where it is discussed by specialists, to include "everyday people," like the students we teach in our schools. In order to contribute to the development of purpose, values, efficacy, and self-worth in students' lives, what mathematics is as a discipline has to matter to students.

The Case of Humanizing Mathematics Education

The Canadian educational theorist Kieran Egan (1986, pp. 81–2) provides an instructive example for the ingenuity, beauty, and power of mathematical thinking as it is purposively used to tackle a problem people are invested in solving. Egan tells the made-up story of a king's counsellor who tries to address the challenge of counting the number of the king's soldiers. As the soldiers march past him one by one, the counsellor counts them using an invented algorithm that requires only a small number of pebbles and baskets, mimicking our base-ten number system. The story illustrates the power of the base-ten number system for counting and recording large numbers of objects: you only need ten digits, and by using grouping and positioning of digits, these ten digits are all that is needed to count *any* number of objects. The story also illustrates how people develop such core mathematical concepts and ideas in the face of concrete situational problems. If we compare this, for instance, with the tallying system of counting, we see the ingenuity, beauty, and power of the base-ten number system, and thus the power of mathematical thinking about patterns and general processes. The ingenuity and beauty come through its simplicity and its power comes through the fact that it solves *all* counting problems. The story makes this tangible to most of us, because the story puts the mathematical idea behind the base-ten number system in the light of a problem that mattered greatly in the context of a story most of us can easily relate to. It allows us to see the relevance of what characterizes mathematical thinking, namely abstracting from the specifics to capture and manage patterns.

Using imaginative storytelling to teach for conceptual understanding in mathematics education, as Egan (1986) suggests in his book and illustrates through the referenced story, is a way of teaching that is grounded in a humanistic philosophy of mathematics education: It shows mathematics as a way *people* think to solve problems that matter in *people's* lives – and what matters can be the solving of abstract problems. In other words, it shows mathematics as a human endeavour that is guided by human needs and purpose. Other proposals for the teaching and learning of mathematics in school that build on a humanistic philosophy of mathematics education include approaches that consider mathematics education as citizenship education (e.g., Jacobsen & Mistele, 2011; Simmt, 2001; Skovsmose & Valero, 2001), as value and moral education (e.g., Bishop, 2012; Falkenberg & Noyes, 2010), as well as those approaches to mathematics education that emphasize the importance of attitude and affect in mathematics education (e.g., Goldin, 2014; Grootenboer & Marshman, 2016; McLeod, 1992).

What all these humanistic philosophies of mathematics education have in common is that they suggest to students a humanistic philosophy of mathematics. In Egan's approach of using imaginative stories to teach mathematical concepts, students come to see mathematics as a way of thinking that humans engage in with all that makes them human, namely with interest invested in certain types of problems rather than other types, in having impact on others for a variety of reasons, in making helpful and less helpful as well as good and bad decisions, and in striving after success that is internally or externally defined. Egan's story approach to the teaching and learning of mathematics illustrates how mathematics teaching that is grounded in a humanistic philosophy of mathematics education can provide students with experiences that suggest to them a view of mathematics as a discipline akin to a humanistic philosophy of mathematics.

With reference to Egan's humanistic approach to the teaching and learning of mathematics, I now illustrate how this view of mathematics as a discipline can contribute to addressing the four needs for meaning identified in the MIL_{WB2} framework: the needs for purpose, values, self-efficacy, and self-worth. To this end, I will first restate each of these needs in light of the task to explain how an understanding of mathematics as a discipline (here: a discipline built upon a humanistic philosophy of mathematics) provides ways for students to address these four integrated needs and, thus, to derive meaning in life.

Developing a humanistic philosophy of mathematics can support addressing a student's *need for purpose* if the student understands how a short-term and long-term engagement with mathematics provides present and future life options, and the student is motivated to pursue such options. Egan's example illustrates how a student who experiences humanistic mathematics might develop purpose in life in engaging with mathematics such understood, because mathematics such understood is a way of dealing with the world and problems we encounter in the world, and mathematical thinking helps us do so in ingenious, beautiful, and powerful ways. Experiencing mathematics as a human endeavour allows students to link mathematical thinking to their own life in ways that contribute to their life's purpose. For instance, it may contribute to developing meaning in working as an engineer, because it allows one to engage mathematical thinking to solve engineering problems in an ingenious, beautiful, and/or powerful way. For a professional, it can also be the way in which one engages in one's job that provides purpose to their life.

Developing a humanistic philosophy of mathematics can support addressing a student's *need for values* if the student understands what value system is needed to justify a life in which engaging with humanistic mathematics is a worthwhile life option for the present and future, and the student is motivated to live their life in accordance with these values. The story – used as part of "teaching mathematics humanistically" (Brown, 1996, p. 1308) – suggests to students that mathematics is a discipline that helps us cope with problems we face as we live our life purposefully, and as such, learning mathematics humanistically may help us value mathematics as a life tool. This goes beyond the typically mentioned examples of the usefulness of simple mathematical skills like being able to calculate percentages to give a proper tip at a restaurant or to use ratios to compare prices of various items we intend to buy in a store. Rather, it is about valuing mathematics as a powerful tool to address all kinds of life problems that we pursue with purpose and value, including purely mathematical problems that mathematics has struggled with over generations (see, for instance, Stewart, 1987). For someone for whom these kinds of problems are meaningful, mathematics as a discipline provides a system of values that can contribute to that person's meaning in life.

Developing a humanistic philosophy of mathematics can support addressing a student's *need for efficacy* if the student understands what capabilities are required for making their engagement with humanistic mathematics a present and future life option, and the student is motivated to develop, engage, and get better with these capabilities. Egan's story talks about an "ingenious counsellor" (Egan, 1986), and stories about the life of mathematical geniuses like Gauss and Ramanujan (see, for instance, Smith 1996) enforce the notion that mathematics is a discipline that requires inborn talent that you either have or don't have. For our purposes, this notion ignores two important points. First, it ignores that outstanding people in a field, including in mathematics and theoretical physics, require years and years of engagement with relevant problems to develop what to the limited view of the outside world looks like nature-given genius. Second, for mathematics as a discipline to contribute to someone's efficacy as an aspect of their meaning in life, it is not at all needed that the person is "a genius" in mathematics. One just has to be efficacious enough in one's own eyes in one's engagement with mathematics to find meaning in life through such efficacy. The implications for mathematics education for MIL_{WB2} are twofold. First, that helping students understand the importance of mathematical efficacy relies on helping students understand *efficacy* in this context as *relative to the respective* values and purpose they connect with mathematics as a discipline. Second, that linking the teaching and learning of mathematics to MIL_{WB2} provides an opportunity to help students understand the importance of mathematical efficacy for the way they meaningfully live their lives. For instance, if a student understands that mathematics as a discipline provides us with such powerful tools for addressing problems *because* it is a discipline that abstracts from the concrete and focuses on patterns and structures rather than on specifics, then it is much more motivating for the student to develop efficacy in abstract thinking and thinking about patterns.

Developing a humanistic philosophy of mathematics can support addressing a student's *need for self-worth* if the student understands that engaging competently and in line with the corresponding value system with humanistic mathematics provides them with a sense of self-worth, and if the student is motivated through this sense of self-worth to pursue the present and future life options provided through engaging competently with humanistic mathematics in accordance with the corresponding value system. The king's counsellor in Egan's story has good reasons for having a sense of self-worth as someone who solved in a very ingenious way a problem that mattered to all involved. Such self-worth can be an aspect of the counsellor's meaning in life (MIL_{WB2}, more precisely) as characterized above. In the context of teaching and learning of mathematics in school, this aspect of the concept of MIL_{WB2} would mean the following: students can get a sense of self-worth from which they draw meaning in their life as they engage efficaciously with problems that they value as worthwhile mathematical problems in light of their understanding of mathematics as a humanistic discipline.

Conclusion: MIL_{WB2}-Based Mathematics Education in Schools

Drawing on what has been presented in this chapter, what can I say about MIL_{WB2}-based mathematics education in schools? It is mathematics education that frames educational experiences around potential contributions to students' MIL_{WB2}. In order to make such contributions, it draws on meanings of elements of mathematics education (table 12.2). The previous section has illustrated how a particular meaning given to mathematics as a discipline, that is, a humanistic philosophy of mathematics, in conjunction with an aligned philosophy of mathematics education, encourages experiences in the learning of mathematics that can help students develop the understandings and motivations needed to address the four needs that are of building blocks of MIL_{WB2}: need for purpose, need for values, need for efficacy, and need for self-worth.

NOTE

1 For a discussion of other philosophies of mathematics, such as formalism and intuitionism, see Ernest (1991) and Hersh (1997).

REFERENCES

Baumeister, R.F. (1991). *Meanings of life*. Guilford Press.

Bishop, A.J. (2012). From culture to well-being: A partial story of values in mathematics education. *ZDM Mathematics Education, 44*, 3–8. https://doi.org/10.1007/s11858-011-0379-5

Brown, S.I. (1996). Towards humanistic mathematics. In Allan J. Bishop et al. (Eds.), *International handbook of mathematics education* (2 vols., pp. 1289–321). Kluwer.

Courant, R., & Robbins, H. (1996). *What is mathematics? An elementary approach to ideas and methods*. Oxford University Press.

Egan, K. (1986). *Teaching as story telling: An alternative approach to teaching and curriculum in the elementary school*. The Althouse Press.

Ernest, P. (1991). *The philosophy of mathematics education*. The Falmer Press.

Falkenberg, T. (2014). Making sense of Western approaches to well-being for an educational context. In F. Deer, T. Falkenberg, B. McMillan, & L. Sims (Eds.), *Sustainable well-being: Concepts, issues, and educational practices* (pp. 77–94). ESWB Press. www.ESWB-Press.org

– (2019). *Framing human well-being and well-becoming: An integrated systems approach*. http://wellbeinginschools.ca/paper-series/

Falkenberg, T., & Noyes, A. (2010). Conditions for linking school mathematics and moral education: A case study. *Teaching and Teacher Education, 26*(4), 949–56. https://doi.org/10.1016/j.tate.2009.10.036

Frankl, V.E. (2006). *Man's search for meaning* (I. Lasch, Trans.). Beacon Press. (Original published 1946)

Goldin, G.A. (2014). Perspectives on emotion in mathematical engagement, learning, and problem solving. In R. Pekrun & L. Linnenbring-Garcia (2014). *International handbook of emotions in education* (p. 391–414). Routledge.

Grootenboer, P., & Marshman, M. (2016). *Mathematics, affect, and learning: Middle school students' beliefs and attitudes about mathematics education*. Springer.

Hersh, R. (1997). *What is mathematics, really?* Oxford University Press.

Howson, G. (2005). "Meaning" and school mathematics. In J. Kilpatrick, C. Hoyles, & O. Skovsmose (Eds.), *Meaning in mathematics education* (pp. 17–38). Springer.

Hoz, R., & Weizman, G. (2008). A revised theorization of the relationship between teachers' conceptions of mathematics and its teaching. *International Journal of Mathematics Education in Science and Technology, 39*(7), 905–24. https://doi.org/10.1080/00207390802136602

Jacobsen. L.J., & Mistele, J. (2011). Mathematics education: What is the point? In B. Atweh, M. Graven, W. Secada, & P. Valero (Eds.), *Mapping equity and quality in mathematics education* (pp. 555–68). Springer.

Lakatos, I. (1976). *Proofs and refutations: The logic of mathematical discovery*. Cambridge University Press.

McLeod, D.B. (1992). Research on affect in mathematics education: A reconceptualisation. In D.A. Grouws (Ed.), *Handbook of research on mathematics teaching and learning* (pp. 575–96). National Council of Teachers of Mathematics.

Nussbaum, M.C. (2011). *Creating capabilities: The human development approach*. Harvard University Press.

Ryff, C.D. (1989). Happiness is everything, or is it? Explorations on the meaning of psychological well-being. *Journal of Personality and Social Psychology, 57*(6), 1069–81. https://doi.org/10.1037/0022-3514.57.6.1069

Seligman, M.E.P. (2011). *Flourishing: A visionary new understanding of happiness and well-being*. Free Press.

Sen, A. (2009). *The idea of justice*. Harvard University Press.

Simmt, E. (2001). Citizenship education in the context of school mathematics. *Canadian Social Studies Journal, 35* (3). https://canadian-social-studies-journal.educ.ualberta.ca/content/articles-2000-2010#ARcitizenship_education23

Skovsmose, O., & Valero, P. (2001). Breaking political neutrality: The critical engagement of mathematics education with democracy. In Bill Atweh, H. Forgasz, & B. Nebres (Eds.), *Sociocultural research on mathematics education* (pp. 37–55). Lawrence Erlbaum.

Smith, S.M. (1996). *Agnesi to Zeno: Over 100 vignettes from the history of math*. Key Curriculum Press.

Stewart, I. (1987). *The problems of mathematics*. Oxford University Press.

Thompson, A.G. (1984). The relationship of teachers' conceptions of mathematics and mathematics teaching to instructional practice. *Educational Studies in Mathematics, 15*, 105–27. https://doi.org/10.1007/BF00305892

Wong, P.T.P. (Ed.). (2012). *The human quest for meaning: Theories, research, and applications* (2nd ed.). Routledge.

Yalom, I.D. (1980). *Existential psychotherapy*. Basic Books.

13 Making Meaning of Science Curriculum through Ecojustice and Place-Based Education: Looking through the Lens of Well-Being and Well-Becoming

MICHAEL LINK

What if our students, well trained to ask critical questions, ask us this question? "So, you say that today's world everywhere is constructed by the modern scientific knowledge and technologies. But look how terrible and terribly troubled the world is today. You have been in fact telling us that according to many scientists, our world may not continue, cannot be sustained, beyond the next few decades, at the rate we humans are consuming and destroying the world. If modern science and technology is what constructed such a world, then why should we continue to study them?" What would be our answer?

(Beavington & Bai, 2017, p. 473)

In the face of mass extinction and climate collapse, the youth-led global environmental movement has adopted a host of unifying ideas, including Einstein's familiar maxim, "Problems cannot be solved with the same mindset that created them." Modern science is dominated by a mindset that regards the world as existing primarily for humans, sometimes referred to as *anthropocentrism*. Harari (2016) has suggested that while *Homo sapiens* has elevated itself to a godlike status, it has been most cruel and merciless in the treatment of its animal subjects. Hierarchal thinking governs human interactions, including human-over-human dynamics, to a large extent. Just as the lives of non-human animals are devalued, so too – with regard to nationality, race, gender, sexuality, and social class – are some human lives valued more than others. What the human-over-human and human-over-nature mode of thinking have in common is a sense of disconnection and imposed alienation.

If mass extinction and climate collapse are to be addressed, a mindset of disconnection and alienation will not suffice. Our schools have, to varying degrees, uncritically perpetuated the dominant, hierarchal way of relating to each other and to the natural world. In reference to the damaging impact of Canadian residential schools on Indigenous peoples and culture, Murray Sinclair, Commissioner of the Canadian Truth and Reconciliation Commission, remarked, "Education got us into this mess, and education will get us out of this mess" (Watters, 2015). Schools can be a place where students can critically reflect on harmful societal norms and act in ethical ways that value life for their intrinsic worth, and not merely for their use to humans.

In light of the threat of extinction of up to a million species, including our own, a rapid shift to an ecologically-centred curriculum, grounded in the development of capabilities for well-being, is proposed here. People, especially young people, are driven by meaningful pursuits. What could be more meaningful than to be a part of a transition to a just and sustainable world that values well-being?

This chapter offers an approach to science curriculum design that empowers students to act toward a just and sustainable world in ways that benefit well-being. Such curricular design begins with opportunities for students to reflect and critique the mindset that "got us into this mess." In this way, students may avoid an anthropocentric approach to addressing local issues that regards and benefits only humans (or certain humans).

While there are many approaches to education, very few of them engage students in both *reflection* and *action* to tackle ecological and social injustice. Drawing from the fields of place-based and ecojustice education, I argue science curriculum may be taught in a meaningful way by providing opportunities for students to become actively involved in reflecting on the roots of eco-social dysfunction and then addressing or communicating local problems.

But why should humans be concerned with ecological and social injustice and how would such a concern be linked to living well? To address this question, I draw from an ethical conception called *sustainable well-being*, under the umbrella of the Well-Being and Well-Becoming (WB2) Framework (Falkenberg, 2019, 2020). Sustainable well-being describes what it means for a person to live in harmony within the human community and the ecological world (of which humans are embedded). To live sustainably we need to be concerned for the well-being of all humans of the present and future generations at the centre of our life ethic. Sustainable living also means cultivating a life ethic that is based on respect for the natural world. To live sustainably *well* involves a reorientation that is grounded in the reality of living well and living in a just and ethical manner. In other words, to live sustainably well means aligning what we think we need to live well within the realm of what allows for an ecologically sound and equitable present and future world. Sustainable well-being does not mean adopting a puritanical attitude of self-sacrifice and misery, but rather orienting one's agency to choose experiences and dispositions that contribute to one's well-being without diminishing the that of other present and future beings or ecological systems.

The following example highlights the importance of social connection for our well-being. Let's say you are a person with more money than you know what to do with. Every year, you and all of your friends fly to Las Vegas for a get-together. You drink, eat, gamble, and socialize. Through the lens of sustainable well-being, you recognize that the social connection is what contributes most to your well-being. If you went alone to Las Vegas, the experience would be greatly diminished. You also recognize the ecological impact of you and all of your friends flying on a plane, as well as the cost to present and future generations. So what do you do? Rather than deprive yourself of what it means to live well, in this case having social connections, you change the once-a-year social gathering in a far-flung place to a once-a-week party in your backyard. You drink, eat, gamble (play poker), and socialize. In this example, sustainable well-being involves the ethical act of recognizing both what it means to live well and what experiences are ecologically sound.

I argue that education's primary purpose should be to provide students with the motivation and opportunity to live a good and just life, for themselves, for others, and for the ecological systems that sustain all life. In this chapter let's consider approaches to ecological and social justice education through the lens of sustainable well-being and the development of capabilities to live sustainably well, specifically through the WB2-Framework. Looking at two pedagogical approaches, place-based and ecojustice education, we explore the question: How might students be provided opportunities to develop the types of capabilities to live in a way that contributes to social and ecological well-being?

The pages that follow will describe an approach that offers students an opportunity to develop capabilities to meaningfully engage with ecological and social issues not only by learning about them, and reflecting on the values that inform them, but also by working toward solutions (Martusewicz et al., 2020; Sobel, 1996). By engaging students in action that is meaningful in order to improve our world (at however small a scale), they may develop capabilities that in turn will impact their well-being.

The Two Elephants in the Room: Ecological and Social Injustice

Ecological Injustice

While the COVID-19 pandemic has been and is a serious threat to many, one that may last well into the current decade (Kissler et al., 2020), and has the potential for resurgence in additional waves (Xu & Li, 2020),

COVID-19 does not represent a lasting existential threat to humans and other countless species. The issues of climate crisis and mass extinction, however, are interconnected long-term existential problems (Díaz, 2019; Gills & Morgan, 2019). The United Nations' Intergovernmental Science-Policy Platform on Biodiversity and Ecosystem Services (IPBES) released a report that identified approximately one million animal and plant species currently threatened with extinction (Bongaarts, 2019). Many of the species identified are predicted to become extinct within decades. This amounts to the greatest mass extinction in human history – a critical issue that must be addressed.

Social Injustice

During the spring of 2020, the headlines were dominated by stories of COVID-19. That all changed on 25 May, when George Floyd, having been arrested for allegedly passing a counterfeit $20 bill at a Minneapolis grocery store, was brutally killed by a police officer (Furber et al., 2020). A video recording showed the police officer kneeling on Floyd's neck for nearly eight minutes (Bennett et al., 2020). Floyd's death sparked global protests against racism, the use of excessive force by police against Black people, and lack of police accountability.

As with other systemic forms of discrimination, racism has a profound impact across all institutions, including education. While the roots of discrimination and oppression are complex and have a long history, it has been argued that the paradigm of discrimination and oppression is based on attempts to maintain power structures (Kreisberg, 1992). Rather than a participatory "power-with" paradigm, there exists across our institutions a widespread "power-over" ideology. This power-over paradigm leads to behaviours of social injustice and abuse. Some have argued that Western civilization is dominated by a culture of abuse (e.g., Jensen, 2000). The abuse and injustices perpetuated by those with power follow a pattern of domination of human-over-human, as well as human-over-nature. This pattern of control and supremacy may be observed in human-to-"lesser"-human and human-to-nature perceptions of what sociologists and ecopsychologists refer to as "the other," that is, those beings and matter that are perceived by the dominant group as being separate from and of less inherent value than the dominant group or its members (Kahn, 2010). Just as ideas about race and gender are socially constructed, so too are perceptions that put humans above, and disconnected from, the life systems in which they are embedded. This hierarchal way of thinking and behaving in the world is at the root of gender, racial, and other forms of social discrimination.

In the same way, this power-over mindset is linked to a separation from nature, resulting in behaviours that lead to, for example, widespread indifference in the face of mass extinction (IPBES, 2019).

Scientists warn of an existential crisis in which our future will be drastically diminished if action to curb emissions is not taken. Our detached relationship with our fellow humans and other forms of life and matter is at the heart of the current crisis. As discussed, social inequity is born of the same hierarchal thinking that perpetuates the deeply engrained patterns of perception in which non-human life and matter are ranked as inferior. The value of people is defined by socially constructed ideas about race, gender, class, sexuality, and other attributes, and non-human life and matter are defined by their aesthetic or material utility. This way of thinking is at the core of the social and ecological injustices that exist today and it is thinking that needs to be challenged within an educational setting. Hierarchal thinking, in all of its forms, needs to be examined, reflected upon, critiqued, and challenged.

Education plays a critical role in engaging the current generation of students to undertake the massive cultural and structural change that is urgently needed. It has been argued that an ethical mandate of schools should be to prepare students for the future as engaged citizens (Westheimer & Kahne, 2004). Ecological approaches to curriculum design and teaching, discussed below, will be of interest to educators and scholars pursuing such change. In the following section, place-based and ecojustice education will be framed to address ecological and social injustices through a well-being lens. We begin by considering a particular approach to well-being in schools: the WB2-Framework.

Well-Being and Purpose: The Well-Being and Well-Becoming (WB2) Framework

The following section outlines the WB2-Framework approach to conceptualizing human well-being and well-becoming (Falkenberg, 2019)[1] and how well-being through purpose-driven curricular design may be fostered in a school setting. The WB2-Framework holds that human needs must be met in order for humans to live a life of well-being. Humans are also constantly "becoming," involved in a continual interaction between with their environments and each other (p. 13). Further, the dynamic aspect of well-being and well-becoming is "integral to understanding the quality of a person's present state (well-being)" (p. 5). Succinctly put, "*well-becoming* expresses the dynamic aspect of well-being and *well-being* expresses the momentary state of well-becoming" (p. 14).

In the WB2-Framework, human well-being develops as a property of striving to have experiences, and dispositions for experiences, including:

1. having agentic capabilities linked to human needs;
2. experiencing situational opportunities to engage one's agentic capabilities in relevant life domains;
3. enjoying life;
4. living a meaningful life;
5. experiencing personal and communal connections that contribute to one's well-being. (Falkenberg, 2019, pp. 15–16)

When humans exert their agency to live their lives in a certain way, they do it in order to have the kinds of experiences and dispositions represented by these five components. Considering the nature of this chapter, the first and fourth component will be the focus of what follows.

Frankfurt (1971/1988, p. 12) proposes that what differentiates humans from other animals is the ability to have *second-order desires*, namely desires to have certain desires. In the WB2-Framework, second-order desires arise as desires to develop certain capabilities that allow us to fulfil our fundamental human needs and to live according to an ethic of sustainability:

> Living within an ethic of sustainable well-being means to orient our agency toward living sustainably well. The kinds of experiences and dispositions for experiences we are striving for in our effort to live well need to be *attuned to and in line with* a way of living that allows for all humans of the current and future generations to flourish (live well) and for a sustainable development of the Earth's ecosystem. (Link & Falkenberg, 2021, p. 346)

How might schools play a role to prepare students to both fulfil their fundamental human needs and live according to an ethic of sustainability and social justice? Falkenberg (2019) proposes providing educative opportunities to develop capabilities that are linked to human needs. A component of Falkenberg's (2019) WB2 conception brings together Nussbaum's (2011) capabilities development approach and the fundamental human needs model proposed by Max-Neef (1991).

Nussbaum (2011) is concerned with what opportunities are equitably available to individuals in order for them to live a life they consider worthwhile. In order to have such opportunities, people need to develop and exercise agentic capabilities. Nussbaum (2011) proposes the following as central capabilities: being able to have good health, being able to engage in critical reflection about the planning of one's life, being able to engage in various forms of social interaction, and being able to participate effectively in political choices that govern one's life. In a school setting, it is easy to imagine how a teacher might provide opportunities to develop such capabilities, and how meaningful the development of those capabilities would be for students.

Nussbaum sees the equitable distribution of opportunities necessary to live a good life as a matter of social justice. For example, a child may have an innate curiosity to explore natural spaces (an inner feature), but no external opportunity to experience natural spaces due to conditions of poverty and lack of access (external features). In order for suitable capabilities to develop, opportunities must be available. Further, by allowing students agency over the development and enactment of capabilities, a sense of purpose and well-being may follow. Schools may play an important role in providing such meaningful opportunities for students to develop capabilities. An example of this approach, combined with Max-Neef's model, is shared below.

If capabilities are to be meaningfully developed in order to fulfil human needs, then it is necessary to identify what basic human needs are required to live well. Max-Neef (1991) offers a list of nine: subsistence, protection, affection, understanding, participation, idleness, creation, identity, and freedom. These needs are addressed in the form of "needs satisfiers." The fulfilment of any of the needs contributes to well-being, while a deficiency in any of the needs results in a "poverty" of that aspect of well-being.

Drawing on Falkenberg's synthesis of Max-Neef's fundamental human needs model and Nussbaum's capabilities approach, I have described a nature-based framework called the Capabilities-Development-With-Nature (CDWN) approach (Link, 2018). In the CDWN approach, students are provided opportunities in nature to develop and enact capabilities that have been identified as necessary to meet fundamental human needs, for example, to ask and voice questions and ideas about what they encounter. These questions are recorded by the teacher and then may form the basis for a student-led investigation. The development of the capability *to ask questions* may also lead to, or overlap with, other capabilities. As children are provided opportunities to ask questions, they are also afforded opportunities to develop the capability to explore and discuss the ideas and questions they have about nature, and to care for, appreciate, and connect with the natural world. In this way, students have meaningful opportunities to develop and enact agentic capabilities that contribute to their well-being.

Approaches to Ecological and Social Justice Education through a Well-Being Lens

In this section, two approaches to ecological and social justice education will be discussed through the lens of well-being: place-based and ecojustice education. Through these pedagogical approaches, well-being and socio-ecological justice are linked. Place-based and ecojustice education are fundamentally about the importance of relationships within social and ecological systems. Present and future generations may flourish only in relation to the health of our natural environment and the social systems in which we are embedded.

As in the CDWN approach discussed above (Link, 2018), the natural world and local community offer opportunities for students to develop needs-linked capabilities, including, for example, the capability to see oneself as part of a community of people embedded within life-giving natural systems. To live sustainably well, students require capabilities that will allow them to meet their own needs and the needs of the socio-ecological community.

The WB2-Framework (Falkenberg, 2019) offers an approach to design opportunities that contribute to a flourishing life. Ecojustice and place-based education can provide the focus for meaningful curricular initiatives, including those offering opportunities to reflect on destructive cultural assumptions and to act in the service of the local human and ecological community. Consider now ecojustice and place-based education through the lens of the WB2-Framework. From a place-based perspective, what needs-linked capabilities would you as a teacher see as appropriate for your students? Drawing from Max-Neef's model, perhaps you would select the need for understanding. A corresponding needs-linked capability might include the capacity to interview community members in order to gather perspectives and understanding, or perhaps the capability to observe and record various aspects and phenomena of nature within the wider ecosystem. As a teacher of ecojustice education, you might select the need to participate. A corresponding capability may be to voice questions and ideas, and to listen to others' questions and ideas about cultural assumptions that contribute to social and ecological injustice.

In the design of a WB2 curriculum, the needs and capabilities are determined first and the creative work of crafting opportunities to develop capabilities come second. However, for the sake of illustration, let's work backwards and draw on the examples described earlier in this chapter from ecojustice and place-based education in order to see what needs-linked capabilities each case provides.

Ecojustice Education through a Well-Being Lens

Ecojustice education looks to challenge what it means to be a citizen and what it means to be educated as a citizen. This approach argues that the purpose of education should not be limited to job preparation and economic development. Just as schools tend to perpetuate cycles of poverty, racism, misogyny, homophobia, and other forms of injustice (hooks, 1994), so too do schools tend to help "reproduce a culture and economic system whose short-term profit motive and ideology of unlimited growth have created a society that dangerously overshoots the carrying capacity of the bio-systems depended upon for life" (Martusewicz et al., 2020, p. 22).

This section describes ecojustice education, an approach to critical pedagogy that challenges the systems of injustice related to ecological destruction and social injustice (Martusewicz et al., 2020; Plumwood, 2002). The section also addresses the anthropocentric and hierarchal structure of our school system (Kahn, 2010) as well as human supremacy as a cultural construct (Lupinacci & Happel-Parkins, 2016).

ECOJUSTICE EDUCATION: AN APPROACH TO CRITICAL PEDAGOGY

Ecojustice education provides opportunities for students to critically reflect on the cultural roots of ecological breakdown and social injustice and then to take action in local projects (for a comprehensive description see Martusewicz et al., 2020). Ecojustice education is built upon the premise that humans are utterly reliant and integrated within nature. The life systems that sustain us are also inherently valuable in themselves, outside of their utility to people. Human values and behaviour should reflect an integrated view of the human within nature and the inherent worth of nature.

Building upon the work of C.A. Bowers (1997, 2001), Martusewicz et al. (2020) have developed six interconnected elements to describe ecojustice education.

1. The analysis of dominant cultural assumptions that undermine local and global ecosystems essential to life.
2. The analysis of entrenched patterns of domination that unjustly define people from racialized communities, women, people living in poverty, and other groups of humans as well as the natural world as inferior.
3. An analysis of globalization, hyper-consumption, and commodification that have led to the exploitation of the southern hemisphere.

4. The recognition of the necessary interdependent relationship of humans with the land, air, water, and other species with whom we share this planet, and the intergenerational practices and relationships among diverse groups of people.
5. An emphasis on Earth democracies: the idea that decisions should be made by the people who are most affected by them, and that these decisions must include consideration of the right of the natural world to regenerate and the well-being of future generations.
6. An approach to pedagogy and curriculum development, emphasizing cultural analysis and community-based learning, that encourages students to identify the causes, and remediate the effects, of social and ecological violence in the places in which they live. (Adapted from pp. 12–13)

Ecojustice education focuses on an understanding of local and global contexts, values and attitudes, as well as opportunities to practise skills and work toward curricular goals that include and go beyond science. Action-oriented projects that attempt to address real problems are cross-curricular in nature and experiential in practice. Ecojustice education provides students with opportunities to engage and interact with community, understand local concerns and contexts, and take part in experiences that potentially have a transformational impact on the learner and the community.

Through ecojustice education, students are actively engaged as informed citizens who strive for a world that is socially and ecologically just. Students are encouraged to reflect on the ethics of dominant attitudes and behaviours linked to our current state of social and ecological degradation. At its foundation, ecojustice education is guided by the premise that the ecological crisis is a crisis of culture. It is "a crisis in the way people have learned to think and thus behave in relation to larger life systems and toward each other" (Martusewicz et al., 2020, p. 10). Our current path can be shifted through a change in thinking about our human relationship to each other and to our place within the web of life. Such belief systems that integrate humans within the natural world exist in many cultures, most notably in the many Indigenous ways of being and perceiving the world. Teachers and students can look to the diverse cultures that have lived in a balanced existence with nature. In the following section, an example of ecojustice education is illustrated.

ECOJUSTICE EDUCATION IN ACTION

We look now to Miller and Cardamone's (2021) example of ecojustice education through an integrated science and art project with Grade 9 students. The goals of the project included building students' capabilities to:

- explore environmental issues of interest [to the students];
- care and connect to the local environment through first-hand experiences in nature;
- research and reflect on how their actions [and the perceptions of the dominant culture] can positively or negatively affect the environment; and
- take action by raising awareness and funds through the creative design of rain barrels, traditional water catchment systems to aid in water conservation. (p. 40)

The students were provided opportunities to reflect on any disconnected feelings toward the natural environment, and to reconnect, care, and design communicative art to positively impact their communities.

The Grade 9 students were invited to reflect on ecojustice issues in their neighbourhood. Watershed ecology was identified as an area of concern, and a partnership with a nature centre was forged. This collaboration led to the creation of a unit that provided opportunities for students to develop community-based art education capabilities. The example offered here focuses on an art lesson that brought together community members to collaborate and work toward improving local watershed ecology. Through local ecology research, a partnership between the school and community organizations, and ecojustice art-making, the project addressed the way rainwater, as it filters through the land, impacts the local watershed and the interconnected systems of life that are dependent on the watershed.

Students began the project by identifying, researching, and expressing concerns about the environment. Students were first given the opportunity to connect with nature by observing and drawing trees and then reflecting on their connections to trees. Students then researched ecological issues by reading newspapers and magazines, cutting out words and images, and reflecting on their findings and concerns. Students created a collage of the words and images that they collected around their tree drawings to express their concerns.

After their preparatory research and collaboration focused on watershed issues, students embarked on a project to design rain barrels. Part of the preparatory work involved researching the ancient method of collecting water to make it available for use and to reduce soil runoff from the land. A partnership with a local nature centre and a naturalist was developed in order to provide opportunities for students to deepen their understanding and connection to a local nature reserve, the greater watershed, and the impact of water collection.

> With their journals in hand, the junior high students took time to explore the land, hiking through the nature reserve. The students were tasked with finding inspiration in nature to use for decorating rain barrels through avenues of drawings, photos, notes, texture rubbings, and found objects. Our goal became to create nature-based decorations on the rain barrels to serve two ecojustice purposes. First, the barrels would be auctioned off to support the nature reserve's work, and second, the rain barrels would be eye-catching enough to continue conversations about our ecological concerns in their new homes and communities. (Miller & Cardamone, 2021, p. 43)

Once the rain barrel designs were complete, the students revisited their tree collages. At the outset of this art project, the students had been directed to fold back three inches of the bottom of the drawing paper in order to leave space for the roots. This space allowed students the opportunity to express how the project impacted them by selecting a representative word or symbol and to integrate into the roots of their creation. In this final summative assignment, students expressed "feelings of empowerment and inspiration to make positive changes with local impact" (Miller & Cardamone, 2021, p. 45).

ECOJUSTICE EDUCATION THROUGH THE LENS OF THE WB2-FRAMEWORK

As outlined above, Miller and Cardamone's (2021) example of ecojustice education provided opportunities for students to investigate "environmental issues of interest, examine how human impact is affecting the local ecosystem, care for the environment, and use artmaking [in their design of rain barrels] to educate local community members" (p. 41). In this example, the opportunities to develop and enact capabilities for well-being are written into the teacher-researcher goals for the project. The capabilities listed below are linked to the following fundamental human needs: understanding, freedom, affection, identity, participation, and creation (Max-Neef, 1991).

– Understanding and Freedom (to choose):
  • explore environmental issues of interest [to the students]
– Affection (for the natural world) and Identity:
  • care and connect to the local environment through first-hand experiences in nature

- Understanding and Identity:
  - research and reflect on how their actions (and the perceptions of the dominant culture) can positively or negatively affect the environment
- Participation and Creation:
  - take action by raising awareness and funds through the creative design of rain barrels, traditional water catchment systems to aid in water conservation. (Miller & Cardamone, 2021, p. 40)

Typically, in the design of a project with the goal of well-being and well-becoming for students and the social and ecological community, the curriculum designer (teacher), in collaboration with significant community members (e.g., parents), begins by identifying the needs and capabilities of students in their context and community. Once these needs-linked capabilities are identified, the curriculum designer's task is to create experiences that allow the students the opportunity to develop the selected capabilities. For example, in the watershed project, the capability *to connect to the local environment through first-hand experiences in nature (linked to the human need for affection and identity)* was addressed through the teacher-designed experience of connecting students with nature; students were provided the opportunity to observe and draw trees and then to reflect on their own connections to trees.

We now will look to an example from the field of place-based education.

Place-Based Education

There are many attributes that place-based and ecojustice education share. Both are concerned with providing students with opportunities to address local issues and problems. Both include an examination of the ecological, cultural, and historical aspects of the community. And both view the local community as the focal point for curricular pursuits. In the past, place-based education has shied away from "controversial" issues, such as racism or ecologically unsound business practices; however, place-based education has now emerged as a braver and more active pedagogy among scholars and practitioners alike (e.g., Malone, 2016). Place-based and ecojustice education differ in that the latter puts more emphasis on reflecting on the root causes of social and ecological injustice. While an overarching goal of place-based education is to foster stewards of nature and active citizens in the community, ecojustice education complements this goal by providing opportunities for students to critique the cultural assumptions underpinning destructive and unjust human actions and beliefs. By starting with opportunities to critique and challenge harmful cultural assumptions, the actions that students take to address local problems are less likely to perpetuate the dysfunctional thinking that initially created the problems. Students may begin by reassessing and critiquing ways of thinking tied to colonialism, for instance, those reflected in the mindset that it is unnecessary to involve the local community that "we" are attempting to "fix" because "we" have all of the answers. In this way, students dissect the cultural assumption that the perspectives and wisdom of those in the community have little value, and that we, as the learned and superior ones, will sweep in and save the day. With this understanding, students may realize the importance of engaging with community, working collectively, and, through the diverse voices, gain some understanding of the reality of a situation in all of its complexity. In a practical sense, this understanding may lead students to engage with elders, community organizations, business owners, and conservation and advocacy groups in order to reach a deeper appreciation of pertinent issues and to create a network of relationships in working toward shared goals for the community.

PLACE-BASED EDUCATION IN ACTION

Grade 6 students from a small urban elementary school in Thunder Bay, Ontario, participated in a cross-curricular daily examination of their classroom community through a Circle of Power and Respect (CPR) framework (Radbourne, 2016).

> The Circle of Power and Respect is part of Ogden School's commitment to using restorative practices to build community within the school. Based in Indigenous worldviews, restorative practice encourages the use of talking circles to build and support community ... students also investigate issues in the larger community as well as [how local issues connect to] the national and international contexts. (pp. 108–9)

One example of this connection between place-based issues and the global community was motivated by the Dhaka garment factory fire in Bangladesh on 24 November 2012. In response to this tragedy, the students investigated the root causes of sweatshops and child labour. This exploration led to the discovery of the fair trade economic model, which supports labour practices that offer a fair wage and safe working conditions. Students determined that encouraging the purchase of fair trade consumer products locally was a way in which they could address unfair labour practices globally. The project began through a student-hosted Mother's Day fair trade tea and grew to a mission to lobby the Thunder Bay city council to become a fair trade city, committed to purchasing and providing goods that could be identified as fair trade. This mission led subsequent Grade 6 classrooms at Ogden School to carry on with these projects. One class furthered the cause by requesting that the local school board consider a fair trade designation as well. Another went on to address local food security and related issues of poverty and health. It is important to consider that all of these reflective and action-oriented student-led initiatives are fundamentally cross-curricular in nature.

While not a typical example of place-based pedagogy (the local community and environment is usually the sole focus), the project described above highlights the reality of our interconnected world and the rich opportunities afforded to students as they seek to address a complex issue.

The reader may ask, What does this have to do with science? In answer to that question, this example provides a strong illustration of how various disciplines, not just in science, merge when addressing authentic problems. For example, this project involved social justice issues discussed in social studies curricula; subsequent incarnations discussed science- and physical education–related outcomes connected to health but also inequity (social studies again); the language arts curriculum is invoked in writing persuasive scripts in preparation for the rehearsal of public speaking to be delivered to city council; the arts curriculum is integrated through the design of awareness-building advertisements concerning the Mother's Day fair trade tea and the lobbying of council for fair trade city status.

PLACE-BASED EDUCATION THROUGH THE LENS OF THE WB2-FRAMEWORK

As described earlier in the chapter, Radbourne's (2016) place-based education case study saw Grade 6 students participate in a daily restorative justice practice that encouraged the use of talking circles to research, reflect, voice, and take action on issues in the school and local communities, and to also research, reflect, voice, and take action on issues that connect with local and global crises. The particular example highlighted opportunities for students to address the tragedy of the Dhaka garment factory fire, as a representation of unjust labour practices throughout the global economy. This led the students to research and reflect on causes and local solutions to this complex problem, including their lobbying city council to designate Thunder Bay a fair-trade city. The capabilities listed below are linked to fundamental human needs: freedom, understanding, and participation (Max-Neef, 1991).

Freedom

- select and explore local problems of interest (and their connections to global issues of inequity)
- brainstorm and choose ways to address issues of inequity

Understanding

- research, reflect on, and voice issues in the school and local community
- research, reflect on, and voice specific issues that connect local and global problems

Participation

- take action on issues in the school community and local community
- take action on specific issues that connect local and global problems

As with the ecojustice education example, the design of a place-based project in pursuit of a well-being and well-becoming agenda begins with the identification of the needs and related capabilities by invested community members. The educator then designs the appropriate experiences that provide opportunities to develop and enact the capabilities. For instance, the capability *to take action on specific issues that connect local and global problems* is addressed through the many steps undertaken to lobby local city council in promotion of the idea of a fair trade city designation, some of which are connected to other capabilities listed above. As with these other capabilities, the teacher-designer would need to break down the *take-action* capability into additional subcategories, such as the capabilities to:

- bring together an organizing committee of people (students, in this case) with the same interest in the topic of inequity;
- facilitate or be part of an organizing committee to plan a lobbying initiative;
- write a persuasive argument in the form of a script;
- argue a point in public; and
- contact media sources to promote awareness of the initiative and engagement with city council

There are, of course, many more capabilities that could be added to this list. Again, by way of illustration, students wishing to develop the capability *to argue a point in public* could begin by speaking in front of a small group of peers, then progressing to the whole class, an assembly of students, and finally city council. Much creative and invigorating work is involved in planning such opportunities for well-being and well-becoming.

By designing ecojustice and place-based education through the lens of the WB2-Framework, we can imagine many ways to contribute to a student's sense of purpose and well-being. We can see schools as places of possibility for cultivating meaningful opportunities that contribute to a flourishing life, as places that allow our students to live well, in balance with the natural world.

Conclusion

Meaning is a fundamental aspect of well-being. Science curriculum, as well as the mandate of schools generally, may be designed with meaning and well-being in mind. Such a design may be undertaken through the provision of opportunities to develop capabilities that contribute to well-being (Falkenberg, 2019). The fields of place-based and ecojustice education are considered here through the lens of Falkenberg's WB2-Framework. A WB2 focus leads us to:

1. a curriculum that is grounded in the context of the local community through ...
2. the provision of purpose-driven opportunities to develop capabilities that ...
3. benefit student well-being and the socio-ecological community.

By engaging in meaningful endeavours that address current environmental crisis students are empowered to contribute not only to their own well-being but also to that of their communities and the planet as a whole.

NOTE

1 See also the discussions of the WB2-Framework in chapters 5, 6, and 14 (this volume).

REFERENCES

Beavington, L., & Bai, H. (2017). *Science education in the key of gentle empiricism*. In L.A. Bryan & K. Tobin (Eds.), *13 Questions* (pp. 473–84). Peter Lang. https://www.peterlang.com/view/9781433144967/xhtml/chapter33.xhtml

Bennett, D., Lee, J., & Cahlan, S. (2020, 30 May). The death of George Floyd: What video and other records show about his final minutes. *Washington Post*. https://www.washingtonpost.com

Bongaarts, J. (2019). [Review of *IPBES, 2019. Summary for policymakers of the global assessment report on biodiversity and ecosystem services of the Intergovernmental Science-Policy Platform on Biodiversity and Ecosystem Services*]. *Population and Development Review*, 45(3), 680–1. https://doi.org/10.1111/padr.12283

Bowers, C. (1997). *The culture of denial: Why the environmental movement needs a strategy for reforming universities and public schools*. State University of New York Press.

– (2001). *Educating for eco-justice and community*. University of Georgia Press.

Díaz, S., Settele, J., Brondizio, E., Ngo, H., Agard, J., Arneth, A., Balvanera, P., Brauman, K., Butchart, S., Chan, K., Garibaldi, L., Ichii, K., Liu, J., Subramanian, S., Midgley, G., Miloslavich, P., Molnár, Z., Obura, D., Pfaff, A., … Zayas, C. (2019). Pervasive human-driven decline of life on Earth points to the need for transformative change. *Science*, 366(6471). https://doi.org/10.1126/science.aax3100

Falkenberg, T. (2019). *Framing human well-being and well-becoming: An integrated systems approach*. http://wellbeinginschools.ca/paper-series/

– (2020). The ethics of sustainable well-being and well-becoming: A systems approach to virtue ethics. In H. Bai, D. Chang, & C. Scott. (Eds.), *Eco-virtues: Living well in the Anthropocene* (pp. 157–77). University of Regina Press.

Frankfurt, H.G. (1988). Freedom of the will and the concept of a person. In H.G. Frankfurt, *The importance of what we care about: Philosophical essays* (pp. 11–25). Cambridge University Press. (Original work published 1971)

Furber, M., Burch, Aurdras, B., & Robles, F. (2020, May 29). George Floyd worked with officer charged in his death. *New York Times*. http://www.nytimes.com

Gills, B., & Morgan, J. (2019). Global climate emergency: After COP24, climate science, urgency, and the threat to humanity. *Globalizations*, 1–18. https://doi.org/10.1080/14747731.2019.1669915

Harari, Y.N. (2016). *Homo deus: A brief history of tomorrow*. Joosr.

hooks, b. (1994). *Teaching to transgress: Education as the practice of freedom*. Routledge.

Intergovernmental Science-Policy Platform on Biodiversity and Ecosystem Services (IPBES). (2019). *Summary for policymakers of the global assessment report on biodiversity and ecosystem services of the Intergovernmental Science-Policy Platform on Biodiversity and Ecosystem Services* (S. Díaz et al., Eds.). IPBES Secretariat. https://ipbes.net/sites/default/files/2020-02/ipbesglobalassessmentreportsummaryforpolicymakersen.pdf

Jensen, D. (2000). *A language older than words*. Context Books.

Kahn, R. (2010). *Critical pedagogy, ecoliteracy, & planetary crisis: The ecopedagogy movement*. Peter Lang.

Kissler, S.M., Tedijanto, C., Goldstein, E., Grad, Y.H., & Lipsitch, M. (2020). Projecting the transmission dynamics of SARS-CoV-2 through the postpandemic period. *Science*, 368(6493), 860–8. https://doi.org/10.1126/science.abb5793

Kreisberg, S. (1992). *Transforming power: Domination, empowerment, and education*. State University of New York Press.

Link, M. (2018). *Nature, capabilities, and student well-being: An evaluation of an outdoor education approach* (Doctoral dissertation). http://hdl.handle.net/1993/33289

Link, M., & Falkenberg, T. (2021). Teacher leadership in education for sustainable well-being and well-becoming. In K. Walker, B. Kutsyuruba, & S. Cherkowski (Eds.), *Positive leadership for flourishing schools* (pp. 341–53). Information Age Publishers.

Lupinacci J., & Happel-Parkins A. (2016). (Un)learning anthropocentrism: An ecojustice framework for teaching to resist human-supremacy in schools. In S. Rice & A.G. Rud. (Eds.), *The educational significance of human and non-human animal interactions* (pp. 13–30). Palgrave Macmillan.

Malone, K. (2016). "Dapto Dreaming": A place-based environmental education project supporting children to be agents of change. In K. Winograd (Ed.), *Education in times of environmental crises: Teaching children to be agents of change* (pp. 113–28). Routledge.

Martusewicz, R.A., Edmundson, J., & Lupinacci, J. (2020). *Ecojustice education: Toward diverse, democratic, and sustainable communities*. Routledge.

Max-Neef, M.A. (1991). *Human scale development: Conceptions, applications and further reflections*. Apex Press.

Miller, W., & Cardamone, A. (2021). Educating through art, ecology, and ecojustice: A rain barrel project. *Art Education (Reston)*, 74(1), 40–5. https://doi.org/10.1080/00043125.2020.1825595

Nussbaum, M.C. (2011). *Creating capabilities: The human development approach*. Harvard University Press.

Plumwood, V. (2002). *Environmental culture: The ecological crisis of reason*. Routledge.

Radbourne, C. (2016). Acts of resistance: Decolonizing classroom practice through place-based education. In K. Winograd (Ed.), *Education in times of environmental crises: Teaching children to be agents of change* (pp. 102–12). Routledge.

Sobel, D. (1996). *Beyond ecophobia: Reclaiming the heart of nature education*. Orion Society and Myrin Institute.

Watters, H. (2015, 1 June). *Truth and Reconciliation chair urges Canada to adopt UN declaration on Indigenous Peoples*. https://www.cbc.ca/news/politics/truth-and-reconciliation-chair-urges-canada-to-adopt-un-declaration-on-indigenous-peoples-1.3096225

Westheimer, J., & Kahne, J. (2004). What kind of citizen? The politics of educating for democracy. *American Educational Research Journal*, 41(2), 237–69. https://doi.org/10.3102/00028312041002237

Xu, S., & Li, Y. (2020). Beware of the second wave of COVID-19. Lancet, 395(10233), 1321–2. https://doi.org/10.1016/S0140-6736(20)30845-X

14 Kitchen Table and Greenbelt Writers: Flourishing Writing in English Language Arts and Beyond

JENNIFER WATT

> Here is what I hope you get from this ... Ten years from now, I hope you will be sitting up some night at midnight under the light at the kitchen table – writing. Not because you have a paper due the next day or because someone has given you an "assignment" – but because you are hurting or grieving or confused, or because you are collecting some of the small joys of your day, or because you need to let go of some anger. Whatever the reason, you'll be sitting at the table writing because you are a writer. My wish is for you to be a lifelong writer. My hope is that writing will be a tool – an emotional, intellectual, and spiritual tool – to help you survive and grow and find meaning and purpose and peace in your life.
>
> (Nelson, 1994, p. 13)

I have learned a lot about myself as a writer over the years. Like the writer in the quote above, I have spent many a night (or morning or afternoon) under the light at the kitchen table – writing. I write my sorrows, my longings, my grief, my terror, and my joy. I write with the hope that I can become curious about why I am feeling furious. Unlike the above writer, my writing rarely takes place at midnight, because I turn into a pumpkin at ten in the evening (and we all know that pumpkins, while beautiful and useful in many ways, are not the best writers). My most sacred times to write are in the suspended stillness of the morning before my household fully wakes or just after I return from a walk, when my ideas have had a chance to meet the fresh air and the momentum of my steps carries me back to the page with renewed bravery (or at least until I try to capture those elusive, slippery ideas into concrete, steadfast sentences). I have learned that I am a lifelong writer (even when it is painful) and a dedicated teacher of writers (even when I am uncertain that I know how). I continually experience how writing helps my students and myself "survive and grow and find meaning and purpose and peace" in our lives.

As a writer and teacher of writers, I am deeply committed to exploring and illustrating how and why English language arts (ELA) classrooms are alive with opportunities for students, teachers, and communities to cultivate well-being and well-becoming. As a former middle- and senior-years ELA teacher, and now as a teacher educator and educational researcher, I have experienced profound moments when I recognize my own and others' flourishing while immersed with students, fellow teachers, or the wider community in the context of ELA curriculum-making. I am inspired by the theoretical framing and pedagogical stances of the innovative curriculum framework for English language arts in the province where I live and work:

> Tapping into students' identities and communities along with co-creating meaningful and rich contexts or experiences in English language arts can provide a focus for language learning and give students opportunities to explore significant ideas that have enduring value beyond the classroom. If Manitoba students are to understand, develop, and deepen their sense of identity/self, draw upon and harness multiple ways of knowing, thinking, and doing, and live well together in an interconnected world, students need opportunities to explore questions about themselves and the world. (Manitoba Education, 2020, p. 25)

I believe this curricular directive to explore "significant ideas that have enduring value beyond the classroom" points us back toward caring for and encouraging the lifelong writers at the kitchen table. Educators are thus encouraged to ask expansive "what if" and "what happens when" questions: what if teachers co-designed curricular opportunities with students that bring the kitchen table to the classroom and the classroom to the kitchen table? What happens when curriculum-making expands beyond what happens in classroom spaces, and how it can contribute to our students' well-being and well-becoming throughout their lives?

Just as there are writers sitting up at kitchen tables making sense of their lives, there are also readers curled up under the covers with a flashlight reading one more chapter after lights out, aspiring bakers with their phones open to a website trying out new recipes, creators exploring and designing films and video games, and social justice advocates analysing important issues from multiple perspectives. The list goes on endlessly. Language arts are living practices that contribute to human flourishing both in the present moment and in the imagined future. As Leland and Harste (1994) argue, "a good language arts program is one that expands the communication potential of all learners through the orchestration and use of multiple ways of knowing for purposes of ongoing interpretation and inquiry into the world" (p. 339). Although English language arts curriculum-making in schools focuses on multiple ways of knowing, this chapter explores what might happen if/when writing in K-12 schools is approached through a well-being and well-becoming (WB2) framework (Falkenberg, 2019). I examine how "greenbelt writing" (Fletcher, 2017) is one possible promising writing pedagogy that exemplifies how the components of the WB2-Framework contribute to greater flourishing in the classroom and beyond for both writers and teachers of writers.

Being and Becoming Well through Writing in School Contexts

It is through our writing that we "make our thinking visible, both to ourselves and to others. Through research and feedback, we engage with the ideas of others and then sharpen our own, draft by draft" (National Writing Project, n.d.a). It is no wonder that students spend so much of their time in all school content areas writing. Teaching students to write well and to communicate their thinking clearly is a priority in K-12 schooling, one that is especially thrust upon and taken up in English language arts classrooms. The desire to help students write well is often connected to succeeding in school assessment practices or meeting future goals in their adult lives: "For students, writing is a make-or-break practice as they navigate assignments, tests, college essays, and job applications. Without guided practice in writing, students face limits in their social, academic and professional lives" (National Writing Project, n.d.a). ELA teachers strive to figure out the most promising ways to encourage students to develop as writers who can negotiate the variety of writing demands in their current and future lives.

In the past, the landscape of writing in many Canadian schools has been quite different from that of our American counterparts, with its demands of high-stakes, standardized assessments, and the lockstep requirements of the Core Curriculum. However, Canada has recently seen a rise in government-led, public discourse and policy decisions that demand "improvement" in literacy levels (especially those measured in international standardized tests), "accountability" of the teachers within the system to raising those test scores, and the preparation of "future-oriented" students expected to directly contribute to the economy as soon as possible in many provinces (see, for instance, Manitoba Education, 2021). This kind of discourse and the impact of the policy decisions that follow may change how ELA teachers prioritize and spend time in their classrooms —{ focusing on teaching writing that

— gov't push

will help students achieve higher scores on tests, rather than exploring writing that helps them grow as critical thinkers and imaginative, empathetic human beings.

University writing instructor and author John Warner (2018) warns against the "well-meaning" but "terribly misguided" turn to standardizing writing and practices like the long-hailed five-paragraph essay:

> By trying to guide students toward "proficiency" or "competency," we wind up providing them with rules and strictures that cut students off from the most important and meaningful aspects of writing. In order to be judged "proficient," students are coached to create imitations that pass muster on a test a grader may take all of three minutes to read, or even worse, a test that's assessed by a computer algorithm on the lookout for key words and phrases. (p. 6)

For students learning in these conditions, writing becomes a set of boxes to be checked or hurdles to be jumped in the pursuit of individual success. The writing that happens in schools becomes increasingly distanced from the more authentic purposes, audiences, and personal agency of the writing that happens in life. Warner notices how "increasingly writing is a public and even collaborative act, but school often keeps ideas walled off from the world, shared only between students and teachers, and sometimes only between student and an anonymous grader" (pp. 16–17). He describes how educational systems that have focused too much on a "failing-schools narrative" lurch from one pedagogical fad to another (p. 129), arguing that "trying to fix schools while not paying sufficient attention to the people who populate those schools has only led to a system increasingly antithetical to learning, and even toxic to students' mental and physical well-being" (p. 129). In this context, the medicine becomes a poison – the dull instruction and extra pressure prescribed to help students write well on manufactured assessment tasks contaminate students' engagement and joy of writing for authentic, meaningful purposes. Instead, Warner suggests that rich, authentic, and engaging writing emerges when we "spend much less time worrying about the writing as demonstrated through largely meaningless assessments and *instead pay attention to the writers themselves*" (p. 132, italics added). Not denying that most parents and society members hope children will grow into productive and contented adults, Warner issues an important reminder: "Life is to be lived, including the years between five and twenty-two years old. A world that suggests those years are merely preparation for the real stuff, and the real stuff is almost entirely defined by your college and/or career, is an awfully impoverished place" (p. 138). Teachers of writers are encouraged to create writing experiences that pay attention to the writers themselves right in front of them, right in the moment – contributing to the enjoyment, exploring possibilities, and making meaning in students' immediate lives.

In the K-12 context, Ralph Fletcher (2017) explores shifts and changes to the "writing process movement" (p. xii) due to the increasing demands of accountability and reform measures. Fletcher describes how a shift in writing pedagogy was ushered into ELA classrooms in the 1970s and 1980s through the work of teacher-writers such as Donald Graves, Donald Murray, Lucy Calkins, Nancy Atwell, and others as "a reaction against the repressive writing practices of the 1950s and 1960s in which so many young writers felt disengaged" (p. xii). These leaders in writing pedagogy encouraged teachers to focus on the writing process, rather than discrete and often disconnected grammar and composition exercises, proposing "a refreshing change, a bold new vision: Let's allow young writers to do what real writers do" (p. xii). The heart of the writing process movement was to create space within the ELA curriculum to design and implement writing workshops, which Fletcher describes as follows:

> The writing workshop was both elegant and stunningly simple. At its core, it still is. You gathered a group of kids, encouraged them to write about what was important to them, and turned them loose. While those children wrote, you moved around the classroom and met with them in one-to-one encounters (writing conferences). During this time, teachers listened carefully to students and, if there was time, read their writing. They enjoyed it, affirmed what they were doing well, asked a few questions and – if the situation called for it – nudged the young writer with a suggestion or challenge. Skilled writing teachers understood that writers break easily, so they tried to use a gentle touch when doing that nudging. (p. 4)

The writing workshop, in its essence, was and is about paying attention to the writer, and then attending to the writing as an extension of the respect and compassion the teacher holds for the student as meaning-maker.

The writing workshop model was embraced by many teachers of writing throughout the K-12 system in North America and beyond, especially in early- and middle-years ELA classrooms. Fletcher (2017) explains how the writing workshop "put writing on the curricular map, giving it a permanent home, a definite slot in the daily class schedule, a subject with its own sovereign importance" (p. 5). However, since Fletcher has been part of the writing process movement over the decades, he has a long-range view of how the writing process has been affected by increasing external demands. Using a powerful metaphor, Fletcher describes the writing workshop model as a hot air balloon. At the beginning of the movement, "for roughly an hour each day the kids and the teacher would climb in and – *whoosh!* – up they'd go" (p. 5). The writing workshop – which students and teachers enjoyed immensely – thrived because it offered freedom, opportunities to take risks, and authentic, agentic writing. In Fletcher's words, "our hot-air balloon (the writing workshop) was simple, efficient, and dependable. So, naturally, people couldn't leave it alone" (p. 6). Since it was an example of something that was working well within the curriculum, increased demands began to be placed on the writing workshop – preparation for state writing exams, Common Core requirements for specific types and genres of writing, and the stuff that would help students write college entrance essays: "And so we added that weighty cargo. The balloon still rose, sluggishly this time. But things felt different" (p. 7). Teachers and students no longer anticipated the writing workshop with as much joy as they once had. What was once student-led exploration became instead another space for "covering the curriculum" or "teaching to the test." Sadly, Fletcher identifies a heavy cost for this trade-off: "Writing was a lot less fun than it used to be. It felt more like work – the not-fun kind. We finally got to the point where our beautiful balloon remained earth-stuck and no longer rose out of the sky" (p. 7). The once buoyant experience of authentic student engagement in their own writing and in their own well-being and well-becoming was grounded in the weight of too many external expectations. The pressures of writing to *perform well* in academic tasks and assessments took away opportunities for writing to *become well* as a human being.

Connecting the WB2-Framework for Well-Being and Well-Becoming to Writing

As captured in the soaring hot air balloon metaphor (Fletcher, 2017), when the teaching of writing in school focuses on the writers themselves, there is greater potential for students to experience a sense of flourishing. Most teachers of writers will instinctively recognize a connection between a vibrant writing classroom and students experiencing increased agency and voice, more joy and spark in what they are doing, a deeper sense of meaning-making, and more authentic connections to themselves and others. Explicitly connecting the curriculum-making involved in designing rich writing experiences to a framework for well-being and well-becoming can give teachers of writers more ways to articulate why this work needs to be prioritized and the ways it needs to be protected. As Falkenberg (2019) argues: "Any school education system that is concerned with students' quality of life – be it at present as students within the system or be it in the future as adults – needs to ground its work in an understanding of human well-being and the WB2-Framework could provide such needed understanding" (p. 25). This also holds true for ELA teachers – we need to root our curriculum-making in understandings of human flourishing, so we can continue to advocate for why writing and all other literacy practices matter.

The WB2-Framework proposed by Falkenberg (2019) is "based on the notion that the term *well-being and well-becoming*" captures "what humans are striving for when exerting their agency as they live their lives" (p. 16).[1] He identified the following components that "capture clusters of motives and drives for a human being to live their life one way rather than another" (p. 16): having the capacity for and/or experiencing agency; enjoying life; living a meaningful life; and experiencing personal and communal connections. The table below shows how Falkenberg has organized a framework based on Veenhoven's (2000) categorical dimensions of the good life (p. 22). One dimension differentiates between the inner aspects (what we experience within ourselves) and outer aspects (what we experience in relationship to others) of the good life; while the other dimension draws a distinction between "life chances" (what opportunities and freedoms are available to us) and "life results" (what we accomplish, achieve, or contribute) (Falkenberg, 2019, p. 22).

Writing also has inner and outer dimensions, which teachers of writing strive to make visible to their students. On the one hand, writing is a profoundly internal process – the ideas come from within. As Warner (2018) articulates:

> Writing is a skill, but it is a skill that lives inside the person and that often develops through idiosyncratic and individually driven processes. The best ways to demonstrate that skill may vary from occasion to occasion and person to person. We want writers to understand what's appropriate in a given rhetorical situation, but we should value writers who are able to express some aspect of themselves inside those situations. (p. 138)

On the other hand, writing is a public act – the ideas are brought into conversation with a wider audience. We write to take what is internal and make it external: "When we have an idea worth expressing, the

Table 14.1. The WB2-framework components for conceptualizing well-being and well-becoming

	inner aspect		outer aspect
life-chances/ freedom	having agentic capabilities linked to human needs		experiencing situational opportunities to engage one's agentic capabilities
life-results/ achievement	enjoying life	living a meaningful life	experiencing personal and communal connections that contribute to one's well-being and well-becoming

Note. The table is taken from Falkenberg (2019); reprinted with permission.

desire to share it provides the necessary intrinsic motivation to find the precise language to do so" (Warner, 2018, p. 144). As Fletcher (2017) notes, "the deep roots of the writing process can be found in the constructivist philosophy put forth by Jean Piaget: *humans learn best through direct experience of the world*" (p. 4). Our internal ideas come from our direct interactions and experiences of the world and our external writing can further connect us to others as well as back to our inner selves. The writing process exemplifies the inner and outer aspects of well-being and well-becoming but is also a tool for navigating the inner and outer aspects of living a good life.

The other dimension, of life chances and life results, is also connected to writing. As discussed earlier in this chapter, writing is often connected to life results and achievements, so there is significant pressure on teachers to create opportunities within schooling for students to develop specific communication skills needed to thrive in a variety of academic, professional, and personal situations. Imagine if we momentarily renamed the aspects of the dimension "writing chances/freedoms" and "writing results/achievements." If approaching designing rich curricular experiences through this framework, teachers would be encouraged to offer students as many opportunities to try as many different genres, modes, and forms of writing as possible and offer them as much freedom as possible to decide what writing best suits their needs, purposes, and audiences. Students would be given multiple chances to read like writers and write like readers, gaining exposure to rich mentor texts from diverse others, including their teachers, published authors, and other students (Chavez, 2021; Cullham, 2014; Gallagher, 2011; Kittle, 2008; Wood Ray & Cleaveland, 2018; Young & Ferguson,

2021). The greater opportunity for students to write about what is most important to them would likely result in more writing and, hopefully, more of a sense of confidence and achievement within their writing practices. With more opportunities to write within the curricular spaces of ELA classrooms, students might discover that they can head to the kitchen table to write for the rest of their lives to "survive and grow and find meaning and purpose and peace" (Nelson, 1994, p. 13). The components that contribute to human well-being and well-becoming – agency, enjoyment, meaning-making, and connections to self and others – can be explored and experienced through writing, as exemplified in Fletcher's (2017) "greenbelt writing" approach to teaching writing.

Designing Greenbelt Writing: An Illustration of the WB2-Framework in Action

As a long-time writer and teacher of writers, Fletcher (2017) is a self-confessed lover of metaphors (p. 38). Along with the powerful metaphor of the writing workshop as a hot air balloon, Fletcher harnesses another metaphor for a concept he calls "greenbelt writing." Drawing upon his knowledge of community planning and urban management, Fletcher describes the devastating impact of human populations and urban sprawl on the world's natural resources and wildlife (p. 38). To address these issues, many community planners design urban spaces to include greenbelts, which Fletcher defines as an "invisible line designating a border around a certain area, preventing development of that area, and allowing wildlife to return and be established" (p. 38). He further elaborates that "in a community the greenbelt plays an important role not only for what it is (wild), but also for what it is not (developed)" (p. 69). Greenbelts are purposefully designed as spaces that are left alone to flourish on their own without intervention.

Fletcher (2017) then suggests that this concept of undeveloped, wild writing spaces be embraced by curriculum-makers:

> I'm proposing a new concept: *greenbelt writing*. Writing that is raw, unmanicured, uncurated. I'm talking about informal writing. Writing that is wild, like the pungent skunk cabbage that sprouts haphazardly along the edge of a swamp. I'm talking about low-stakes writing, the kind of comfortable composing kids do when there's no one looking over their shoulder. (p. 39)

Alongside more developed and structured writing instruction, which may include more formalized versions of writing workshops complete with mini-lessons, peer editing, and teacher assessments, Fletcher proposes that teachers also make sure that students have dedicated "spaces and opportunities to experience the pleasure of writing" (p. 40). Although he admits that "some kids, like some species, may be able to survive and even thrive" in a "more developed workshop atmosphere" (p. 39), many other students find the confines of this kind of instruction "too narrow and constricting for them to generate any enthusiasm for writing" (p. 40). Fletcher argues that teachers should make dedicated time for students to write in ways that are free and unguided. He suggests that greenbelt writing time may include opportunities for students to create their own writer's notebooks and/or collaborate with others to co-author projects of interest. Within the greenbelt, teachers need to embrace the role of co-explorer and commit to allowing writing to unfold without teacher influence:

> The operative phrase for a natural greenbelt is not to *keep out* but *hands off*. We might decide to walk through an area like this to savor the quiet, maybe to sample a few wild blackberries growing there. But nobody ever visits a greenbelt hoping to improve it by pruning, weeding, clearing brush, and so on. These areas are, by design, unmanicured. (pp. 40–1)

Greenbelt writing, in all its unmanicured glory, has the potential to illustrate the components of the WB2-Framework (Falkenberg, 2019): agency, enjoyment, meaning-making, and connection to self and others.

Agency

> Two of the most important traits for students to succeed at education in general, and writing in particular, are agency and resilience. Agency is simply the ability to act and think under one's own initiative. Resilience is the ability to get up when you've fallen down, to learn from your own failures. (Warner, 2018, p. 49)

Many of us who have sat under the light at a kitchen table or wandered in greenbelt writing spaces know that "to write is to make choices, word by word, sentence by sentence, paragraph by paragraph. Writers choose what they want to write about, whom they want to write to, and why they're writing" (Warner, 2018, p. 5). Yet much of the writing that is done in school is not about *student* choice, but instead is dominated by *teacher* decisions. Teachers often decide what writers will write about, whom they will write to, why they are to write, and even make demands of what words should be included, how sentences will be structured, and how many paragraphs will be considered acceptable. What happens to student agency when teachers make all the choices? How do students learn about their own writing process, build their own voices as writers, or make decisions about whether their writing is working effectively or not if they only experience teacher-controlled writing assignments?

The beauty and power of greenbelt writing is that it is a low-stakes, risk-friendly, student-directed space for the student to develop and practise agency, both as a writer and as a human being:

> Many students – more than we might imagine – will find their stride through greenbelt writing. That's where they will (re)discover the passion of writing, the thrill of saying exactly what you want to say and how you want to say it, savouring how it feels when you create every word, comma, exclamation point and can say with proud confidence, "This is what I wrote – and it's all mine." (Fletcher, 2017, p. 97)

In greenbelt writing, students choose what they write, how long they stick with it, who they are writing for, and what they think will be the most effective way to communicate for their chosen purpose. They can write about what matters to them, explore what they already know a lot about (or something they know nothing about), or explain why they think something should change or be made better. Writing offers students situational opportunities to engage in their agentic capabilities (Falkenberg, 2019, p. 21).

Enjoyment

> And if writing isn't going to be fun, at least most of the time, what's the point of being a writer? (Fletcher, 2017, p. 69)

By its very design, greenbelt writing is meant to be more playful and exploratory than other kinds of school-based writing. It gives students "time, place, and opportunity to teach themselves to write by actually writing about what interest them in the way they want to write about it" (Fletcher, 2017, p. 95). Students can push their desks together and co-create a series of comics, a screenplay, or a menu and marketing plan for the bubble tea café they plan to open. Or they can put in their ear buds and write page after page of fan fiction, doodle the design of an avatar they would add to a video game, or release rage in fiery slam poetry. The greenbelt can help students discover that writing can become an enjoyable life-long pursuit – a craft and a calling:

> Writing is not all sweetness and light for me – I certainly have my struggles – but overall, I consider it a pleasurable activity. A craftsperson enjoys the process of making a piece of furniture: the smell of the wood, the sound of the miter saw, the way a three-dimensional drawing gets transformed into a chair that's both functional and beautiful. In a similar way I love the "smell" of words, the crunch of sentences, the little jolt of satisfaction that comes when a strong sentence snaps cleanly into a paragraph. When I'm in my writing groove, I feel like a kid with a pile of blocks, mucking around in sentences, trying to build my city of words. (Fletcher, 2017, p. 4)

Greenbelt writing offers writers a glimpse into the highs and lows of writing that is pursued for play and passion. As Warner (2018) argues, "Writing is a highly challenging, endlessly frustrating pursuit that delivers lasting pleasure and knowledge. This aspect of writing should not be reserved for professional writers. It should be available to anyone who must write for any occasion" (p. 150). Greenbelt writing can be a reserve for joy – even if that joy will, at times, be hard-earned.

Meaning Making

> To get students writing, we have to put them to work making meaning. (Warner, 2018, p. 145)

In its essence, writing is about making and sharing meaning. But let's be honest, not all writing in school feels meaningful. Writing often feels transactional. Students write to show that they understand (or can at least reproduce) the ways someone else (an author, scientist, historian, even their teacher) has previously made meaning for them within some content area. Writing is frequently used to fulfil an assigned task that may or may not feel relevant or connected to other aspects of students' lives. Although there is a place for transactional writing and it serves many purposes, it may not necessarily inspire flourishing writing or flourishing writers. Warner (2018) suggests that "students find writing meaningful when they understand how the writing fits inside the larger picture of their lives and experiences" (p. 151). Writing that is meaningful and that contributes to well-being and well-becoming is writing that *matters to the writer*. This kind of writing can happen in carefully designed assignments and in more formal curricular spaces. However, there may also need to be other, adjacent, wilder spaces within the curricular landscape where students can explore and discover what matters to them as writers and as human beings, without having to share their works-in-progress for assessment. Fletcher (2017) reminds us that greenbelt writing is "meaning based, not meant for public consumption. It's private and personal. It's not presentation, and it shouldn't be treated as such. Writing teachers need to think carefully about how to create conditions that will encourage and not squelch it" (p. 77). When students are given agency to choose what they explore and the freedom to play with their ideas, they can become lost (and found) in the process of making meaning.

Connections to Self and Others

> On the first day of class I tell students that writing is a pathway to being a better and more contented human being. I tell them writing will make them capable of experiencing empathy for others while also acting with personal agency inside a complex and contradictory world. I believe that. I believe that because writing is a route towards the joy of discovery, of using writings as a tool to understand myself and the world. (Warner, 2018, pp. 149–50)

Greenbelt writing invites students to connect to their own identities as writers and to connect with others as a community of writers. In these unstructured writing times, individual students will encounter opportunities to say about themselves, "I am a writer," but also look around and realize, "We are *all* writers." Warner suggests that "students find writing meaningful when they view is as a 'social act,' and as part of an 'environment' much larger than the assignment" (Warner, 2018, p. 151). Writing can become part of the culture of the classroom – a way to connect to one another and a way to connect beyond to imagined or real audiences. When more of the kinds of writing that students do on their own for their own purposes becomes embedded practices within the classroom, there also becomes more of a connection between home and school. Teachers may begin to hear, "We were working on our next chapters at our sleepover on Friday" or "I read my comic to my little brother." As Fletcher (2017) observes, "When they write at home, they're giving us important information. They're letting us know that writing has become part of who they are" (Fletcher, 2017, p. 96). Writing can facilitate connections that contribute to our students' sense of well-being and well-becoming. When students realize that they have an audience they can write to and write for (even when that is the important audience of themselves), they also become more aware of how interconnected they are with others.

Inviting Teachers of Writing to the Kitchen Table and Greenbelt

It is not just students who can benefit from engaging in writing to increase agency, enjoyment, meaning-making, and connection. Teachers of writers also can experience more flourishing in their personal and professional lives if they dedicate time to their own writing practices, venturing into the greenbelt or sitting under the light of the kitchen table as writers themselves. High school English language arts teacher Penny Kittle (2008) has written extensively about the importance of writing alongside the students in her classrooms: "I believe you can't tell kids how to write; you have to show them what writers do. I believe you have to be a writer, no matter how stumbling and unformed that process is for you; it's essential to your work as a teacher of writing" (p. 8). Teachers who write have more compassion for the writers in their classrooms – they understand the struggle, the resistance, the thrill, and the solace of writing because they are regularly engaged in the process themselves. They become part of the interconnected community of writers – not just a guide at the side, but as another writer right in the messy middle of it all.

The idea of supporting teachers of writing to become writers themselves is a foundational principle of the National Writing Project, which is an almost 50-year-old network of over 175 sites in the United States that are co-directed by teacher-leaders from universities and K-12 schools (National Writing Project, n.d.b). I am proud to be one of the co-directors of the Manitoba Writing Project (MBWP), which is the first and only Associated International Site in Canada: "The goal of the MBWP community is to contribute directly to educating and empowering young people to think critically, develop passion about human rights issues, and identify as writers who can effectively communicate and offer their voices in public dialogue as citizens" (Manitoba Writing Project, n.d.). In all our efforts, whether is building a network of teacher-leaders, supporting student writing contests or innovative school-based writing projects, or offering our biannual Summer Writing Institute for teachers of writing, we approach writing through an inquiry stance and as a form of teacher research: "We believe teacher inquiry contributes to a profession that values teachers as theorists, as producers of curriculum and materials, and as activists for their students and communities" (Manitoba Writing Project, n.d.). We strive to contribute to developing agentic capabilities for students and teachers, while also offering writing experiences that contribute to the other components of well-being and well-becoming – enjoyment, meaning-making, and connection.

And so, I keep coming back to the light of my kitchen table – writing my sorrows, my longings, my grief, my terror, and my joy. I hope my students (who are the teachers of writers) do the same and I hope their students do the same. I hope English language arts curriculum, both in its more formal writing workshops and in its more informal greenbelt writing spaces, can continue to contribute to the well-being and well-becoming of individuals and the community, as we "survive and grow and find meaning and purpose and peace" (Nelson, 1994, p. 13) in our lives.

NOTE

1 See also the discussions of the WB2-Framework in chapters 5, 6, and 13 (this volume).

REFERENCES

Chavez, F.R. (2021). *The anti-racist writing workshop: How to decolonize the creative classroom*. Haymarket Books.

Cullham, R. (2014). *The writing thief: Using mentor texts to teach the craft of writing*. Stenhouse Publishers.

Falkenberg, T. (2019). *Framing human well-being and well-becoming: An integrated systems approach*. http://wellbeinginschools.ca/paper-series/

Fletcher, R. (2017). *Joy write: Cultivating high-impact, low-stakes writing*. Heinemann.

Gallagher, K. (2011). *Write like this: Teaching real-world writing through modeling and mentor texts*. Stenhouse Publishers.

Kittle, P. (2008). *Write beside them: Risk, voice, and clarity in high school writing*. Heinemann.

Leland, C.H., & Harste, J. C. (1994). Multiple ways of knowing: Curriculum in a new key. *Language Arts, 71*(5), 337–45. https://www.jstor.org/stable/41961975

Manitoba Education. (2020). *English language arts curriculum framework: A living document*. https://www.edu.gov.mb.ca/k12/cur/ela/framework/

– (2021). *Better education starts today: Putting students first*. https://bettereducationmb.ca/

Manitoba Writing Project. (n.d.). *Ongoing efforts*. https://manitobawritingproject.weebly.com/ongoing-efforts.html

National Writing Project. (n.d.a). *Why writing?* https://www.nwp.org/why-writing

- (n.d.b). https://www.nwp.org
Nelson, G.L. (1994). *Writing and being: Taking back our lives through the power of language.* Innisfree Press.
Veenhoven, R. (2000). The four qualities of life: Ordering concepts and measures of the good life. *Journal of Happiness Studies 1*(1), 1–39. https://doi.org/10.1023/A:1010072010360
Warner, J. (2018). *Why they can't write: Killing the five-paragraph essay and other necessities.* Johns Hopkins University Press.
Wood Ray, K., & Cleaveland, L. (2018). *A teacher's guide to getting started with beginning writers: Grades K-2.* Heinemann.
Young, R., & Ferguson, F. (2021). *Writing for pleasure: Theory, research, and practice.* Routledge.

15 Conclusion: Where to Go from Here

THOMAS FALKENBERG

In the introductory chapter (chapter 1), I sketched major ideas (and by no means all of them) from the scholarly literature on well-being in schools, and structured them into five domains of study: purpose of school education, conceptualizing educational concepts, school ecology, teaching and learning, and curriculum. Then I provided a framework of statements (table 1.1 in chapter 1) that listed and linked (integrated) core ideas from the chapters in the different parts of this book that – in my view – contribute to these domains of study. Now that the authors have presented their respective chapters – and after the introductory chapter has attempted to pull those ideas into a larger scholarly context and framework – what can this concluding chapter offer the reader?

I see two possibilities. First, there is the possibility – the need, I would say – to engage the ideas of the different chapters within and across the parts of the book with each other to demonstrate in what way these ideas can be integrated with each other to generate a more comprehensive understanding of well-being and well-becoming in schools. While the framework of well-being and well-becoming in schools provided in chapter 1 provides a list of core ideas from the chapters from each section, those ideas are not systematically connected across chapters and parts, because the elaboration of these ideas was still to come in the respective chapters. Now, at the end of the book, such engagement of ideas could happen in this conclusion chapter. However, the chapter authors have decided that such an engagement can more fruitfully take place by having the authors themselves "at the table," and that is literally what we have agreed to do, that is, to meet, engage in a dialogue on our different chapter ideas and how these ideas connect, complement, and sometimes conflict with each other. To this end, all chapter authors have agreed to such a real-life dialogue, to have this dialogue audio-recorded, and for the audio-recording to become part of a podcast series entitled *Well-Being in Schools*, which will be posted online at https://umfm.com/series at the time of the publication of this book. The podcast series is intended to complement this book.

That leaves the second possibility for this conclusion chapter, namely the question of what can meaningfully follow this book project for the team of scholars who have contributed to it. How can the ideas presented in the different parts of the book and in their different chapters be expanded upon? What areas of study might be missing from what is presented in this book? What could the team of scholars who contributed to this book explore further? This concluding section will respond to these questions. What needs further exploration, however, depends on the overall purpose, and so I want to take as the purpose for what follows a possible follow-up research project that involves the different chapter authors in order to build, extensively and intensively, a comprehensive structure of ideas for school education for well-being and well-becoming that expands on the ideas presented in this book. Thus, for what follows in this concluding section, I will go back to the integrative framework for well-being in schools presented at the end of chapter 1 (table 1.1) and use the structure and ideas presented in this framework, as well as the development of those ideas in the chapters, to create a list of questions that could form the basis for a follow-up research inquiry.

One foundational matter that any concern for human well-being and well-becoming has to engage with is the conceptualization of the core concept of "well-being and well-becoming." Initially, how to define the concept itself matters less than the need to be specific about *the type of* concept we have in mind in our concern for well-being and well-becoming in schools. Each type of concept comes with different commitments, as Magnuson and Krepski (chapter 2) have demonstrated. Knowing what the implied consequences of each kind of concept are will help us decide on the concept whose consequences aligns best with our values and commitments. In their classification of types of definitions of human well-being, Magnuson and Krepski have drawn on the received views within academic analytic philosophy. Some of the questions that arise from their inquiry are as follows:

- Does this philosophical categorization of conceptions of human well-being capture definitions that are prominent in other academic disciplines, like psychology and sociology? If not (or not quite), how would the categorization need to be expanded, and what are the consequences associated with types of conceptualizations that fall into these other categories?

- Does this categorization of approaches to human well-being in Western philosophy capture definitions that are prominent in the work undertaken within non-Western contexts? If not (or not quite), why not, and can these different conceptions of human well-being still be integrated?
- How do approaches to human well-being from non-Western traditional knowledge systems (including Indigenous traditions) relate to the conceptualizations captured in the categorization presented in chapter 2?
- How does a concept like "human well-becoming" relate to the conceptualizations of well-being captured in the categorization in chapter 2?

Of importance is also the question of the impact of culture on the understanding and conceptualization of well-being and well-becoming. Can we work with a culture-transcending concept of well-being and well-becoming in the face of both individual-oriented and collective-oriented societies in the contemporary world? Three book chapters in particular have spoken to this question. Heringer and Falkenberg (chapter 4) have argued that, in general, the individual-focused definitions of well-being that were categorized in Magnuson and Krepski's chapter (chapter 2) need to be complemented by an ethic of well-being in order to foster the social and communal connections essential to our well-being and well-becoming. Further, Kerr (chapter 9) has argued that something akin to communal flourishing should be seen as an integral part of our understanding of human well-being and well-becoming, because as humans we are inextricably embedded and enculturated into a community. Deer and Trickey (chapter 5) have exemplified this challenge to individual-centred understandings of well-being and well-becoming from an Indigenous perspective on well-being. These qualifications and challenges to an individual-focused conceptualization of human well-being and well-becoming, as is currently prevalent in the academic literature on well-being and well-becoming, raise the following questions for future research:

- What are community-centred conceptions of human well-being and well-becoming and how are they distinct from individual-centred conceptions?
- Can an individual-centred concept be sustained in light of an understanding of the existential importance of social and communal connections for human living? If yes, what are the conceptual

relationships between individual-centred and community-centred conceptions of well-being and well-becoming?
- Can the concept of an ethic of well-being and well-becoming complement an individual-centred concept of well-being and well-becoming to accommodate the notion that as individuals we are still an integral part of a social network, and that the quality of the relations in this network are integral to an individual's well-being and well-becoming?

While these questions are focused on issues around the *content* of the concept of human well-being and well-becoming, there is also the question of the *form* of the concept. This question has two versions: (1) Can and must the definitions be formally so general that they have room for culturally specific versions of the respective definition? (2) Do all definitions of well-being and well-becoming need to be specific to a particular culture? The WB2-Framework for Conceptualizing Human Well-Being and Well-Becoming, outlined in chapter 6, proposes a general definition of well-being that leaves space for culturally specific versions of the definitions of the components of well-being and well-becoming. On the other hand, Deer and Trickey (chapter 5), who explore the WB2-Framework from an Indigenous perspective, challenge the possibility of such a general definition. This raises interesting questions concerning the culture-specificity of conceptualizing human well-being and well-becoming for future research:

- Can and must a definition of human well-being and well-becoming be general enough to allow for cultural-specific versions of this definition for any practical use of the definition?
- If yes, how general does a definition have to be to be flexible enough across cultural specificities without losing substance and usefulness as a definition?

Once we decide upon a concept or type of concept for human well-being and well-becoming, we have to make the value commitment to student well-being and well-becoming – in the defined sense – as a goal of school education. To do so thoughtfully, we need to go back to the foundational issue of needing to understand that basic commitment, and what such a goal would require in additional value commitments for the educational goods that we consider relevant and important in working toward such a goal. This is what Krepski has argued for in her chapter (chapter 3). She makes reference to a discourse around educational goods that raises the following general questions that need further exploration:

- What are the nature and the role of educational goods in school education that have well-being and well-becoming as a goal? For instance, are educational goods the knowledge, skills, attitudes, and competencies that subject-specific curricula are concerned with, or are educational goods a more abstract, value framework for the learning outcomes of such curricula?
- Are there specific educational goods for particular concepts of well-being and well-becoming as a central goal of school education? If yes, how would they apply to particular conceptions?

The term educational *goods* suggests something that can and needs to be *distributed* to be of value to students. Krepski (chapter 3) has discussed the issue of distribution of educational goods across student populations. This brings "the subjects" of well-being and well-becoming to the forefront – ultimately well-being and well-becoming is always the well-being and well-becoming *of someone*. Once the decision has been made to make well-being and well-becoming a central goal of school education, the focus on the subjects of well-being raises two issues. First, there is the issue that Krepski (chapter 3) has discussed, namely the question of how the educational well-being and well-becoming goods are and should be distributed to students. Krepski's chapter lays the groundwork for the following inquiries:

- What are the actual distributions of educational goods linked to specific conceptualizations of well-being? Are those distributions desirable from a social justice standpoint? If not, what does a socially just distribution look like? How can it be achieved and sustained?
- How does a socially just distribution of educational goods in a school education system that has student well-being and well-becoming as a core goal help achieve that very goal?

The second issue linked to a focus on the subjects of well-being and well-becoming concerns *who* is included as subjects in schools. Tze and Brekelmans (chapter 7) have argued for the importance of giving due consideration to the well-being of school psychologists and school counsellors. They discuss the impact of the well-being of school staff on that of students, and the question arises whether the well-being and well-becoming of school staff need to be an integral concern for schools as workplaces. Expanding on the work done by Tze and Brekelmans, the following questions need further research:

- What is the connection between well-being and well-becoming of school staff and that of students?

- Should our concern for well-being and well-becoming in schools go beyond a focus on schools as educational institutions for children to include schools as places of work for adults?
- What are the workplace conditions that are conducive to the well-being and well-becoming of school staff?

This focus on schools as places of work, as well as that on the purpose question of education, suggests another theme that needs exploring in the context of well-being and well-becoming in schools, namely the social-political role of schools as organizations. Three chapters in particular have explored this theme: chapters 8, 9, and 11. Eblie Trudel (chapter 8) has inquired into well-being in schools through an organizational lens, suggesting that well-being can be the driving focus of and concern for all organizational aspects of school education, from the purpose and educational priorities of the organization to the legislative framework for school education, and from the organizational systems components to the larger community in which a school as an organization is embedded. In this regard a single chapter can only scratch the surface, but what the chapter does is provide a roadmap for making well-being and well-becoming the guiding principles of all aspects of schools and school divisions as organizations. Tasks for future research and inquiry include:

- Can the concern for human well-being and well-becoming be *a* or even *the* foundational principle for schools and school divisions as organizations? If yes, what does it mean and how is it feasible for this principle to be foundational to all aspects of the organization? How can this be accomplished and what obstacles can be expected? What role do communities in which a school or school division is embedded play in making this principle foundational to the school or school division as an organization?
- How can such concern for human well-being and well-becoming be justified as a/the foundational principle for school and school divisions as organizations? What role do human rights principles and legislation play in such justification? What role do community values play in and for such justification?
- What legislative and policy frameworks need to be in place for making the concern for human well-being and well-becoming a/the foundational principle for schools and school divisions as organizations, and what role does the community play in establishing such frameworks?
- How can and should the adoption of the concern for human well-being and well-becoming as a/the foundational principle for schools and school divisions as organizations become a systems

initiative that impacts all aspects of the organization (including educational priorities and the understanding of organizational/ educational leadership)?

Falkenberg et al. (chapter 11) have argued that schools and school divisions more broadly should be understood as complex adaptive social systems, following a systems framework for the organizational perspective presented by Eblie Trudel (chapter 8). This gives rise to the following questions:

- How are organizational aspects of schools and school divisions, as discussed by Eblie Trudel, represented in a complex adaptive social systems framework? Can a complex adaptive social systems framework adequately capture the dynamics inherent in organizations and organizational change?
- How is the concern for human well-being and well-becoming as a/ the foundational principle for schools and school divisions as organizations shaping the understanding of schools and school divisions as complex adaptive social systems?

One central feature of complex adaptive systems is that they are constantly adapting to environmental and internal disturbances, as systems-internal experiences of the systems-external environment are called in general systems theory. In other words, social systems have a history, and the present is the result of that history. Kerr (chapter 9) brings that very point to bear: she has argued that a historical perspective is crucial when considering well-being and well-becoming in schools, especially in countries, like Canada, with a colonial past. This past still reaches into the present through the continued existence of colonizing social structures and a capitalist economic system that leaves many people materially impoverished and politically powerless – a concern that is directly connected to the distribution issue of educational goods discussed by Krepski (chapter 3). This raises the following for further inquiry:

- How can history, cultural differences, inequities, power structures in general, and colonizing social structures in particular be framed as phenomena of complex adaptive social systems?

If schools and school divisions are understood as complex adaptive systems with a past that needs to be understood in order to understand the present, how does one inquire into the adaptation process in order to influence this very process in ways that align with the school educational purpose and larger social concerns like decolonization, equitability, and democratic commitment? A parallel question arises from the discussion by Eblie Trudel (chapter 8): If schools and school divisions are understood as organizations within a complex adaptive social systems framework, how do we inquire into organizational change and how do we initiate and sustain organizational change toward desired outcomes? The chapter by Hauseman et al. (chapter 10) has suggested one such approach to inquiries addressing the two kinds of questions: assessing the development of the system relative to intended outcomes through the use of developmental evaluation, an approach to program evaluation that is specifically useful for complex systems environments. While Hauseman et al. have illustrated the use of developmental evaluation using data from their support of a school divisional change process intended to upscale well-being initiatives in that school division, more general research questions arise:

- What is the potential for developmental evaluation as a means to understand systemic change processes and to impact systemic change in schools and school divisions as complex adaptive social systems in which the concern for human well-being and well-becoming is a/the foundational principle?
- How does developmental evaluation as a means to understand systemic change processes and to impact systemic change in schools and school divisions as complex adaptive social systems change or reconceptualize our understanding of organization, accountability, and so on?
- What are the limitations of developmental evaluation as a means for impacting desired change in complex adaptive social systems and what other means are available?

Up to this point, everything considered concerns school education as an institutional project: its purpose, its socio-political and socio-cultural context and embeddedness, and its organization. However, school education is in the end always about intended student learning and student development. Such learning and development happen generally in the classroom, where a professional educator purposefully engages students in activities that are intended to see students develop skills, knowledge, attitudes, and competencies in accordance with learning outcomes prescribed in grade and subject-specific curriculum documents. From this book's perspective, the question that arises is how can the core purpose of school education – to help students with the skills, knowledge, attitudes, and competencies needed for their well-being and well-becoming – be achieved in the kind of teaching, learning, and curriculum contexts just described? The chapters by Falkenberg (chapter 12), Link (chapter 13), and Watt (chapter 14) illustrate such possibilities by demonstrating how a student well-being and well-becoming lens fits within the teaching of three subjects that are generally considered the core subject areas in school education: mathematics, science, and language arts (here English). Considering the many elements in teaching of subject matter in general – lesson planning, assessment, textbooks, learning activities, to name just a few – the three chapters can only scratch the surface of their respective topics. Further questions for exploration include:

- What do we need to create school curricula that are guided by a concern for student well-being and well-becoming, and what would these curricula look like?
- What do we need to create learning activities and teaching that are guided by a concern for student well-being and well-becoming, and what would these activities and teaching look like?
- Is separation of content into distinct subject areas an adequate curricular approach to structure teaching and learning in terms of student well-being and well-becoming, or are more holistic approaches more suitable?

In summary, the chapters of this book not only offer grounded, state-of-the-art discussions on their respective topics, but also point to future directions for exploration and expansion of the work that needs to be done to enhance well-being and well-becoming in schools.

Index

actor, social. *See* complex adaptive social system
affordance. *See* complex adaptive social system
agency. *See* complex adaptive social system
aims of school education. *See* purpose of school education
Alberta, 148
Anishnaabe education, 3
Anishinaabe people, 85, 90, 92
assessment, 35
Australia, 10, 85, 88, 123, 128

behaviour, 202–3, 210
bio-ecological systems approach, 8
British Columbia, 171

capabilities and well-being/well-becoming, 8, 86, 107, 119
Capabilities-Development-with-Nature approach, 241–2
change dynamics, 198, 212–14, 278; success, 213
change of school systems, 197
classrooms, safe and caring, 10
communication. *See* complex adaptive social system
community, flourishing, 13, 273, 276

complex adaptive social system, 14, 198–206, 277: actor in, 199, 200–3, 205, 207–9, 213–14; affordance in, 200–5, 209, 212; agency in, 202–3, 205–6, 208–9, 211, 213; and well-becoming, 212–14; closure of, 205–6, 211; co-evolution, 206, 212–13; communication in (*see* interaction in); constraints in, 200–5, 209, 212; coupling in, 201, 208–9; dynamics of, 203, 205–6, 211–12, 277; emergence in, 200, 204–5, 209–12; emergent, ephemeral/stable, 200, 204, 209–12; environment of, 200, 207–8; interaction in, 199–206, 209, 213; open, 211; perturbations of, 205–8, 211, 213–14; power structure in, 209; school system as, 180, 206–12, 278; structure in, 201, 203–5, 209, 212. *See also* system
constraint. *See* complex adaptive social system
coupling, structural. *See* complex adaptive social system
COVID-19, 69, 159, 192, 237
curriculum: ecologically-centred, 236; English language arts, 255; holistic, 11, 279; science, 236, 251;

282 Index

curriculum (*cont.*)
  student-chosen, 11. *See also* well-being and curriculum

Dakota people, 83, 163
Dene people, 92
developmental evaluation, 178, 180–2, 213, 278, 191–3; activities in, 183–5; benefits of, 185–9; challenges of, 189–91
differentiated instruction, 34–5

educational goods, 13, 46–50; and trade–offs, 50–1
emergence; emergent. *See* complex adaptive social system
England, 128
English language arts education, 279
enjoying life, 107
equality of opportunity. *See* well-being and distribution of opportunities
ethic of hospitality, 62–6, 69–71. *See also* well-being and ethic of hospitality
experience, 202

flourishing life, 60–1, 71, 101, 117, 159, 164, 219
flow, 7

good life, the, 3, 79
goods, educational, 41, 275; distribution of, 41, 275
greenbelt writing, 262–7

hidden curriculum, 52
hope, 7
hospitality. *See* ethic of hospitality

Indigenous (perspective on) well-being, 79–80, 93–5, 161–5, 273; and agency, 81–6; and artwork, 87; and Circle of Courage, 162–3; and community, 83–4, 91, 162; and cultural traditions, 87; and enjoyment, 87; and family, 90–1, 162; and holism, 88–90, 162; and integrationist approach, 95–6; and land, 91–2; and meaningfulness, 87–90; and Medicine Wheel, 92, 163; and parallelist approach, 94–5; and reconciliation, 94–5; and relational worldview, 162–3; and self-determination, 86; and social connections, 90–3; and spirituality, 88, 92–3; and Truth and Reconciliation Commission of Canada, 94; and two-eyed seeing, 89; and WB-Framework, 81–93
inner-city, 160
Inuit people, 81, 85, 90–1
IQ testing, 44

Kashwenta, 94–5

Lakota people, 163

Manitoba, 4, 84, 125, 139, 145–6, 150, 160, 162, 169–70, 178, 182
Manitoba Writing Project, 267
mathematics as a discipline, 224–6, 231; humanistic view of, 225–6, 230–2; Platonic view of, 224–6; and well-being, 227–32
mathematics education, 10, 220, 222–4, 279; attitude and affect in, 229; as citizenship education, 229; humanistic approach to, 226, 228–32; learning in, 223; and meaning in life, 227–32; meanings in, 222–4, 228; philosophy of, 226, 232; as value and moral education, 229

meaning in life: conceptual structure of, 101–4; and cosmic meaning, 102; dimensions of, 103; having meaning, 104; levels of meaning, 102–3; and mathematics education, 227–32; and the need for efficacy, 104, 220–1, 227–8, 231; and the need for purpose, 104, 220–1, 227–8, 230; and the need for self-worth, 104, 220–1, 227–8, 232; and the need for values, 104, 220–1, 227–8, 230–1; objective meaning, 103; and purpose, 103–4; and school education, 115–17; seeking meaning, 104; situational meaning, 102; sources of, 104–5; subjective meaning, 103; and terrestrial (personal) meaning, 102; and understanding, 103–4, 220; and well-being, 101; ultimate/global meaning, 102; versus meaning of life, 102
mino-bimaadizwin, 3, 15

Native Hawaiians, 91–2
New Sociology of Childhood, 6

Ontario, 36–7, 140
Organization for Economic Co-operation and Development (OECD), 60

Pan-Canadian Assessment Program, 44
parents, 44
perception, 203
perturbation. *See* complex adaptive social system
positive psychology, 7, 11, 59, 149
Program for International Student Assessment (PISA), 44

purpose of school education, 5–7, 11, 23, 41–6, 68–9, 119, 274

Reggio Emilia, 10, 33

school: climate, 9; ecology of, 8–10; as organization, 276–8; as social system, 6, 206–14
school division. *See* school
science education, 235–51
Scotland, 10
self-determination theory (SDT), 120, 128, 130
self-understanding, 203
student voice, 8, 9, 35
system: bio-psychic, 202–3, 206–8, 211, 213; complex adaptive, 198; complex, 198, 202; social interaction, 199, 200; social, 199, 202, 214. *See also* complex adaptive social system

trade-offs. *See* educational goods and trade-offs

United States, 128
universal design learning (UDL), 34–5, 141

WB2-Framework, 80–1, 96, 106–8, 117, 118, 220, 236–7, 239–42, 251, 256, 260, 274; and ecojustice education, 246–7, 251; five conceptual components of, 107–8; and Indigenous well-being, 81–93; and meaning in life, 108–15, 220–1; meta-characteristics of, 106–7; and place-based education, 249–51; and writing in English language arts, 259–66
well-becoming, 4, 107, 118, 197, 198, 214, 273

well-being: of administrators, 7; and capabilities/competencies, 8, 141, 149, 236; and colonialism, 166–72; and community, 83, 145–7, 159, 168–9; and comprehensive school health, 144; conceptualization of, 7–8, 13, 25–31, 139–40, 144, 161–5, 179, 272–3; and curriculum, 11, 169–71, 279; desire fulfilment theories of, 28–30, 34–6; and distribution of opportunities, 51–6; and ecojustice education, 237, 239, 242–7; and ecological injustice, 236–7; and educational goods, 46–50; and ethic of hospitality, 60, 67–8; ethic of, 60–2, 67–71, 273–4; formal/explanatory theories of, 25; hedonistic theories of, 25–7, 33–4, 61; and holism, 163, 168–71 (*see also* Indigenous (perspective on) well-being and holism); and human rights, 61–2, 139, 142–4; individual, 59–62, 67, 70–1, 273; and inequality, 165–72; integrative framework for, 12–14, 272; and legislation in Canada, 142–4; measurement, 147–9; objective list theories of, 30–2, 36–8, 59; organizational perspective on, 139; and pedagogy, 171–2; and place-based education, 237, 239, 247–51; and poverty, 166–72; and purpose of school education, 5–7, 42, 45, 237; of school staff, 7, 13, 120, 276; and social injustice, 236, 238–9; subjective, 59, 61; substantive/enumerative theories of, 25–6; and sustainability, 236–7; of teachers, 7, 120–1, 140–1, 149–51, 267; theories of, 23–32, 59; theories of well-being and school education, 32–8; virtue-based approaches to, 59; and well-becoming, 4, 107, 161, 274; and writing, 256–9. *See also* Indigenous well-being; well-being of school counsellors; well-being of school psychologists

well-being of school counsellors, 120–6, 275; and autonomy, 131; and burnout, 121, 123–5; and role confusion, 123–5; and self-care, 125; and student well-being, 121, 125; and support, 124–5

well-being of school psychologists, 121, 126–30, 275; and autonomy, 131; and emotional toll, 127–8, 130; and ethical dilemmas, 127; and mindfulness, 129–30; and self-care, 130; and support, 128–30

Winnipeg, 160, 165–72, 182